Better English, by Norman Lewis, teacher and author of numerous books on the language, is a sensible and authoritative guide to grammar, pronunciation and spelling—a book that takes the pedantry out of correct English.

GRAMMAR
Twenty-six comprehensive chapters. Each opens with a realistic problem, discusses enough grammar to make the solution easy to understand and remember, closes with a simply worded rule and finally puts you through an exacting test to make certain you can apply all you have learned.

PRONUNCIATION
Six chapters, including a glossary of troublesome words, discuss pronunciation in terms of a sound, functional principle: Correct pronunciation is the pronunciation used by the majority of educated people throughout the country.

SPELLING
Some very famous people have been poor spellers, but here you can correct your own weaknesses by learning the thirteen hardest words to spell and putting to use a list of easy spelling rules and tricks for remembering special words.

Better English

(Revised Edition)

BY NORMAN LEWIS

A LAUREL BOOK
Published by
Dell Publishing Co., Inc.
1 Dag Hammarskjold Plaza
New York, New York 10017

Laurel ® TM 674623, Dell Publishing Co., Inc.

ISBN: 0-440-30548-9

Reprinted by arrangement with Thomas Y. Crowell,
a division of Harper and Row, Publishers, Inc.

Printed in the United States of America
Previous Laurel edition
Seventeen printings
New Laurel edition
First printing—September 1981
Third printing—July 1984

CONTENTS

PART 1

How to Make Grammar Work for You

OPINIONS ON SPECIFIC POINTS

PART 2

Correct Pronunciation

PART 3

Correct Spelling

PART 1 *How to Make Grammar Work for You*

A Personal Record Sheet for Part 1

chapter 1 WHAT IS GRAMMAR?

Grammar is what you say.

Grammar is how you put words together to fashion a thought. And thoughts are expressed, either in speech or writing, for the purpose of communicating an idea to a listener or a reader.

So grammar is, quite simply, the architecture of ideas as expressed in words.

That is not half so difficult as what you remember from your school days, is it?

(Nor, I trust, half so dismal?)

Does Marilyn Monroe have a tremendous *effect* on you —or is it a tremendous *affect*?

Do you speak of a murderer's being *hung* or *hanged*?

Is it a secret between you and *I*—or between you and *me*?

Do you *lay* down—or *lie* down—for a nap after lunch?

Who—or *whom*—would you like to be if you weren't yourself?

Has—or *have*—either of your children come home yet?

Do you ever say: "It is *me*"—"It makes me *mad*"—"I *got* sick"—"*Can* I have another helping, please?"—"It will be a *nice* day if it doesn't rain"—"That child *aggravates* me"—"I've *got* an *awful* cold"? And, if so, are you speaking "bad" English?

Do you know when to use *continual* instead of *continuous*? *Let* instead of *leave*? *Incredible* instead of *incredulous*?

15

Imply instead of *infer? Uninterested* instead of *disinterested?*

These are vital, contemporary, and recurrent problems. And grammar offers you a solution to all of them.

If you understand the basic principles of English grammar, you can be assured that your speech will never get in your way. You will know not only *what* to say, but, perhaps more important, *why*.

The world often forms its first impression of you by the way you put words together. And so I expect to explore with you—minutely, specifically, intensively, exhaustively—the proper methods of putting words together, the principles of expressing your ideas in correct English.

No one in his right mind, you will admit, ever stops you at a busy intersection during lunch hour to ask: "Quick, what's an adverb?" Or, "What case of the personal pronoun is used after a preposition?" Or, "When do you make a verb plural?" But if you know the answers to these and similar questions, you have come a long way toward attaining a feeling of complete self-confidence whenever you open your mouth to voice a thought.

And so, the first part of this book is planned as follows:

We will be far more interested—chapter after chapter—in actual problems of correct usage than in theoretical principles of grammar. Each chapter opens with a realistic problem, discusses enough grammar to make the solution to that problem easy to understand and easy to remember, closes with a simply worded rule to guide you whenever the problem occurs in your daily speech, and finally puts you through a searching test to discover whether you understand and can successfully apply all that you've learned.

Between chapters you will find a rambling section labeled optimistically, but, I think, correctly: "As Easy as A B C!" Under *A* we will discuss problems in the grammar of meanings. How does *alumnus* differ in meaning from *alumna?* How does *childish* differ from *childlike?* What is the distinction between *optometrist, oculist,* and *optician?* Between *allude* and *refer?* Between *sensual* and *sensuous?*

16

You have probably often wondered. Now you can be sure.

Under *B*, the grammar of allowable "errors," we will explore the standing of such controversial expressions as "I feel *badly*," "Let's not walk any *further*," "There are *less* people than I expected," and "He is different *than* I thought." Maybe you use such expressions—and feel that you shouldn't. Now you will have ample evidence bearing on the question of their acceptability, and you will be able to speak naturally without feeling a vague sense of guilt.

An allowable "error," as the term will be used throughout Part One, refers to an expression which some old-fashioned grammar texts and many handbooks of speech sweepingly, unrealistically, and stubbornly condemn, despite the wide and general currency which such an expression may have in educated speech. Since the final criterion of correct English is current, educated, usage—not the arbitrary "laws" of grammar manuals—any expression which is commonly used on the cultivated level of language and which can be found in the works of reputable writers is, of course, correct English, puristic and pedantic objections to the contrary notwithstanding.

Let me warn you, however, that you will have to approach this section in a truly scientific and objective spirit.

I shall suggest that the various items coming under the heading of allowable "errors" are perfectly acceptable on the colloquial level—that is, they may be used in everyday conversation, and there is nothing sinful or ungrammatical about them. You do not have to use them, and you may, if you wish, restrict yourself to their more formal equivalents. If you are in the habit of using *mad* with the meaning of *angry*, you will not, the grammar of allowable "errors" will tell you, be speaking "bad" English. On the other hand, if you wish to play safe and avoid such use of *mad*, you have every moral, legal, and linguistic right to do so. What you do not have the right to do, this section will contend, is look down upon an honest citizen who reports that he is *"mad* at his mother-in-law."

Understand, then, that the usages under the grammar of allowable "errors" are not recommended to the exclusion of stricter forms; they are merely offered to you as completely acceptable in your everyday speech.

But you must be scientific and objective. So I shall offer you evidence both pro and con, and you will, as an intelligent adult, exercise your democratic right to make a free choice. To gather this evidence, I sent personal letters to a number of people whose business it is to use the English language as effectively as they know how—editors, authors, radio stars, professors of English, linguists, newspaper columnists, and the like. Some of them have answered that of course the expressions under consideration are good English, that they would have no hesitation in using them in their own speech. Others, on the contrary, have expressed varying degrees of horror. Their replies will be spread out for your consideration and you will be able to decide for yourself whether or not you wish to use these controversial expressions.

Under *C*, the grammar of correct usage, we will talk about a number of specific but isolated questions: "What's the sense (in, of) arguing?" "What (kind of day, kind of a day) is it?" "All I need (is, are) more pictures"? "Two (spoonfuls, spoonsful)"? "The data (is, are) most interesting"?

Our approach to grammar, then, is entirely functional. What mistakes do literate speakers make? What grammatical information do they need in order to avoid such errors? How can they avoid using bad grammar on the one hand, and still steer clear, on the other hand, of a much worse danger—the danger of sounding pedantic, puristic, or "schoolmarmish"? These are the questions which intimately dictate the organization and atmosphere of this book.

I have been fortunate, in the last few years, to be able to work directly, face to face, with a large number of educated people who wish to improve their grammar, their use of their native tongue. My work with these students, adults who have taken my courses at New York University, has taught me what problems most frequently afflict the average

18

literate American. These problems are broadly divisible into four major categories:

1. How to know when to use *me* or *I, he* or *him, she* or *her, we* or *us, they* or *them.*
2. How to be sure of the distinctions between *who* and *whom.*
3. When to say *lay* and when to say *lie.*
4. When to make verbs plural and when to keep them singular. (*Is* or *are? Has* or *have? Was* or *were?*)

The fact that most literate adults are especially confused by these four broad problems of English usage is what makes our study of grammar particularly easy. For the aspects of English covered by such problems are the ones we will hit again and again, the ones we will spend most of our time studying and discussing and exploring and analyzing—to the end that most of the problems which *you* now have in English will eventually vanish.

And we will study only those aspects of formal grammar which will help us to understand and solve the problems of everyday speech.

Understanding and solving these problems will, I must confess, bring to our attention such abstractions as verbs and nouns and the future perfect tense and the subjunctive in conditions contrary to fact; not to mention such matters as case and number and person. But don't be alarmed. The abstractions of grammar are easy enough to understand so long as they are tied up with problems of correct usage, so long as they are not studied just for themselves.

Are you sold on studying grammar?

Then let's begin. . . .

chapter 2 A TEST OF YOUR PRESENT
GRAMMATICAL ABILITY

First I want to test your present grammatical knowledge—
your ability to solve problems of correct usage. I have for
you one hundred questions which will explore your speech
habits, which will probe deeply and mercilessly into the
language patterns you now use.

This is the test with which I confront my students during
the opening session of the course. And how do they make
out? On the average, they come through with a grade of
35 to 50 per cent. You may do about the same. If you do,
that will mean one thing only: not that your English is
"bad," but that your problems are the same as everyone
else's.

At the end of the course I test my students once again.
How much have they learned? Enough to make an average
score of 93 to 98 per cent in the retest. (The retest covers
essentially the same problems but in different contexts.)
When you try the retest at the end of your work, you will
probably do as well.

This is incontrovertible proof, I maintain, that grammar
is easy—if studied properly.

A Pretest of Your Grammatical Ability

Check, in each sentence, the word that you believe is grammatically preferable.

    1. Why does Marilyn Monroe have such a tremen-
       dous (affect, effect) on you?
    2. How does one go about (effecting, affecting) a rec-
       onciliation between husband and wife?
    3. You come up here at least twice a week to see me;

why do you make such (continuous, continual) demands on my time?

4. What with our high income taxes, I can't see the sense (in, of) trying to make an honest dollar any more.
5. I wish you would (let, leave) me go.
6. What (kind of, kind of a) fool do you think she is?
7. The Colonial Diner is one of the (principle, principal) eating places in town.
8. The murderer will be (hung, hanged) at dawn.
9. (Mother-in-laws, Mothers-in-law) are probably the most unpopular of all relatives.
10. Doris Garn told an (incredulous, incredible) story of her experiences in book publishing.
11. Take two (spoonsful, spoonfuls, spoons full) of arsenic, mix with an ounce of cyanide, stir well in a glassful of orange juice, and drink before retiring.
12. Are you trying to (imply, infer) that Charlotte is flirting with Mimi's husband?
13. (It's, Its) the first hundred years that are the hardest.
14. No one but (she, her) could possibly love such a man.
15. I've spoken to everyone except (he, him).
16. Between you, (I, me), and the lamppost, she's making a fool of you.
17. Is this book for Helen and (I, me)?
18. Why did you (rob, steal) that money?
19. (Those, That) data (are, is) inconclusive.
20. Harry Simon has a little (stationery, stationary) store on North Avenue.
21. Vitamins are thought to be an excellent (preventative, preventive) of disease.
22. Bea is a most naïve and (ingenious, ingenuous) person.
23. Do you really think that Jules speaks just like (I, me)?
24. The cost of new houses (is, are) dropping every day.

25. There (was, were) a man and a woman waiting for you.
26. One of his cousins (comes, come) from Boston.
27. The senator, with his clerks and secretaries, (draw, draws) a whacking salary from the treasury every week.
28. Your appearance as well as your personality (is, are) against you.
29. Florence, like her sisters and parents, (has, have) red hair.
30. (Has, Have) either of your friends come in yet?
31. Each of the men (was, were) given thirty lashes.
32. Boatload after boatload of refugees (was, were) stopped.
33. Neither of your answers (is, are) correct.
34. Allan, unlike his rich relatives, (has, have) to live economically.
35. A captain and a lieutenant (is, are) coming to see you tonight.
36. The manager or his assistant (is, are) always in the store.
37. Neither your money nor your influence (is, are) of any use to you now.
38. Either Dr. Jaffe or one of our other podiatrists (is, are) coming up to see you tomorrow.
39. He's very (childish, childlike); if he doesn't get his own way, he sulks.
40. I think one or two of the men (is, are) here already.
41. Myrtle and (I, me) would like to pay you a visit tonight.
42. Can you visit Estelle and (I, me) some evening?
43. I'm (uninterested, disinterested) in hearing about your personal troubles.
44. A number of cases (was, were) settled out of court.
45. Please (lie, lay) down.
46. (Lie, Lay) the baby in the crib.
47. His genius (lay, laid) dormant all during his marriage.

22

48. You've (laid, lain) the rug on the floor of the wrong room.
49. If she had (laid, lain) quiet, she would not have been hurt.
50. He (lay, laid) his hand on my shoulder and spoke in a confidential tone.
51. If you would (lay, lie) down for a while, you might feel better.
52. When you (lie, lay) in a new store of canned goods, let me know.
53. He was (lying, laying) down for a nap when the phone rang.
54. His (fiancée, fiancé) has red hair.
55. Three-quarters of the rent (is, are) due when you sign the lease.
56. A majority of the members (has, have) promised to vote for you.
57. It was (she, her) I was referring to, not you.
58. George, together with his whole family, (is, are) coming up the steps.
59. Was it (she, her) who lost her husband?
60. (Who, Whom) do you think you are, anyway?
61. (Who, Whom) are you looking at?
62. I want to speak to (whoever, whomever) answers the phone.
63. His brother, (who, whom) I met in Istanbul, is much richer than you think.
64. (Who, Whom) would you rather be, if you weren't you?
65. He has finally found a teacher (who, whom) he believes can handle that class.
66. (Who, Whom) do you want to see?
67. Your brother is shorter than (I, me).
68. I'm just as good as (he, him).
69. Neither he nor I (am, is, are) your friend.
70. We have (swam, swum) for over an hour.
71. Have you (drank, drunk) all your milk?
72. Young children are generally (sensuous, sensual) in their approach to life.

73. You should (of, have) come on time if you wanted to see him.
74. He talks as if he (was, were) my keeper.
75. I'm not thinking of her lack of beauty; it's just that I wish she (was, were) richer.
76. If your husband (was, were) more considerate, he wouldn't talk that way to you.
77. If the doctor (was, were) in all morning, why didn't he phone me?
78. What would you like for (dessert, desert)?
79. Why do you continue to (prosecute, persecute) me so?
80. I'm not very hungry; (beside, besides) I don't like fish.
81. She's one of those women who never (say, says) die.
82. She doesn't live here (any, no) more.
83. That (ain't, isn't) the way to act.
84. We (have, haven't) hardly any money left.
85. I'm going (irregardless, regardless).
86. (This, This here) book doesn't help me any.
87. Have you got a (better, more better) one?
88. I thought you (was, were) a gentleman in every sense of the word.
89. Did you get an (invitation, invite) to her party?
90. If I (hadn't, hadn't of) seen it with my own eyes, I wouldn't have believed it.
91. He (don't, doesn't) act the way he should.
92. I'm going to give you some (council, counsel).
93. It is I who (am, is) the only friend you've got.
94. The most striking thing about Eden is her (luxurious, luxuriant) black hair.
95. Let (he, him) who is without sin cast the first stone.
96. Some economists are (prophesying, prophecying) a continuing period of prosperity.
97. What we need (is, are) bigger salaries for the working classes.
98. Two thousand dollars (is, are) too much for that car.

99. (Who, Whom) did you believe him to be?
100. The memoranda (is, are) on your desk.

ANSWERS

1. effect
2. effecting
3. continual
4. in
5. let
6. kind of
7. principal
8. hanged
9. mothers-in-law
10. incredible
11. spoonfuls
12. imply
13. it's
14. her
15. him
16. me
17. me
18. steal
19. those, are
20. stationery
21. preventive
22. ingenuous
23. me
24. is
25. were
26. comes
27. draws
28. is
29. has
30. has
31. was
32. was
33. is

34. has
35. are
36. is
37. is
38. is
39. childish
40. are
41. I
42. me
43. uninterested
44. were
45. lie
46. lay
47. lay
48. laid
49. lain
50. laid
51. lie
52. lay
53. lying
54. fiancée
55. is
56. have
57. she
58. is
59. she
60. who
61. whom
62. whoever
63. whom
64. who
65. who
66. whom
67. I

68. he
69. am
70. swum
71. drunk
72. sensuous
73. have
74. were
75. were
76. were
77. was
78. dessert
79. persecute
80. besides
81. say
82. any
83. isn't
84. have
85. regardless
86. this
87. better
88. were
89. invitation
90. hadn't
91. doesn't
92. counsel
93. am
94. luxuriant
95. him
96. prophesying
97. is
98. is
99. whom
100. are

SCORING

Each correct choice counts 1 point.

YOUR SCORE ON THE PRETEST:................ (Record the result on page 13.)

Your grammar has been tested and you know where you stand.

Now let's get to work.

chapter 3 HOW TO DELIVER THE MESSAGE TO GARCIA

1. The Problem

What is the difference between *effect* and *affect?*

2. The Solution

The essential difference is this:
Affect is usually a *verb*.
Effect is usually a *noun*.
But what is a verb?
A verb is one of the eight different categories into which all the words in the English language are grammatically divisible.

These eight categories are:

1. noun	4. adjective	7. conjunction
2. verb	5. adverb	8. interjection
3. pronoun	6. preposition	

Every one of these terms is an inheritance from Latin, a language used two thousand and more years ago by a comparatively small segment of the human race inhabiting a boot-shaped peninsula, a projection of the south end of Europe—a peninsula which we now call Italy.

The people who spoke this ancient tongue were Romans, so called after their capital city, *Roma*, or Rome.

The Romans were no slouches. You have, of course, heard of Caesar and Cicero. If you are of a literary bent of mind, you have perhaps also heard of Horace and Pliny and Livy and Marcus Aurelius. And Brutus.

The Romans left their mark on the world. The eighth month of the year is named after one of the emperors, Augustus Caesar. July is named after another emperor—Julius Caesar. To say nothing of roads and laws and codes of justice—for all of which we are in debt to the ancient Romans.

A good half of the Latin vocabulary found its way, at one time or another, into English. And some of the Latin rules of grammar.

The Latin language was imposed, by the conquering Romans, on a number of their defenseless neighbors. And today French, Italian, Spanish, Portuguese, and Rumanian are Latin tongues in modern dress.

But not English. English is a Germanic language, the modern version of the tongue spoken by the invading Angles, Saxons, and Jutes, the Teutonic hordes which swept Britain centuries ago.

The language you speak today is a variant of Germanic—but the grammatical terminology is almost wholly Latin.

The eight categories into which English words are divided are identical with the categories of Latin words—and the names for these divisions are English renditions of Latin terms.

These categories are called *parts of speech.*

Noun is from the Latin *nomen,* name.

Pronoun adds the Latin prefix *pro,* meaning *for.* As we shall discover, a pronoun is used for, or in place of, a noun.

An *adjective,* by literal translation from the Latin, is a word thrown (*ject*) toward (*ad*) a noun.

An *adverb* is thrown toward a verb.

A *preposition* is a word placed (*posit*) before (*pre*) a noun.

A *conjunction* acts to join (*junc*) words together (*con*).

An *interjection* is literally a word thrown (*ject*) between (*inter*).

And the *verb?* Verb is from the Latin *verbum,* word.

That a verb is simply called *a word* attests to its importance.

That is why we start our study of English grammar by analysis of the verb.

(And, incidentally, you cannot intelligently appreciate the distinction between *effect* and *affect* without understanding the function, the atmosphere, the appearance of a verb.)

An important part of every idea is the verb.

It is the verb that delivers the message to Garcia—it is the verb that gets your idea across.

In one of the most electrifying statements of World War II, "Sighted Sub, Sank Same," two of the four words are verbs—and the message of that statement is wrapped up in, and stems from, those two verbs.

You can best appreciate the importance of the verb by examining the front page of your daily paper. The headlines are designed to get messages to you in the quickest, most economical, most dynamic form. And every headline is built around a verb.

Let us look at some headlines from an issue of *The New York Times:*

Atom Bomb *Sinks* Battleship in Second Test
Soviet Flatly *Rejects* Baruch Control Plan
Robber *Kills* Wife of Banker in Home

In each headline, the italicized word is the verb. *Sinks, rejects, kills*—these are the pivots on which the headlines swing.

The verb is the pivotal word of the sentence.

Actions speak louder than words, claims the old proverb. And of the eight different kinds of words in the English language, verbs speak the loudest—because verbs are words of action. You can understand then how easy it is to spot the verb in a sentence—look for the word of action.

Study these headlines from the *Times*. Again each verb is italicized.

Asks Job Freedom in the Constitution
Plane Barely *Misses* Empire State
City Board *Faces* a Heavy Calendar

DO YOU GET THE POINT?—*test 1*

Action, completion, movement, fulfillment—these are the attributes of the verb. If you will look for these qualities, you will successfully spot the single verb in each of the following headlines. Underline the verb in each case.

1. Vegetarian Shouts "Foul" over Shaw Dinner's Fowl
2. College Gets Army Check
3. Ships Bob Around in Blast like Toys
4. British Fear Move for Ouster in Iran
5. Philippine Envoy Hails U.S.

Advertisements are carefully planned, by highly skilled and highly paid writers, to get a message across to you as forcefully as possible. As you would suspect, most ads also rely heavily on verbs. Can you spot the single verb in each of the following?

6. Protect Your Fine Summer Lingerie in Dainty Cotton Cases   (Henri Bendel)
7. Outwit Boredom at Dinnertime
      (Longchamps)
8. Night and Day, You'll Talk about "Night and Day"
      (Hollywood Theater)
9. Use in Place of Wax
      (Surface-Nu)
10. Wait for the New Canaday Frigidaire Water Coolers
      (Canaday Cooler Company)

CHECK YOUR LEARNING—*answers to test 1*

Here are the answers. Did you make at least eight proper choices?

1. shouts	3. bob	5. hails	7. outwit	9. use
2. gets	4. fear	6. protect	8. talk	10. wait

The ability to spot a verb will stand you in good stead throughout your study of English grammar. I shall not pretend that, because you have successfully identified the verbs in the preceding sentences, you are *ipso facto* (more Latin influence) an expert on verbs—there is much more to learn about this part of speech before you can qualify for such a rating. But you have come far if you can correctly identify the verb of a sentence. To make sure you are beginning to get your hand in, try one more test of your ability to recognize English verbs.

DO YOU GET THE POINT?—*test 2*

Check the single verb in each of the following sentences.

1. Senator Bilbo ran for the office of U.S. Senator.
2. The people of Mississippi elected him to that office.
3. But Senator Taft challenged Bilbo's right to the seat.
4. Certain Southern Democrats threatened a filibuster.
5. Taft invoked the law of cloture.
6. Upon a roll-call vote, the Senate refused admittance to the Mississippian.
7. Such action came as no surprise—except, perhaps, to Bilbo.
8. With his death, Bilbo may now be forgotten.
9. The other Mississippi Senator, James O. Eastland, still holds his seat.
10. *The Saturday Evening Post* published an interesting article about John E. Rankin, a Mississippi Congressman, in the spring of 1947.

CHECK YOUR LEARNING—*answers to test 2*

1. ran	5. invoked	8. may be
2. elected	6. refused	forgotten
3. challenged	7. came	9. holds
4. threatened		10. published

In sentence 8, the verb is made up of several words, *may*, *be*, and *forgotten*. Such an instance is called a *verb phrase*.

The word *now*, which splits the parts of the verb phrase, indicates *time* and is an adverb.

To get back to *effect* and *affect:*

Affect is usually a *verb*.

Note its verbal force in the following sentences:

His actions *affect* me strangely.
How *does* the weather *affect* your business?
Prices *will be* adversely *affected* by declining demand.
Has your income *been affected* by the relaxation of federal controls?
Your action cannot help but *affect* your standing in the community.

Note that there were verb phrases in some of the preceding sentences: *does affect; will be affected; has been affected*. A verb phrase is made up of one or more *auxiliaries*, or helping verbs, and the main verb. *Does, will be, has been* are auxiliary verbs.

Can you appreciate that in each of the preceding sentences *affect* is used as a verb? If you now have a feeling for verbs, you are ready to go on to an understanding of *effect*, the noun. That will be our central problem in chapter 4.

as easy as A B C

A. What is the difference between *continual* and *continuous?*

B. Is it correct to say, "He *got* sick"?

C. Which is preferable: "What's the sense *of* arguing?" or "What's the sense *in* arguing?"

A. The Grammar of Meanings

Continual, Continuous

Continual bickering goes on, with few breaks, over a period of time. There may be occasional cessations, but not for long.

Continual warfare implies successive battles, skirmishes, raids, attacks and counterattacks, again over an extended period.

Continual rain indicates a series of rains, with short spells of fair weather intervening between the frequent storms.

Continual refers only to time, and indicates a series of successive actions.

Continuous, on the other hand, implies unbroken, uninterrupted movement.

Continuous bickering allows for no moment of peace.

Continuous warfare indicates no cessation of fighting.

Continuous rain means that the rain never stops.

Continuous may refer to space as well as time—a *continuous* line, a *continuous* stretch of narrow land, a *continuous* expanse of desert.

The two words are close in meaning, but the distinction in *implication* is very strong. *Continual* describes one thing after another; *continuous* describes one unending thing.

1. A (continuous, continual) application of hot packs, three or four every hour for two days, will alleviate your congested condition.
2. His (continuous, continual) rejection of the applications from the home office has raised the manager's ire.
3. Her (continuous, continual) criticism of his work, whenever he brought his manuscripts home, completely demoralized him.
4. The rain came down (continuously, continually); not for five minutes did the storm abate.
5. There was a long (continuous, continual) ring on the "intercom" phone, followed by four short rings.
6. Not a sound broke the stillness; the (continuous, continual) silence was unnerving.
7. There were (continuous, continual) fights in the upstairs apartment—at breakfast, lunch, and supper the sounds of conflict came through to the tenants on all sides.

CHECK YOUR LEARNING—*answers to test 3*

1. continual   4. continuously   6. continuous
2. continual   5. continuous   7. continual
3. continual

B. The Grammar of Allowable "Errors"

He *got* sick.

Pedantic grammar maintains that the verb *get* has only one meaning: *to obtain.* In actuality, *get* has over a score of different meanings and uses, as any large dictionary will attest. One of the most acceptable and current of its meanings is as a synonym for *become,* as in "He *got* rich," "You will *get* sick if you overeat," "She *got* well when she took the medicine," "I *get* dizzy when I climb so high." These uses of *get* are perfectly correct in everyday, informal speech.

PRO AND CON

Q. Many modern grammarians maintain that "I *got* sick" is correct, idiomatic English. Do you agree?

Pro

A. I am one of the modern grammarians who maintain "I *got* sick" to be correct and idiomatic English.
—Donald L. Clark

Donald Clark is professor of English at Columbia University, conductor of Writer's Workshop Courses, and co-author of *Magazine Article Writing.*

Pro (with reservations)

A. I would agree that the expression "I got sick" is more or less correct idiomatic English. The degree of education of the people among whom it is established would be open to question. But certainly such usage of "got" is very common these days in America even though it is frowned upon in England. Surely I have nothing against it, and I have always felt that language is made so that people could say what they mean.

For my own part, I don't use that form, but, as I said, I see no real reason why I shouldn't, if I wanted to.
—Howard Fast

Howard Fast is the author of *Freedom Road, The American, Citizen Tom Paine,* and other best-selling novels.

Pro (with reservations)

A. We are not much concerned with the individual characteristics of coins used in the everyday business of life. One nickel will do just as well as another for the purpose for which we have destined it. We may stop to consider the coin if it is newly struck or designed, but only for a brief time. After a little it sinks again into the category of a class of things. Its purpose alone counts, its individuality does not.

The word *get,* in the sense of *become,* as in others of its meaning, is common coin. It is as unobtrusive as a particular nickel in transmitting an idea. It in itself does not catch the eye or thought.

When a boy has *got* sick, he has reached a state different from a previous one. *Get* serves merely in a general way to show that he is not now as he was before. But suppose you wish to call attention to the particular circumstance in which the change occurred. *Get,* the overall term, may turn out to be an inadequate spokesman for your point. The boy *turns* sick to his stomach at a *sudden* realization of adversity. He *grows* sick with fear as the hours of anxiety *wear on.* As he *becomes* sick he has to play less and exercise less *in the process. Get* will serve in each of these cases, but it will do no more than serve. It does not particularize, and so does not somehow evoke the same feeling as the other words in the individual instance. It is not the *mot juste.* In short, it lacks color in the sense that it does not command attention by narrowing down the situation.

All this does not mean that *get* is a disreputable item in the English vocabulary or in good usage. It is a "utility tool" and not a "precision instrument." It should be used as such and not disdained. You will find it in the dictionary defined as "to become," and you will meet it frequently in this sense even in a most casual perusal of good English writing.

—Bernard Levy

Dr. Levy is a professor of romance languages at the College of the City of New York, and director of the Adult Education Program of City College. He is the author of a number of college textbooks.

C. *The Grammar of Correct Usage*

> What's the sense *of* arguing? *or*
> What's the sense *in* arguing?

Idiomatically, *sense*, meaning *logic* or *sensibleness* (as it does in this sentence), is followed by *in:*

He has no sense *in* his head.
There's no sense *in* your going out.
What's the sense *in* talking to such a man?
Where's the sense *in* doing that?
I don't see any sense *in* acting that way.

However, if *sense* signifies *meaning,* it is followed by *of:*

Can you get the sense *of* that poem?

PREFERABLE FORMS:

What's the sense *in* arguing?
There's no sense *in* walking if you can ride.

chapter 4 HOW TO CALL A NAME

1. *The Problem Repeated*

What is the difference between *effect* and *affect?*

2. *The Solution Continued*

Affect is usually a verb.

Effect is, with an exception to be noted shortly, a *noun.*
But what is a noun?

Look about you—everything you see is a *noun.*

Recall the names of your friends, relatives, business associates—they are all *nouns.*

Pore over a map—every city, state, and country; every village, county, and town; every river, bay, and inlet; geographical divisions large and small, from Kennebunkport, Maine, to Los Angeles, California, from London to Yalta, from Nagasaki to Pinsk—all these are *nouns.*

Everything is a *noun.*

Persons are nouns:

Chester Bowles	Protestant	man
Harry S. Truman	Catholic	woman
George Bernard Shaw	Jew	child

Places are nouns:

Speonk	Tallahassee	Champs Élysées
Broadway	Coral Gables	Mastic Beach
Dubuque	Stebbins Avenue	City College

Things are nouns:

cigarettes	television sets	white shirts
prime ribs of beef	brassieres	inlaid linoleum
Chevrolets	wrist watches	typewriters

Abstract qualities, ideas, emotions, concepts, and activities are nouns:

sex	the Democratic and Republican parties
politics	
war	fascism and antifascism
food	The Unit System in Georgia and the Kulak System in Russia
clothing	
shelter	
fear, hate, courage, love	

You are a noun, and I am a noun, although the words *you* and *I* are not generally nouns, but *pronouns*. *Word* itself is a noun, although not every word in the language is a noun.

If all this sounds a little mixed up, don't worry. Nouns and verbs are the sort of things you soon develop an instinct for. If you bear in mind that verbs are words that show action, and nouns are the names of persons, places, things, ideas, concepts, or activities, you will shortly be able to spot nouns and verbs without half trying.

Study this paragraph from *The New York Times* (the nouns are italicized):

During the German *occupation* of *Denmark* a *novel* was published in *Copenhagen* with the unsuspicious *approval* of the Nazi *censors*. Since it was a quaint and romantic *story* of two innocent young *girls* and their mysterious *adventures* in the *year 1840* it is hardly surprising that to German *eyes* it seemed unpolitical. It wouldn't be surprising if it seemed so to *Danes* or to *Americans*, either. But the *Danes* must be more subtle *folk* than is generally their *reputation*, or else *life* beneath German *rule* must marvelously quicken allegorical *sensitivity*, for in *Denmark* "*The Angelic Avengers*" by *Pierre Andrezel* was greeted with *joy* as a neat *thrust* of *irony* at the *Germans'* *expense*. The *question* then was:

did the *Germans* fail to get it, or were they smart enough to refuse to admit that it concerned them?

—Orville Prescott, "Books of the Times," January 3, 1947

In these five sentences there are twenty-eight different nouns—names of people, things, places, ideas, concepts, or activities.

PEOPLE	PLACES	THINGS	IDEAS, CONCEPTS, OR ACTIVITIES
censors	Denmark	novel	occupation
girls	Copenhagen	eyes	approval
Danes			story
Americans			adventures
folk			year
Pierre Andrezel			1840
Germans			reputation
Germans'			life
			rule
			sensitivity
			"The Angelic Avengers"
			joy
			thrust
			irony
			expense
			question

The same five sentences contain seventeen verbs, as follows:

Sentence 1: was published
Sentence 2: was, is, seemed
Sentence 3: would be (*a verb phrase*), seemed
Sentence 4: must be, is, must quicken, was greeted
Sentence 5: was, did, fail, to get, were, to refuse, to admit, concerned

Verbs like *was, must be, would be, seemed* may not appear to you to show very much direct action. As a matter of fact, there is one type of verb, called *copulative* (another Latin-born term) which shows *a state of being* rather than action, and *is, was, must be, seem* are, among others, verbs of this type.

Is your instinct for nouns and verbs beginning to develop? Try a test to make sure.

DO YOU GET THE POINT?—*test 4*

Check twenty-two nouns in the following paragraph. Count each noun even if it is repeated in two or more sentences or phrases.

At first all went well. Mr. Pennhollow taught the girls Latin and history. But soon vague suspicions began to infest the atmosphere. Was the old man as benevolent as he seemed? What had become of the other young girls he had befriended? Why was Clon, the moronic servant boy, so frightened? Why did the provincial judge charge so benign a person with such preposterous wickedness? When all these questions were suddenly answered stark terror overcame the girls. Mr. Pennhollow was evil incarnate, a murderer, white-slaver and worshiper of the devil himself.

—Orville Prescott, *ibid.*

Now look for the verbs.

1 verb in sentence 1 ....
1 verb in sentence 2 ....
2 verbs in sentence 3 ...., ...
2 verbs in sentence 4 ...., ...
2 verbs in sentence 5 ...., ...
1 verb in sentence 6 ....
1 verb in sentence 7 ....
2 verbs in sentence 8 ...., ...
1 verb in sentence 9 ....

1. Mr. Pennhollow	9. Clon	17. Mr. Pennhollow
2. girls	10. boy	18. evil
3. Latin	11. judge	19. murderer
4. history	12. person	20. white-slaver
5. suspicions	13. wickedness	21. worshiper
6. atmosphere	14. questions	22. devil
7. man	15. terror	
8. girls	16. girls	

1. went	6. was
2. taught	7. did charge
3. began, to infest	8. were answered, overcame
4. was, seemed	
5. had become, had befriended	9. was

How did it go? If you made any errors, they were of two possible kinds:

1. You may have failed to recognize a few of the nouns and verbs in the paragraph; or
2. Perhaps you checked words which are not nouns and verbs.

Study carefully your sins of omission or commission. Let your errors help you to get a more certain feeling for nouns and verbs. And in any case, understand that if your work was 50 per cent accurate or better you are doing very well—you have developed a sufficient instinct for nouns and verbs so that we can intelligently proceed with a further analysis of *effect*, the noun, and *affect*, the verb.

This is still early in the game, but your mind is gradually becoming attuned to seeing differences in function between nouns and verbs. Note in the following sentences how *effect*, the noun, is used as the name of a concept, while *affect*, the verb, is used to show a kind of action.

42

NOUN: The *effect* of the war was widespread.
VERB: Everyone *was affected* by the war.

NOUN: What *effect* does education have on the mind?
VERB: How *does* education *affect* the mind?

NOUN: The tremendous *effect* of the atom bomb on the people of Hiroshima has been graphically chronicled by novelist John Hersey.
VERB: How the atom bomb *affected* the people of Hiroshima has been graphically chronicled by novelist John Hersey.

As a noun, *effect* generally means *result* or *influence*.
As a verb, *affect* generally means *to influence* or *to change*.

There is, in addition, one special instance in which *effect* is a verb. In this instance it does not mean *to influence* or *change*, but *to bring about*. For example:

1. We must *effect* better relations with Russia if we wish to avoid another war.

Are better relations with Russia now in existence? No—we must bring them about; we must *effect* them. (But there are many different conditions which will *affect* our relations with Russia.)

2. Doctors have not yet learned to *effect* a cure for cancer.

Is there now a cure for cancer? No—doctors must learn to bring one about, to *effect* one.

3. He will try to *effect* a reconciliation between Tommy Manville and his latest estranged wife.

Is such a reconciliation now in existence? No—he will try to bring it into existence.

Affect, the verb, has an additional meaning to the one we have been discussing, namely *to make a pretense of,* as in "He *affects* a British accent."

With the grammatical background you now have, you will find the rule about *effect* and *affect* easy to understand.

3. The Rule

Is a *noun* required? Use *effect.*
Is a *verb* required? Use *affect.*
However, is a *verb* required with the meaning of *bring about* or *cause?* Use *effect.*
In general usage, affect is never a noun.[1]

4. The Test

Now if you have followed the material in these pages step by step, you should have no difficulty in making a perfect score in the next exercise, which tests your ability to avoid errors in using *affect* and *effect.*

DO YOU GET THE POINT?—*test 5*

Check the correct word in each sentence.

1. What (effect, affect) did a Republican congress have on Truman's program?
2. How would a new round of strikes (effect, affect) the general business picture next year?
3. The picture (effected, affected) him deeply.
4. Penicillin can (effect, affect) a cure within twenty-four hours.
5. Do you think doctors will ever (effect, affect) a cure for polio?
6. His illness has (effected, affected) him in many ways.
7. Why does he (effect, affect) such effeminate mannerisms?

[1] There is a noun *affect,* with a specialized technical meaning, in psychological parlance. You need not concern yourself with it.

44

8. His presence had a tremendous (effect, affect) on the audience.
9. Do you think Edmund Wilson's *Memoirs of Hecate County* has a libidinous (effect, affect) on adolescents?
10. And how do you think the same book (effects, affects) adults?

CHECK YOUR LEARNING—*answers to test 5*

1. effect
2. affect
3. affected
4. effect

5. effect
6. affected
7. affect

8. effect
9. effect
10. affects

You should have made a perfect score on this test. If you were guilty of any errors, study your mistakes, review the pertinent information in the chapter, and then check yourself once again on the following test.

DO YOU GET THE POINT?—*test 6*

1. Your insults do not (effect, affect) me.
2. Dr. Bruno Furst, the eminent memory expert, has a dynamic (effect, affect) on his students.
3. *Forever Amber* created an (effect, affect) that was felt throughout the country.
4. The picture contains many lovely scenic (effects, affects).
5. Ann Matteo's story (effected, affected) us all deeply.
6. The war has (effected, affected) every family in the city.
7. If we can (effect, affect) a certain measure of economic security for all families, this nation will be a much happier one.
8. Why do Syd and Mimi (effect, affect) that silly pseudo-Southern accent?
9. Your plan will have far-reaching (effects, affects).
10. What you say will never (effect, affect) our decision.

11. If you can (effect, affect) a reconciliation between Doris and Bernard, you are a miracle man.
12. How does the weather (effect, affect) you?

CHECK YOUR LEARNING—*answers to test 6*

1. affect	5. affected	9. effects
2. effect	6. affected	10. affect
3. effect	7. effect	11. effect
4. effects	8. affect	12. affect

as easy as A B C

A. What is the difference between *let* and *leave*?
B. Is it correct to say, "Don't get *mad* if I tell you the truth"?
C. Which is preferable: "What *kind of day* is it?" or "What *kind of a day* is it?"

A. The Grammar of Meanings

Let, Leave

The distinction between these two words is largely a matter of idiom, though in general *leave* means *to depart* and *let* means *to allow*. Thus:

LET, *to allow:*
Let us go, *not Leave* us go.
Let him work tomorrow, *not Leave* him work tomorrow.
Let us be friends, *not Leave* us be friends.

LEAVE, *to depart:*
We will *leave* the house by two o'clock.
We'll *leave* for the coast tomorrow.
Has he *left* town yet?

Idiomatically, *let* is used in patterns like the following:

Let me alone (*or Leave* me alone).
Let me be.
Let him in.
The dog was *let* loose.

The cat was *let* out of the bag.
Let me off at Fifth Avenue.

Idiomatically, *leave* is used in these patterns:

Leave a tip.
Leave a legacy.
Five minus three *leaves* two.
Leave him alone (*or Let* him alone).
It *leaves* me cold.
Leave your work on my desk.

DO YOU GET THE POINT?—*test 7*

1. (Let, Leave) us not talk about it any more.
2. Why don't you (let, leave) Gary play with Margie?
3. (Let, Leave) him go.
4. (Let, Leave) her be.
5. (Let, Leave) them alone.
6. (Let, Leave) some money for the grocer.
7. He (let, left) the cat out of the bag at that time.

CHECK YOUR LEARNING—*answers to test 7*

1 to 4 = let, 5 = *either* let *or* leave, 6 = leave, 7 = let

B. The Grammar of Allowable "Errors"

Don't get *mad* if I tell you the truth.

Yes, *mad* means insane, when the word is used with that meaning. When we say *mad dog,* we do not mean an angry dog, and when we speak of a *madman,* we do not refer to someone in a fit of pique.

When we report that Jane is *mad* about men, it is true that we imply a mild (but understandable and not at all dangerous) form of insanity, rather than a condition of rage or anger.

In *Alice in Wonderland,* Humpty-Dumpty claims that a word means exactly what he intends it to mean, no more

48

nor less. Such an arbitrary criterion would of course lead to a certain degree of confusion if it were applied to ordinary communication; however, it is a fact that words do mean exactly what people *understand* them to mean, no more nor less.

And one thing people understand *mad* to mean, in addition to *demented*, is *angry*—provided the word is used in certain patterns:

That kind of talk makes me *mad*.
Don't get *mad* if your wife burns your supper.
He's *mad* at his father.

Such patterns are idiomatic, current, and acceptable; and in each instance the hearer understands *mad* to be synonymous with *angry*. The worst that can be said about *mad*, with such a clearly discernible meaning, is that it should not be followed by the preposition *on*. "He's mad on his brother" is an illiterate pattern, and particularly common in childhood parlance. (Typical childhood phrasing of the idea would be as follows: "I'm not mad on him any more. I'm glad on him today." Children, as you've discovered if you have any between the ages of five and eight, are alternately "mad" and "glad on" each other—apparently without any reason comprehensible to an adult. But people of all ages speak of having "a mad on," and women of a certain cast of mind make sure to keep some "mad money" handy—in case of an emergency.)

PRO AND CON

Q. Many modern grammarians maintain that "He is *mad* at his sister" is correct, idiomatic English established by common usage among educated people. Do you agree?

Pro (with reservations)

A. Although "He is mad at his sister" may to some extent be sanctioned by usage, I do not think that a Pater or

49

a Cabell or a Cather or anyone at all punctilious in the use of English would care to use it. In time it may become incorporated in the best English but I do not think that time has arrived as yet.

—William Bradley Otis

William Bradley Otis is professor of English at the College of the City of New York and author of a number of textbooks on English and American literature.

Pro (with reservations)

A. I am willing to concede that "He is mad at his sister" may have become correct English through common usage, but I would never dream of using it myself. I don't like the sound of it.

—Bennett Cerf

Mr. Cerf is president of Random House, book publishers, and is the compiler of innumerable anthologies, including *Anything for a Laugh* and *Try and Stop Me.*

G. The Grammar of Correct Usage

What *kind of day* is it? *or*
What *kind of a day* is it?

The word *a* is considered unnecessary, following "what kind," "what sort," or "what type," and is rarely heard in educated speech, although it is prevalent in illiterate language patterns.

PREFERABLE FORMS:

What *kind of book* do you want?
What *sort of fool* do you think I am?
What *type of dress* should she wear?

chapter 5 HOW TO BE EXPLICIT

1. The Problem

What is the difference between *principal* and *principle?*

2. The Solution

Our new problem involves an understanding of a third part of speech—the *adjective.*

But what is an *adjective?*

The word *adjective,* you recall, is formed from two Latin elements: *ad,* toward; and *ject,* thrown.

An adjective is a word thrown toward a noun.

This description may sound somewhat violent and inelegant, so let us use the correct grammatical terminology. To wit:

An adjective *modifies* a noun.

And what does *modify* mean?

The term *modify,* as used in grammar, is synonymous with *limiting.*

An adjective *limits* a noun. It makes the noun more explicit.

The noun *book* is general; it may refer to any book printed since Gutenberg invented movable type.

Let us limit our classification by calling it "an *obscene* book."

Now we are being more explicit.

An *obscene* book would refer to a more specialized category of reading matter—perhaps *The Memoirs of Fannie Hill, a Woman of Pleasure.* (This is a classic and very famous piece of pornography reputedly written by Samuel Clelland in the reign of Queen Victoria. And, so the story goes, the British government offered its author a pension for life if he would stop writing. The original, profusely illustrated, edition is, as you can imagine, a collector's item.)

The description *obscene* may refer to *The Life and Loves of Frank Harris*, or to D. H. Lawrence's *Lady Chatterley's Lover* (unexpurgated), or to *Memoirs of Hecate County* by Edmund Wilson (banned in New York), or even to *Forever Amber* by Kathleen Winsor (banned in Boston), such classification depending, of course, on your moral and literary point of view.

Hollywood is fond of adjectives. A new picture (noun) may be described by such words as *colossal* (adjective), *sensational* (adjective), *supercolossal* (adjective), *stupendous, thrill-packed, unforgettable* (adjectives). In Hollywood parlance, these adjectives would signify that a picture is tolerably good, or at least it cost a lot of money to produce.

The part of speech of a word depends entirely on its function within the sentence. The word *list*, for example, can be a noun, a verb, or an adjective, according to its use.

NOUN (the name of a concept) : The *list* is complete.
VERB (a conveyor of action) : We will *list* your name.
ADJECTIVE (a modifier of a noun) : The *list* price is high.

Certain words are conventionally considered as static parts of speech, with other forms of the same word assuming the functions of other parts of speech. Thus:

NOUN	VERB	ADJECTIVE
resistance	to resist	irresistible

(But of course *resistance* would be an adjective in: "He is a member of the *resistance* movement.")

player	to play	playful
argument	to argue	argumentative
nation	to nationalize	national

52

Identifying adjectives in a sentence is child's play. In the following short paragraph, study the italicized adjectives. The arrow leads to the noun (or pronoun) which each adjective modifies.

"Mr. Blandings Builds His Dream House" is illustrated, by WILLIAM STEIG, in very much the *same* mood of *quiet* desperation with which it is written. If a book that keeps one *wreathed* in smiles throughout can be described as a *funny* book, that is what *Mr. Blandings* is. But if you want to go and get *philosophical* (we do) it is the story of a *universal* experience. It is the story of a *gentle* creature trying to build its nest in the midst of *whirring* machinery—the machinery of *jungle* ethics and *slaughterhouse* manners that a man encounters dealing with land and landlords.

—An ad by Simon and Schuster in the
Saturday Review of Literature, January 6, 1946

Dream is not italicized, since the full title of a book is usually considered a single noun. However, in any other context, *dream house* would consist of the noun *house* and its modifying adjective *dream*.

Now that you've learned how to find adjectives, find some for yourself.

DO YOU GET THE POINT?—*test 8*

Find seven adjectives in the following paragraph (you

realize, of course, that a noun can be modified by more than one adjective). Draw an arrow to the noun that each adjective modifies.

At *Essandess* there are several amateur country gentlemen who have been staggering through the soul-searing, manic experience of building or remodeling a country home. You can tell them apart from the others by the look of vague pain on their faces.

—Same ad

CHECK YOUR LEARNING—*answers to test 8*

1. *several,* modifies gentlemen
2. *amateur,* modifies gentlemen
3. *country,* modifies gentlemen
4. *soul-searing,* modifies experience
5. *manic,* modifies experience
6. *country,* modifies home
7. *vague,* modifies pain

Note 1: *Country,* which might conventionally be considered a noun, here serves in two instances to limit a noun, hence in each particular sentence functions as an adjective. If we say, "I love my country," *country* is a noun; if however we speak of *country gentlemen, country home, country escapades, country delights,* the word acts as an adjective. The part of speech of any word depends on the way in which that word is used within the sentence.

Note 2: The adjective *soul-searing* is made up of two parts, *soul,* conventionally considered a noun, and *searing,* conventionally considered part of a verb. If a stranger stopped you on Fifth Avenue one morning and said: "Quick, what part of speech is *soul?* And how about *searing?*" you would be justified in answering *noun* and *verb.* But in *soul kiss, soul* is an adjective; in *searing experience, searing is an adjective;* and in *soul-searing experience, soul-searing* is considered as a unit and is an adjective.

Note 3: The words *the* and *a* (also *an*) are additional adjectives in the paragraph you have just studied. Although adjectives, since they modify nouns, they are given the special name of *articles*.

Note 4: *Their*, in the last line, may seem to be an adjective, and indeed some grammarians would call it a possessive adjective, but the more common term applied to the words *my, your, his, her, its, our,* and *their* is *possessive pronoun*. Pronouns will be more fully considered in a later chapter.

DO YOU GET THE POINT?—*test 9*

If your last experience with adjectives was not soul-searing, and if you feel you are becoming more and more expert in spotting these useful parts of speech, find five adjectives in the following paragraph. Again note modification with an arrow. (Ignore the articles.)

Comments from advance readers of *Mr. Blandings* are just starting to come in and fairly burble with the sort of lapel-grabbing enthusiasm that makes a great best-seller. For example, HENRY SEIDEL CANBY writes: "*Mr. Hodgins' invention is extraordinary, his imagination as humorous as any I have encountered.*"

—Still the same ad

CHECK YOUR LEARNING—*answers to test 9*

1. *Advance*, modifies readers
2. *lapel-grabbing*, modifies enthusiasm
3. *great*, modifies best-seller
4. *extraordinary*, modifies invention
5. *humorous*, modifies imagination

Note: Here for the first time you have met adjectives which do not precede the nouns they modify. *Extraordinary* and *humorous* come not only after their nouns, but after the verb of the sentence as well. Such adjectives are called *predicate adjectives*, for reasons which will be made clear in a later chapter.

Now that you have $32, would you like to try for $64? Find any six verbs in the paragraph you have just been working on, and write each verb in the proper space below.

1 ...., 2 ...., 3 ....,

4 ...., 5 ...., 6 ....

CHECK YOUR LEARNING—*answers to test 10*

1. are starting   4. makes   6. is
2. to come   5. writes   7. have encountered
3. burble

Note 1: *Comments,* the first word in the paragraph, can function just as easily as a verb, but not in the type of sentence illustrated, where it is a noun. In the following it is used as a verb: Alan Sack *comments:* "Take that book away. It's too good to read." And here as a noun: "It is to be hoped that such *comments* are facetious." Can you readily appreciate the difference in atmosphere in the two uses of the same word?

Note 2: *Advance,* used in the paragraph as an adjective, can be a verb if verbal force is given to it in a sentence. For example: "The men will *advance.*"

Note 3: *Are starting,* the first verb in the sentence, is made up of two parts, as many verbs are. When a verb has more than one part, you will recall, it is termed a *verb phrase.*

What has all this to do with *principal* and *principle*?
Just this:
Principle (*-ple* ending) is a noun.
It is one of the few nouns that are fairly static. It should never be used as an adjective.
Principal (*-pal* ending) is an adjective. This word too is fairly static. There are two instances, to be noted shortly, in

which *principal* may be used as a noun—otherwise it is always an adjective.

As a noun, *principle* means a rule, a truth, a law of conduct or action.

He is a man of *principle*.
The *principle* of gravity was discovered by Newton.
Aren't you violating your professed *principles* by this action?

As an adjective, *principal* means main, chief, leading.

North Avenue is one of the *principal* thoroughfares of New Rochelle.
What do you think is the *principal* reason why Germany lost the war?

And the exception, mentioned earlier:
Principal may be used as a noun referring:

1. to a sum of money:

This bank will pay 1½ per cent on your *principal*.

2. to a person who is the chief or leading figure of a school, drama, business deal, and the like:

The *principal* addressed the teachers at the faculty meeting.
Lunt and Fontanne were the *principals* in "The Guardsman."
The negotiations were carried on for the *principals* by their attorneys.

3. The Rule

Is an *adjective* required? Use *principal*.
Is a *noun* required? Use *principle*.
However, is a *noun* required which refers to a person or a sum of money? Use *principal*.

How to remember the rule: Principle, the noun, ends in *-le.* So does the word *rule,* which is what a *principle* is. *Principal,* the adjective, ends in *-al.* The word *adjective* starts with *a,* and the word *main* contains an *a; princip*AL is an *adjective* meaning *main.*

4. The Test

DO YOU GET THE POINT?—*test 11*

Check the proper word in each sentence.

1. General Marshall, one of the (principal, principle) figures in the 1946 Chinese negotiations, was appointed Secretary of State.
2. Marshall is a man of deep conviction and (principal, principle).
3. The (principal, principle) problems to confront him were Russia, Poland, and Spain.
4. The (principal, principle) of the school has just left.
5. With a (principal, principle) of $150,000, you can live comfortably on your income.
6. Strict (principals, principles) are expensive; sometimes you must be willing to compromise.
7. Once you master certain basic (principals, principles) in grammar, you need never worry whether you are speaking correct English.
8. The (principal, principle) reason for her refusal is that she doesn't like his personality and approach.
9. Henry Wallace will be the (principal, principle) speaker on the panel.
10. This house will be sold to (principals, principles) only; no agents.

CHECK YOUR LEARNING—*answers to test 11*

1. principal	5. principal	9. principal
2. principle	6. principles	10. principals
3. principal	7. principles	
4. principal	8. principal	

as easy as A B C

A. What is the difference between *hung* and *hanged?*
B. Is it correct to say, "I would like to speak *to* Mr. Sack"?
C. Which is preferable: *mother-in-laws* or *mothers-in-law?*

A. The Grammar of Meanings

Hung, Hanged

Pictures are *hung* on the wall; the stockings were *hung* by the chimney with care (in hopes that St. Nicholas soon would be there); the icicles have *hung* from the window since the snowstorm; the clothes were *hung* out on the line to dry.

Anything which is suspended is *hung.* A person has *hung* from a treetop if he has remained suspended there.

Horse thieves were once *hanged* for their crimes. The judge orders the murderer to be *hanged* by the neck until dead. The army has *hanged* the spy.

Hanged is used to describe *execution by hanging.* A person who is *hanged* is put to death. *Hanged* is, then, synonymous with *killed.* A person who has *hanged* himself has committed suicide. The murderer was *hanged* and his corpse *hung* from the gibbet until it was cut down.

DO YOU GET THE POINT?—*test 12*

1. If you're caught, you'll be (hanged, hung).

2. He (hanged, hung) from the window all morning watching the sights on the street.
3. The rope (hanged, hung) from the top of the building.
4. Despondent and ill, he (hanged, hung) himself.
5. Why have they (hanged, hung) the prisoner?
6. Her stockings (hanged, hung) down over her shoes.
7. If that mob catches the thief, he'll be (hanged, hung).
8. He (hanged, hung) himself before the law caught up with him.

CHECK YOUR LEARNING—*answers to test 12*

1. hanged	4. hanged	7. hanged
2. hung	5. hanged	8. hanged
3. hung	6. hung	

B. The Grammar of Allowable "Errors"

I would like to speak *to* Mr. Sack.

Logically, if you speak *to* Mr. Sack, he listens and you speak; if you speak *with* him, a conversation, rather than a monologue, takes place. As most human speaking is done on a give and take basis (I except the relatively rare instances, such as a wife giving her husband a curtain lecture), *speak with*, or *talk with*, should be, one might assume, the more frequently used expression. English is not, however, always a logical language—and as a matter of fact, *speak to*, despite its implication, is the locution most often employed. Both words, *to* and *with*, are equally correct from a grammatical point of view, but *to* is the more common. (Some people find *speak with* a trifle prissy.)

C. The Grammar of Correct Usage

Mother-in-laws or *Mothers-in-law?*

Certain hyphenated or multiple words form their plurals by adding *s* to the principal part:

mothers-in-law   courts-martial   poets laureate
fathers-in-law   editors-in-chief   attorneys general
brothers-in-law   notaries public   postmasters general
sisters-in-law   hangers-on   sergeants-at-arms
passers-by   maids-of-honor
lookers-on   men-of-war

PREFERABLE FORM:

   mothers-in-law

chapter 6 HOW TO DO ALMOST ANYTHING

1. The Problem

Is *go slow* correct English?

2. The Solution

We are dealing with a two-word sentence: (1) *Go*, a verb, and (2) *slow*, an adjective? a verb? a noun?

Slow is not an adjective; it does not modify a noun or pronoun. (*Slow* used adjectivally: "*Slow* torture is generally unpleasant.")

Slow is not a verb; it does not denote action. (Verbal use: "*Slow* down and live longer.")

Slow is not a noun; it is not the name of a person, place, etc. (*Slow* changes in form to become a noun: "The tortoise's *slowness* is proverbial.")

Then how does *slow* function in the sentence in question?

Slow limits the verb *go*.

It makes the verb more specific.

It makes the verb more meaningful.

Go is general, unspecific.

Slow tells how to go.

By now you have begun to suspect, because of the close association between *slow* and the verb, that *slow* is an *adverb*.

Your suspicion is well-founded.

A word which modifies a verb *is* an adverb.

For example:

Go *slow*.
Go *now*.

Do *not* go.
Go *quickly*.
He listened *attentively*.
We'll go *tomorrow*.

All the italicized words in the preceding sentences are adverbs. Each one serves, in one way or another, to delimit the verb with which it is associated.

Adjectives modify nouns.
Adverbs modify verbs.
Adverbs also modify adjectives.

Her husband was ecstatically happy.

His wife was painfully thin.

Happy, an adjective, describes the noun *husband*.
Ecstatically, an adverb, elaborates upon the meaning of *happy*.
Thin, an adjective, describes the noun *wife*.
Painfully, an adverb, elaborates on the meaning of *thin*.
Painfully and *ecstatically* are adverbs which modify adjectives.

Examine the following sentence:

Alan's finger, not yet completely better, is still giving him a painfully awkward time.

Find the first adjective. .... (first adjective)
What noun does it modify? .... (noun)
Now find three adverbs which modify that adjective.
........................, ..., ... (adverbs)
Next find the two-word verb phrase. ....
(verb phrase)
Write the adverb which modifies that verb phrase. ....
(adverb)
Finally, there is a second adjective. ....
(second adjective)

And a fifth adverb, modifying that adjective. ....
(fifth adverb)

This is the way your chart should look:

better (first adjective)
finger (noun)
not, yet, completely (adverbs)
is giving (verb phrase)
still (adverb)
awkward (second adjective)
painfully (fifth adverb)

If you've come this far without mishap, you're ready for a third point:
First point restated: Adverbs modify verbs.
Second point restated: Adverbs modify adjectives.
Third point: Adverbs also modify other adverbs.
To wit:

You can live more happily . . .

The adverb *happily* modifies the verb phrase *can live.*
The adverb *more* modifies the adverb *happily.*

She speaks less effectively . . .

The adverb *effectively* modifies the verb *speaks.*
The adverb *less* modifies the adverb *effectively.*
So:

An adverb modifies a verb, an adjective, or another adverb.

This rule will help us with a number of problems:

1. Do it *good, or* Do it *well?*
2. Mary arrived home *safe, or* Mary arrived home *safely?*

3. Go *slow, or* Go *slowly?*
4. How *slow* the time goes, *or* How *slowly* the time goes?

Let us consider the problems one by one.

Problem 1: *Good* is conventionally considered an adjective; *well* is the adverbial form of the same idea. Since a modifier of the verb *do* is required, "Do it *well*" is correct. Similarly, "Come *promptly*," "Speak *distinctly*," "Handle it *carefully*," are preferable to "Come *prompt*," "Speak *distinct*," "Handle it *careful*." The adverb in each instance describes the action of the verb.

Problem 2: *Safe,* the adjective form, would limit the noun *Mary; safely,* the adverb, would limit the verb *arrived.* Does the word in question describe Mary when she got home, or does it explain the manner of the arrival? In a pattern such as this, it is generally considered that the condition of the noun is being described by the word *safe.* That is, Mary was safe when she got home. Similarly we say, "The package arrived *damaged*," "He weathered the battle *unscarred*," "He came through the fight *unscathed*," etc., each adjective describing the condition of the noun or pronoun, rather than the manner of action of the verb. "Mary arrived home *safe*" is the preferable form.

Perhaps you are getting the idea that the main difference between adjectives and adverbs is the ending *-ly.* You are partly right.

ADJECTIVE FORM	ADVERBIAL FORM
swift	swiftly
rapid	rapidly
curious	curiously
fleet	fleetly
wistful	wistfully

But not all adverbs end in *-ly,* as the following adverbs attest:

fast (Do it *fast.*)
once (Do it only *once.*)
now (Do it *now.*)
forever (To cherish *forever.*)
today (Do it *today.*)

And not all words ending in *-ly* are adverbs. The following are adjectives:

likely (a *likely* story)
comely (a *comely* face)
seemly (*seemly* behavior)
leisurely (a *leisurely* journey)
manly (a *manly* act)

What is true is that adverbs may be formed from adjectives by the addition of the adverbial ending *-ly.*

ADJECTIVE	ADVERB
sweet	sweetly
happy	happily
cool	coolly

All this is by way of introduction to the third and fourth problems:

Problem 3: "Go *slow*" or "Go *slowly*"?
An adverb is undoubtedly required—we want a modifier for the verb *go.* "Go *slowly*" must be correct—*slowly* is an adverb.
But—
"Go *slow*" is also correct—indeed it is equally correct, and perhaps a good deal less stilted.
Slow, in the expression "Go *slow*" is not an adjective, despite its lack of the adverbial ending.
Slow, in this construction, is an adverb.
It is an adverb because it functions as an adverb within the framework of the sentence.

66

If you will look the word up in any good dictionary (say the Merriam-Webster, the Webster's New World, the American College, or the Thorndike-Barnhart) you will find it listed as both an adjective and an adverb.

Slow is an adjective when it modifies a noun; it is an adverb when it modifies a verb.

Such a distinction could of course be made about any adjective functioning as an adverb. We could take the sentence "Speak *rapid*" and, calling *rapid* an adverb, since it is used to modify a verb, argue that no grammatical rules were being broken. However, the test of good grammar is current educated usage. "Speak *rapid*" is rarely if ever used by educated speakers or established writers; it is not part of the idiom of the language. On the other hand, "Go *slow*," or one of its variations, has been used for years and is still used today. Shakespeare used it in the sentence, "How *slow* the time goes," centuries back; writers have used it over and over again in all the years since Shakespeare; police signs all over the country today (STEEP HILL—GO SLOW; SCHOOL—GO SLOW; CURVE—GO SLOW, etc.) attest to the universality of the acceptance of *slow* as an adverb.

"Go *slow*," then, is correct English.

Of course in less idiomatic usages, the conventional adverbial form of the word, *slowly*, is preferable. To wit:

He *slowly* spelled out the words.
Slowly he began to feel his way along the ledge.

On the other hand, in short, common, expressions, *slow* may be, and often is, used adverbially:

Speak *slow*.
Do it *slow*.
Speak *slower*.
Do it *slower*.
Walk *slow*.

Problem 4: "How *slow* the time goes," by the reasoning used for an analysis of problem 3, is acceptable English.

Similarly, such expressions as "That car is moving so *slow*," "How *slow* the wheel turns," etc., are equally acceptable.

In deciding whether to use *slow* or *slowly* in an adverbial function, be guided by the rhythm, cadence, and commonness of the expression in which the word occurs. If *slow* sounds better and more natural than *slowly*, use the shorter form, and be assured that your grammar is just as good as that of the person who consistently, and perhaps somewhat artificially, uses *slowly* whenever an adverb is required.

3. The Rule

An adverb modifies a verb, an adjective, or another adverb.

An adverb often answers the question *how? when? where?* or *to what degree?* about a verb, an adjective, or another adverb.

For example:

"He speaks *rapidly*." *How* does he speak? *Rapidly*.
"He is happier *today* than *yesterday*." *When* is he happier? *Today*.
"Do it *more* carefully." *How* carefully? *More* carefully.
"Go *home*." Go *where? Home*.

PRO AND CON

Pro

—And it loads *quicker*, works *slicker* . . . because of its open channel!

—Advertisement of Swingline Staplers,
New York Times Magazine

Q. Modern grammarians maintain that "Go slow" is correct, idiomatic English, established by common usage among educated people and completely acceptable in informal conversation. Do you agree? Would you use the expression in your everyday speech?

Pro

A. Sure, it's good. So is "Talk low" and "Look sharp." But then "in everyday speech" I'd use "Stop quick," "Lie quiet!" and to my squads "Dress even!" and "Think fast."

—Thornton Wilder

Mr. Wilder is the author of *Our Town, The Skin of Our Teeth, The Bridge of San Luis Rey* and other best-selling novels and hit plays.

Pro

A. Not only do I use and approve of the idiom "Go slow," but if I find myself with people who do not, I leave quick.

—Rex Stout

Mr. Stout, creator of Detective Nero Wolfe, is the author of *Not Quite Dead Enough, Black Orchids,* and other mysteries. He is president of the Author's League.

4. The Test

DO YOU GET THE POINT?—*test 13*

Underline the adverbs in the following sentences.

1. Never say die.
2. Do not play with fire.
3. She's less homely than you led me to believe.
4. He lives more dangerously than anyone else I know.
5. Why work so hard?
6. When are you coming home?
7. He goes where he's directed.
8. He spoke witheringly about his wife's insanely jealous moods.

9. You work too hard for your salary.
10. You're speaking too rapidly; we can't listen that fast.

There were twenty adverbs in the preceding ten sentences. Did you find them all? Count your results before checking with the answers below.

CHECK YOUR LEARNING—*answers to test 13*

1. never
2. not
3. less
4. more, dangerously
5. why, so, hard
6. when, home
7. where
8. witheringly, insanely
9. too, hard
10. too, rapidly, not (n't), that, fast

as easy as A B C

A. What is the difference between *incredible* and *incredulous?*

B. Is it correct to say, "I'll come *providing* you invite me"?

C. Which is preferable: "Take two *spoonsful* of your medicine every hour," or "Take two *spoonfuls* of your medicine every hour"?

A. The Grammar of Meanings

Incredible, Incredulous

Some stories are *incredible;* some people's brashness, or naïveté, or luck is *incredible.*

We may speak of *incredibly* good fortune, of *incredibly* bad manners.

You listen *incredulously,* you sound *incredulous* when you show your skepticism. Some Democrats may have been *incredulous* when they heard the results of the 1946 election.

An account, a story, a report is *incredible* if it is difficult to believe. A person is *incredulous* if he is inclined to disbelieve what he sees or hears. In addition, a person may be *incredible* if his actions, his personality, or his attitudes cause disbelief. On the other hand, a person is *credulous* if he believes what he hears when there is little evidence to support such belief. (Indeed, if his willingness to believe everything is excessive, he might more effectively be described by the stronger adjective *naïve* or *gullible.*)

A story is *credible* if it warrants belief.

1. You are too (credulous, credible); can you not distinguish fact from fancy?
2. I believe that is the truth; at least it's a perfectly (credulous, credible) story.
3. He stared (incredulously, incredibly) at the strange sight, refusing to believe the evidence of his own eyes.
4. He told an (incredulous, incredible) story of his night's adventures.
5. The climate at the Equator is (incredulously, incredibly) hot.
6. You have the most (incredulous, incredible) luck!
7. He's an (incredulous, incredible) character. It's hard to believe that such a person can exist.
8. Don't look so (incredulous, incredible) when I tell you what happened to me.

CHECK YOUR LEARNING—*answers to test 14*

1. credulous	4. incredible	7. incredible
2. credible	5. incredibly	8. incredulous
3. incredulously	6. incredible	

B. *The Grammar of Allowable "Errors"*

I'll come *providing* you invite me.

There is no essential difference, on any level of speech or writing, between the words *provided* and *providing*.

The Merriam-Webster *Collegiate Dictionary* defines *provided* as follows: "on condition; if"; and *providing:* "in case that." The Funk and Wagnalls dictionary says that *provided* means: "on condition that"; and that *providing* means: "provided; in case that"!

Obviously, the words are interchangeable. Which you use is a matter of entirely free choice, although sticklers for "pure" grammar prefer *provided* in the type of sentence illustrated above.

Say either:

She'll marry you *provided* you ask her, *or* She'll marry
you *providing* you ask her.
Provided you pay for the shipment C.O.D., we'll accept
your order, *or Providing* you pay for the shipment
C.O.D., we'll accept your order.

PRO AND CON

Q. Many modern grammarians maintain that "I'll work,
providing you pay me," is correct, idiomatic English established by common usage among educated people. Do you
agree? Would you use the expression in your everyday
speech?

Pro

A. I consider *providing* a commonly used variant of *provided* or *provided that*. However, I do not use the expression in my everyday speech and writing, since I naturally
prefer the simple *if*. To express stipulation in a legal docu-
ment I would use *provided that*.

—Rudolf Flesch, Ph.D.

Dr. Flesch is the author of *The Art of Plain Talk, Why
Johnnie Can't Read* and other books.

Pro

Every farmer receives free fertilizer, *providing* he works
on the land-use plan.

—Carol Hughes, "The Little Shepherd of
Big Lick," *Coronet,* November, 1947

C. The Grammar of Correct Usage

Take two *spoonsful* of your medicine every hour, *or*
Take two *spoonfuls* of your medicine every hour?

Spoonsful is not an accepted word. *Two spoons full,*
which sounds the same, could be rationalized to mean two

separate spoons, each one full. With dishwashing the onerous task that it is, most sensible people use one spoon and fill it twice. Such action is implied in *two spoonfuls*.

PREFERABLE FORMS:

spoonfuls of medicine
cupfuls of flour
handfuls of rice
glassfuls of coffee

chapter 7 HOW TO END A SENTENCE

1. The Problem

Is it incorrect, as so many adults learned in their elementary and high school days, to end a sentence with a preposition?

2. The Solution

Modern young teachers with a pedagogical sense of humor now tell their students in elementary and high school English classes: A preposition is a word you must not end a sentence *with*.

What once prompted the ban against a preposition as the final word in a sentence? Probably three conditions, each one of them insufficient, pedantic, and unnecessary:

First condition: The Latin origin of the term *preposition*. Preposition, you will recall from chapter 3, is made up of the prefix *pre-* (before) and the root *posit* (placed). A preposition is placed *before* a noun, and if we wish to observe the definition literally, how can we set it at the end of a sentence, with no noun following? (But it is illogical to base grammar on etymology.)

Second condition: In very formal writing, prepositions usually do precede nouns or pronouns. In conversation we might naturally render our thought as follows: "What could he be thinking *of?*" or "Is this the book you referred *to?*" But in very formal style these ideas would be rephrased to: "*Of* what could he be thinking?" and "Is this the book *to* which you referred?" (Purists would like us to speak as if we were writing state papers—an obvious impossibility.)

Third condition: In Latin, a preposition is indeed never found except preceding its noun or pronoun. Purists often reason: Is it wrong in Latin? Then it's wrong in English too. (Here again we see a slight touch of insanity. What makes correct English of course is the common usage of the educated speakers of *our* language, not of Latin or any other language. Educated speakers and writers end a sentence with a preposition whenever they find it natural to do so.)

In some types of sentences, it is quite impossible *not* to end a sentence with a preposition. For instance:

He is not a man to be laughed *at*.
My affections are not to be trifled *with*.
She will not stand being made fun *of*.
They do not enjoy being stared *at*.
That will be taken care *of*.

(Try rearranging these sentences if you think a preposition should not terminate a sentence!)

H. W. Fowler, in his deservedly famous handbook, *A Dictionary of Modern English Usage* (Oxford), has this to say about ending a sentence with a preposition:

Those who lay down the universal principle that final prepositions are "inelegant" are unconsciously trying to deprive the English language of a valuable idiomatic resource which has been used freely by all our greatest writers except those whose instinct for English idiom has been overpowered by notions of correctness derived from Latin standards. The legitimacy of the prepositional ending in Literary English must be uncompromisingly maintained. . . .

(And of course there is the classic example of the child whose parent brought up to the nursery the wrong book for the nightly story. Casting all restraint to the winds, the child inquired in a tone of bruised dignity: "What did you bring that book up for me to be read to out of for?" If you're aiming for a nervous breakdown, just try to eliminate those four terminal prepositions!)

Fowler goes on to list the reputable authors who end sentences with prepositions: Chaucer, Spenser, Shakespeare, Jonson, Burton, Pepys, Swift, Defoe, Lamb, Thackeray, Kipling, and many others.

In natural speech and writing, by all means end a sentence with a preposition if you wish to. Note these examples:

CORRECT AND NATURAL	SOMEWHAT STILTED
People worth talking to . . .	People to whom it is worth talking . . .
What were they thinking of?	Of what were they thinking?
The girl I was talking about . . .	The girl about whom I was talking . . .
The man we were listening to . . .	The man to whom we were listening . . .
The person I have the greatest faith in . . .	The person in whom I have the greatest faith . . .

Margaret M. Bryant, professor of English at Brooklyn College, succinctly stated the case for the terminal preposition in a paper in the January, 1947, issue of *College English*, a magazine published by the National Council of Teachers of English:

From the time of the Old English period, prepositions have greatly increased in number and express many complicated relationships not found in the old idiom. Those who insist that final prepositions are inelegant are taking from the English language one of its greatest assets—its flexibility—an advantage realized and practiced by all our greatest writers except a few who, like Dryden and Gibbon, tried to fashion the English language after the

Latin. One may quickly get an idea of the extensive use of the final preposition by turning to H. W. Fowler's discussion of this matter in his *Dictionary of Modern English Usage,* where he cites a large number of examples, including Chaucer, Spenser, Shakespeare, Jonson, Bacon, the Bible, Milton, Pepys, Congreve, Swift, Defoe, Burke, Cowper, Lamb, Hazlitt, De Quincey, Landor, Ruskin, Mill, Thackeray, Arnold, Lowell, and Kipling. After this array of quotations from our great writers, his parting advice is:

"Follow no arbitrary rule, but remember that there are often two or more possible arrangements between which a choice should be consciously made; if the abnormal, or at least unorthodox, final preposition that has naturally presented itself sounds comfortable, keep it; if it does not sound comfortable, still keep it if it has compensating vigor, or when among awkward possibilities it is the least awkward."

Now that we know that a preposition is a word we may end a sentence with (without committing grammatical suicide), perhaps we ought to be quite sure as to what, specifically and exactly, the preposition is.

In the course of this chapter, nine prepositions, out of the scores of prepositions in the language, have already been mentioned:

with   of   to   at   out   for   about   in   up

A preposition, as its name implies, has a position before a noun or pronoun—unless, of course, it ends the sentence, in which case the noun or pronoun is found somewhere before the preposition.

There is, however we slice it, a very definite relationship between a preposition and a noun (or pronoun), no matter what the order of their position.

That is the principal thing to keep in mind—prepositions are linked with nouns or pronouns—indissolubly, inevitably, every preposition ties in, somehow or other, with its noun or pronoun; whether the noun or pronoun be expressed or implied, it is governed by the preposition.

In itself, a preposition has little meaning.

It is unlike a verb—it shows no action.

It is unlike a noun—it names nothing.

It is unlike an adjective or adverb—by itself it does not serve to describe, limit, or qualify.

A preposition is, rather, a link in the chain of a sentence —it ties a noun or pronoun to the rest of the sentence.

It is easy to get on good terms with prepositions. Study the following paragraph, in which all the prepositions are underlined: [1]

One _of_ the most eminent examples _of_ nineteenth-century British statesmen was Sir Robert Peel. _In_ 1812, _at_ the early age _of_ 24, he was given the post _of_ Secretary _of_ Ireland. _Among_ the vexing questions that confronted him was the preservation _of_ life and property _at_ a time when both were notoriously insecure _in_ the Emerald Isle. Peel solved this problem _by_ creating a strong Irish constabulary, the members _of_ which, _in_ tribute _to_ the founder, were soon called _peelers_. Seventeen years later, Robert Peel organized _along_ similar lines the first modern London police force; and the English, not _to_ be outdone _by_ their Irish cousins, used Peel's first name _to_ call the officers _bobbies_—and the name stuck.

Notice how each of the prepositions in the paragraph you have studied is accompanied by its noun, with two exceptions to be explained shortly.

of . . . examples	of . . . 24
of . . . statesmen	of . . . Secretary
in . . . 1812	of . . . Ireland
at . . . age	among . . . questions

[1] From _This Week;_ copyright by United Newspaper Magazines, Inc.

| of . . . life | in . . . Isle |
| at . . . time | in . . . tribute |

etc.

The two exceptions: *to be* and *to call*. An apparent, but not real exception: *by creating*.

The preposition *to* is used with a verb to form *an infinitive*. Other examples of infinitives: *to see, to have, to know, to use,* and so on.

The *-ing* from of a verb may be combined with a preposition: *by creating, for using, against working, while playing,* and the like. Such a form of the verb when combined with a preposition is called a *gerund*. A gerund, while formed from a verb, is functioning within a sentence as a noun—so we do not have here a full-fledged exception to the rule that prepositions govern nouns or pronouns.

DO YOU GET THE POINT?—*test 15*

Now that you are becoming familiar with the appearance and use of prepositions, try your hand at finding twenty-seven prepositions in the following paragraph: [2]

A Scotsman returned to his native land shortly after the Revolutionary War with a fortune he had acquired by trading in captured ships. He was made road trustee of his district, and at once set about to find some better way of building roads, with the object of improving the very poor highways of the locality. When the taxpayers objected to the cost of the experiments, the trustee went ahead with them anyhow, paying for them out of his own pocket. This research convinced him that the most durable roads were those constructed of layers of broken stones. Some years later he was appointed surveyor general of Bristol roads, and was able to put his ideas into practice. The result was so gratifying that the House of Commons voted not only to reimburse *John L. McAdam*

[2] *Ibid.*

80

for the $40,000 of his own money that he had spent experimenting, but to give him an extra $10,000 as a tribute. The *macadamized* road has proved that it was money well spent.

Here are the twenty-seven prepositions as they occurred in the paragraph, each with its noun, pronoun, gerund, or (forming an infinitive) verb:

1. to . . . land (noun)
2. after . . . war (noun)
3. with . . . fortune (noun)
4. by . . . trading (gerund)
5. in . . . ships (noun)
6. of . . . district (noun)
7. to . . . find (infinitive)
8. of . . . building (gerund)
9. with . . . object (noun)
10. of . . . improving (gerund)
11. of . . . locality (noun)
12. to . . . cost (noun)
13. of . . . experiments (noun)
14. with . . . them (pronoun)
15. for . . . them (pronoun)
16. out of . . . pocket (noun) (an example of a double preposition)
17. of . . . layers (noun)
18. of . . . stone (noun)
19. of . . . roads (noun)
20. to . . . put (infinitive)
21. into . . . practice (noun)
22. of . . . Commons (noun)
23. to . . . reimburse (infinitive)
24. for . . . $40,000 (noun)
25. of . . . money (noun)
26. to . . . give (infinitive)
27. as . . . tribute (noun)

If you have given a creditable account of yourself in the test just completed, we may set down these truths:

You can now spot a preposition.

You can now determine the noun, pronoun, gerund, or verb governed by the preposition.

Such being the case, you should know that a preposition and its noun, together with any modifiers of that noun, make up a *prepositional phrase*. The preposition *to* and its verb make up an *infinitive phrase*.

Here are some of the prepositional phrases from the paragraph about John L. McAdam:

to his native land
after the Revolutionary
   War
with a fortune
in captured ships

by trading
of his district
of the locality
as a tribute

DO YOU GET THE POINT?—*test 16*

Find twenty-one prepositional phrases and three infinitive phrases in the following paragraphs: [8]

When he was the Comptroller General of France, just before the French Revolution, he rashly advocated raising money by taxing the lands of the nobles. He argued that if the rich aristocracy would make some sacrifices, the country would soon be able to lighten its financial burdens. The landed messeigneurs were of course horrified at his radical proposals. Reduce their pensions? Melt down their table plate into money? The Comptroller soon had few friends left in the government.

But the common people took him to their hearts. At the time that the Comptroller General was fighting for his program it had become popular to have profile portraits cut out of black paper and mounted, and it soon was the rage of Paris.

What was more fitting than to give the name of this man to a type of portraiture then so much in vogue? And so it is that Etienne de Silhouette, finance minister of France, interested far more in money than in art, is remembered in connection with the type of picturization that bears his name.

[8] *Ibid.*

Prepositional phrases

1. of France
2. before the French Revolution
3. by taxing
4. of the nobles
5. at his radical proposals
6. into money
7. in the government
8. to their hearts
9. at the time
10. for his program
11. out of black paper
12. of Paris
13. of this man
14. to a type
15. of portraiture
16. in vogue
17. of France
18. in money
19. in art
20. in connection
21. with the type
22. of picturization

Infinitive phrases

1. to lighten
2. to have
3. to give

3. The Rule

A preposition is a perfectly good word to end a sentence *with.*

as easy as A B C

A. What is the difference between *imply* and *infer?*

B. Is it correct to say, "The reason I love you is *because* you are so pretty"?

C. Which is correct: "The cat licked *it's* paws," or "The cat licked *its* paws"?

A. The Grammar of Meanings

Imply, Infer

You *imply* that you do not like your mother-in-law. You could be more direct and come right out and say so, but you prefer to use a certain amount of subtlety—after all, she's your wife's mother. So instead of expressing yourself unequivocally, you make an *implication.*

Your mother-in-law *infers*, from your words, your innuendos, your unmistakable hints, perhaps from your actions, that you do not like her. She draws such an *inference*, and of course is far from pleased about it.

To *imply* is to hint or express indirectly. Only a person speaking or acting can *imply* anything; or his words or actions can make the *implication.*

To *infer* is to draw a conclusion from someone's *implication.* Only a listener or watcher can *infer* anything.

DO YOU GET THE POINT?—*test 17*

1. Your words (infer, imply) that I am a liar.
2. Do you (infer, imply) from what he says that he dislikes you?

3. His actions (infer, imply) that he does not know what he is doing.
4. What (inference, implication) can we draw from the facts that Adelaide and Russell have presented to us?
5. I resent your (inference, implication) that I cheated you.
6. It is unfortunate that you are always making (implications, inferences) about your friend's dishonesty.

CHECK YOUR LEARNING—*answers to test 17*

1. imply	3. imply	5. implication
2. infer	4. inference	6. implications

B. The Grammar of Allowable "Errors"

The reason I love you is *because* you are so pretty.

"The reason . . . is *because*" is perfectly acceptable in informal conversation. The strictly grammatical form, "The reason I love you is *that* you are so pretty" may be preferable on the literary or formal level, but in everyday speech no stigma attaches to using "because" after "the reason is."

PRO AND CON

Q. What is your opinion of "The reason I love her is *because* she is so pretty"? Would you use the expression?

Pro

A. Yes, I certainly would use the expression "The reason I love her is *because* she is so pretty." I wouldn't use it because it was "correct," because I don't like the words *correct* and *incorrect*. It seems to me that they strait-jacket the language. I would rather say that the phrase that you have asked about has been made acceptable by common usage.

I could easily write a book on this general subject if any-body would read it. It is rather amusing that Ralph Waldo

Emerson is on my side, and he certainly could hardly be called a roustabout. Perhaps you have already seen the following quotation from one of his books. If you haven't, it may interest and amuse you. Says the sage:

> The language of the street is always strong. What can describe the folly and emptiness of scolding but the word "jawing"? I feel, too, the force of the double negative, though clean contrary to our grammar rules. And I confess to some pleasure from the stinging rhetoric of a rattling oath in the mouth of truckmen and teamsters. How laconic and brisk it is by the side of a page of the *North American Review*. Cut these words and they bleed; they are vascular and alive; they walk and run. Moreover, they who speak them have this elegancy, that they do not trip in their speech. It is a shower of bullets, whilst Cambridge men and Yale men correct themselves and begin again at every half-sentence.

Now I love words. Yet to me there is nothing sacred about them. Or about pronunciation. Or spelling. Or grammar. True, these departments are all subject to rules. But many of the rules are merely a point in time. That is, they were not the rules yesterday, nor will they be the rules of tomorrow. If the scholars had their way these rules would remain static. Pronunciations would be precise. Grammar standardized. Definitions fixed. And the new words that entered the language would never, never come from the mouths of the unwashed of Ipswich. But bothersome folks who don't know any better are continually changing their ideas about language, and are constantly inventing new terms. And when they do, the scholars have to go into a huddle and retailor the rules to fit.

To my proletarian mind this is just fine. For the language we speak is a fluid phenomenon, and if we allow the dictionary brass hats too much authority, we might find ourselves with a medium of expression that had become as rigid and lifeless as Latin.

If my youngest child should say, "I don't want no spinach," it would be clear to me, in spite of the purists, that she had a double dislike for the vegetable. I will even carry my Declaration of Independence to a greater extreme. It is often my pleasure, during a day's work, to say "It is me" precisely as the wise French say "C'est moi." And despite the purists, I think it is well to wisely split an infinitive now and then. And in my faith there are times when a preposition is the perfect thing to end a sentence with, if for no other reason than to show, by small rebellions, that grammar is our servant and not our master.

—Wilfred Funk

Dr. Funk is a noted lexicographer. He is the publisher of *Your Life,* author of the *Reader's Digest* feature, "It Pays to Increase Your Word Power," coauthor of *30 Days to a More Powerful Vocabulary* and author of *The Way to Vocabulary Power and Culture.*

Con

A. I find the expression "The reason is because" awkward and on a par with "different than" in ear-grating quality.

—Pegeen Fitzgerald

Mrs. Fitzgerald is a famous radio personality. She is the feminine half of "The Fitzgeralds," the popular radio show.

C. The Grammar of Correct Usage

The cat licked *it's* paws, *or*
The cat licked *its* paws?

Its means *belonging to it,* and signifies ownership.
It's means *it is,* and is a contracted form, the apostrophe taking the place of the omitted letter *i.*

The cat licked *its* paws.

The baby has soiled *its* diaper.

(Other possessive pronouns, like *ours, hers, theirs,* similarly omit any apostrophe. The apostrophe to denote possession is found only in nouns, not pronouns: *boy's, girl's, boys', girls',* etc.)

chapter 8 HOW TO SUBSTITUTE

1. The Problem

Which is correct: "Everyone came on time but *she*," or "everyone came on time but *her*"?

2. The Solution

She and *her* are obviously different forms of the same word.

Grammatically speaking, we call these forms *cases*.

She is the *nominative case* of one of the personal pronouns.

Her is the *objective case* of the same personal pronoun.

A large proportion of the grammatical errors that adults make stems from a basic confusion as to the proper uses of these two cases of the personal pronoun.

But what are pronouns?

And what is case?

PRONOUNS

Pronouns are substitute nouns. Instead of saying *the man* (a noun), we may convey an identical meaning by substituting *he* (a personal pronoun).

Instead of saying *all the people* (a noun), we can substitute *everyone* (an indefinite pronoun).

Instead of asking *which man?* (a noun), we can substitute an interrogative pronoun, and say *who?*

A book has come into your hands. You flip through the pages and decide that you would be interested in the contents. So you can say to someone, "The *book* I am holding looks like an interesting book." On the other hand, you could (and probably would) phrase your thought more succintly by eliminating a number of words: "*This* looks like an interesting book." You would then be substituting a demonstrative pronoun, *this,* for the noun *book.*

We have various types of pronouns:

Personal pronouns. Words which substitute for nouns referring to persons:

I	she
you	we
he	they

Interrogative pronouns. Words which substitute for nouns and ask questions:

who?   what?   which?

Relative pronouns. Words which relate to, and substitute for, previously mentioned nouns:

who   which   that

The man who came to dinner

The book which I hold

The telephone that I have

Demonstrative pronouns. Words which substitute for nouns and also function to point out:

this   that   these   those   this one   that one

Indefinite pronouns. Words which substitute for nouns and are vague and general, rather than specific, in meaning:

anyone	either	each one
everyone	neither	any
no one	both	some
someone	none	several
all	much	
few	each	

CASE

There are three *cases* in English—*nominative, objective,* and *possessive.* Since the use of the possessive case presents few, if any, difficulties, we will concentrate on the nominative and objective cases.

NOMINATIVE FORMS OF THE PERSONAL PRONOUNS

I	we
you	
he, she	they

CORRESPONDING OBJECTIVE FORMS OF THE PERSONAL PRONOUNS

me	us
you	
him, her	them

The case of a pronoun is determined by a number of rules, only one of which is relevant to the problem of this chapter. To wit:

The objective case of a pronoun is used in a prepositional phrase.

Speak *to me.*
Go *with him.*
Wait *for her.*
He spoke *of us.*
We'll send the letter *to them* tonight.

The pronoun within the prepositional phrase is known as the *object of the preposition.*

And the object of a preposition, as its name would suggest, is in the objective case.

In the sentence under consideration, "Everyone came on time but (she?—her?)," *but* is a preposition which links the pronoun to the rest of the sentence and forms, with the pronoun, a prepositional phrase. The correct choice, then, would be the objective form—*her*.

GRAMMATICALLY PREFERABLE	GRAMMATICALLY INDEFENSIBLE
No one has thanked you but *me*.	No one has thanked you but *I*.
We understood everyone but *him*.	We understood everyone but *he*.
Everyone but *her* is dressed for the occasion.	Everyone is dressed for the occasion but *she*.
You've insulted everyone but *us*.	You've insulted everyone but *we*.
Why do you trust anyone but *them*?	Why do you trust anyone but *they*?

In these sentences *but* has the meaning of *except*. With such a meaning, *but* is always a preposition.

3. The Rule

Is the pronoun the object of a preposition? Use the objective case. When the word *but* means *except*, it is a preposition and is to be followed by an objective pronoun.

PRO AND CON

Q. Do you ever use the nominative case of a pronoun after the word *except*, as for instance in a sentence like, "Everyone is here *except he*"? Do you ever hear this usage from your friends or associates? What is your opinion of the usage?

A. I never use the nominative case after "except," even when I am writing to my best friends. I have never heard my friends or associates use it in that way, and if they did, I should be inclined to drop them.

—Lester Markel

Mr. Markel is Sunday Editor of *The New York Times.*

4. The Test

DO YOU GET THE POINT?—*test 18*

1. No one but (he, him) can help you.
2. No one can help you except (I, me).
3. Everyone was most agreeable to you except (she, her).
4. Everyone but (she, her) was most agreeable to you.
5. Who but (we, us) has enough money to finance such a venture?
6. Who has enough money to finance such a venture except (we, us)?
7. We spoke to everyone but (she, her).
8. She likes everyone but (he, him).
9. Do you see all your friends here? Everyone except (they, them).
10. They all failed the test but (I, me).

CHECK YOUR LEARNING—*answers to test 18*

1. him	3. her	5. us	7. her	9. them
2. me	4. her	6. us	8. him	10. me

as easy as A B C

A. What is the difference between *stationary* and *stationery?*

B. Is it correct to say, "That dress is different *than* mine"?

C. Which is correct: "He practices *preventive* medicine," or "He practices *preventative* medicine"?

A. The Grammar of Meanings

Stationary, Stationery

Is something fixed, in one place, unmoving? It is *stationary* (with the *a*).

Paper, letterheads, envelopes, and similar appurtenances for correspondence, are *stationery* (with the *e*).

Standing still—note the *a* in st*a*nd: station*a*ry.

Paper, etc.—note the *er* in pap*er:* station*er*y.

DO YOU GET THE POINT?—*test 19*

1. Keep the right hand (stationary, stationery) and move the left along the edge of the slide.
2. We have just ordered some new (stationary, stationery).
3. Your (stationary, stationery) is of a very odd color.
4. Modern houses no longer have (stationary, stationery) walls.

CHECK YOUR LEARNING—*answers to test 19*

1. stationary   2. stationery   3. stationery   4. stationary

B. The Grammar of Allowable "Errors"

That dress is different *than* mine.

Quite a to-do is sometimes made in textbooks and speech manuals over the necessity for using the preposition *from* after the adjective *different* or the adverb *differently*. "He is different *from* me," "That dress is different *from* mine," "The battle came out differently *from* what we had expected" are offered as the *only* respectable forms. To say "He is different *than* I," "That dress is different *than* mine," or "The battle came out differently *than* we had expected" is not only forbidden by such books, but the sentences themselves are variously labeled slang, illiterate, ignorant, ungrammatical, or downright sinful.

One such recent publication offers the following precept: "Lilacs are different *from* (not *than*) peonies, poinsettias, and pansies." In a later chapter in the same book, a test sentence offered to the reader is as follows: "People who show good taste in spech are different (than, from) others." And the answers following the test unequivocally, unqualifiedly, call for *from* as the correct choice.

Yet this same author, addressing the reader on another page of the book, says: "There are five words which are pronounced differently when they are nouns (the name of something) *than* when they are adjectives."

On the next page, the author points out that "there are six more interesting words which are pronounced differently when they are adjectives *than* when they are past participles. . . ." The italics are of course my own, but even without the italics a reader is justifiably confused by an author who sets up a rule and then calmly proceeds to violate it.

Different than (and *differently than*) are well-established, popular, acceptable English idioms, and while not quite as formal or "pure" as *different from* and *differently from*, they are certainly not by any means incorrect English.

The Merriam-Webster *Collegiate Dictionary* has this to

say about *different:* "Usually followed by *from,* but also by *to,* especially colloquially in England, and by *than.*"

And Pooley [1] notes a long list of reputable authors in whose works *different than* may be found: H. G. Wells, De Quincey, Addison, Steele, Defoe, Richardson, and many others. Pooley continues:

> It may be seen then that *different than* is no stranger in literature, past or present, and that it is by no means as reprehensible as the textbook writers would have it. While there is little doubt that *different from* is the currently preferred form, *different than* is a possible substitute to be found in reputable writers and polite conversation.

It is obvious, then, that *different than* and *differently than* are at least permissible, if not necessarily preferable, in informal speech; it is certainly impossible to call them "incorrect."

In the case of the verb *to differ, from* alone is used, as in, "He differs *from* his brother in appearance," unless a difference of opinion is meant, in which case *with* is regularly used, as in, "I differ *with* you on that point."

PRO AND CON

Q. Modern grammarians maintain that "The outcome is different *than* we had expected" is correct, idiomatic English, established by common usage among educated people and completely acceptable in informal conversation. Do you agree? Would you use the expression in your everyday speech?

Pro

A. The particular expression you mention, "the outcome is different *than* we had expected," appears to me to be

[1] Robert C. Pooley, *Teaching English Usage* (Appleton-Century)

about as correct as any expression I ever use. In fact, this particular idiom has been in popular usage for so long I think your point is sort of academic.

If you really do wish to use my opinion on this, let me say seriously that I agree that any phrase of this kind, which most people would fail to recognize as actually incorrect, is certainly acceptable in informal conversation, as you say, and even in "formal" conversation. Only the strictest purist would object to it.

—Jerome Beatty, Jr.

Mr. Beatty is a columnist on the *Saturday Review*.

Pro

A. Yes, I agree with the modern grammarians who believe the sentence you give is correct.

I believe the English language, which is a tool in communication, should be considered in the same light as other tools of present-day living and should be adjusted to the changing times just as are the methods of manufacturing, food cultivation, transportation and the like.

We are talking today about jet-propelled airplanes. Why not talk also of streamlined speaking and writing! I am all for a progressive way of looking at grammar.

—Oscar Dystel

Mr. Dystel is editorial adviser of Parents Institute, Inc.

Pro

Steve is a somewhat chastened boy, different in several subtle ways *than* when we last saw him in action.

—Clifford Odets, *Night Music*

Mr. Odets is the well-known playwright, author of several Broadway successes, including *Waiting for Lefty, Golden Boy, Rocket to the Moon*.

Pro

The "Mirrors of Washington," if it had been written by a Democrat, would have reflected differently *than* the same mirrors from the pen of a Republican.

—Donald L. Laird, in *Increasing
Personal Efficiency* (Harper)

Dr. Laird is professor of psychology at Colgate University and author of numerous popular books on practical psychology.

Q. Would you be willing, in your everyday speech or informal conversation, to use the word *than* after *different* or *differently?*

Con

A. For myself, I habitually use *from* rather than *than* with *different* and it's habit so strongly ingrained by now that I'm afraid any other usage would be a self-conscious and affected one. And affectation in either direction is to me one unforgivable sin of speech.

—Jay Nelson Tuck

Mr. Tuck was formerly the television editor of the New York *Post*.

Pro

A. I certainly would—and do—use *different than*, even though fundamentalists consider it wrong.

English needs a good overhauling, and there are certainly plenty of precedents for it. We have gone a long way from Elizabethan English, for instance, and no one—not even the purists—is crying for its return.

If writing is an art (and I like to believe that it is), then it must progress. Painting and music have progressed to express the modern thought of modern man. The painter

98

is not bound to the primary colors in his tubes. He can mix them as he wills. Only the results count. That goes for words, too. We don't have to be bound by the premixed stuff that has come down to us from God-knows-where.

And when someone in the subway says "We need a man *like* Roosevelt was," I'm not going to correct his English. His meaning is clear.

—Richard A. Yaffe

Mr. Yaffe was foreign editor of the newspaper *PM*.

C. The Grammar of Correct Usage

> He practices *preventive* medicine, *or*
> He practices *preventative* medicine?

Most dictionaries now accept the word *preventative* as a substitute for the older and shorter form, *preventive*, both as adjective and noun. However, careful writers and speakers still show a decided preference for *preventive*.

PREFERABLE FORMS:

He practices *preventive* medicine.
What *preventive* can we use?
Has medical science discovered any *preventive* for cancer?

chapter 9 HOW TO JOIN

1. The Problem

Is it correct to say, "Between you and *I*, she's older than her husband thinks she is"?

2. The Solution

The crucial word in this sentence is *between*.

Between is a preposition.

The words *between you and I* form a prepositional phrase.

In this phrase we have, not one object, but two:

FIRST OBJECT: *you*
SECOND OBJECT: *I*

These objects are joined by the word *and*.

And is a conjunction, a part of speech which, you will recall from chapter 3, serves to join (*junc*) words together (*con*).

But the object of a preposition is in the objective case, according to the rule formulated in chapter 8.

I is a nominative personal pronoun.

On the face of it, then, the sentence which illustrates the problem of this chapter is incorrect—an objective pronoun is required in a prepositional phrase.

Corrected version: "Between *you and me*, she's older than her husband thinks she is."

There are other conjunctions besides *and*. Any word which joins similar parts is a conjunction. Note the following:

JOINING TWO NOUNS: war *or* peace
JOINING NOUN AND PRONOUN: Gerbrand *or* I
JOINING TWO ADJECTIVES: Tired *but* happy

Sometimes a conjunction is in two parts, as in the following:

JOINING TWO NOUNS: *Either* the pen *or* the pencil will do.
JOINING TWO PRONOUNS: *Neither* you *nor* I will ever know.
JOINING TWO NOUNS: *Both* Daphne Pereles *and* Alice Fennell are here.

Either . . . or, neither . . . nor, both . . . and are called correlative conjunctions.

Perhaps we had better pause for a moment to recall that a word may be any one of the eight parts of speech, depending exclusively on its function within a sentence. We have already met *but* (meaning *except*) as a preposition in the sentence "Everyone came on time *but* her." Now we encounter the same word as a conjunction in *tired but happy.* We have already worked with *either, neither,* and *both* as indefinite pronouns. We see in this chapter that they can also be correlative conjunctions. To determine what part of speech a word is you must consider how that word functions within the framework of a sentence. Consider:

THE PREPOSITION *but:* No one *but* him can do it.
(*But him* is a prepositional phrase.)
THE CONJUNCTION *but:* He will come *but* he will be late.
(*But* joins two ideas.)
THE INDEFINITE PRONOUN *either:* Can you use *either* of these books?
THE CORRELATIVE CONJUNCTION *either . . . or:* To succeed, you must be *either* lucky or smart.
Either CAN ALSO BE USED AS AN ADJECTIVE: Hold up *either* hand.

———→

THE INDEFINITE PRONOUN *both:* Do you need *both?*

THE CORRELATIVE CONJUNCTION *both . . . and:* Do you need *both* the Packard *and* the Chrysler tonight?

Both CAN ALSO BE AN ADJECTIVE: *Both* cars are in the garage. ⟶

Besides *and, or, but,* and the correlatives, there are many other conjunctions, most of them functioning as joiners of related ideas into single sentences. Note the following:

I will speak to him *if* he speaks to me first.
Although he is her husband, she does not love him.
When it rains, my rheumatism bothers me.
Since you're so smart, what is the correct answer?

In general, conjunctions are words which join similar parts of speech or related ideas in a sentence.

3. The Rule

Does a prepositional phrase contain two or more objects? All such objects are in the objective case.

4. The Test

DO YOU GET THE POINT?—*test 20*

Check the correct personal pronoun in each sentence:

1. When he sent the letter to my sister and (I, me), he felt he had done all that was possible to do under the circumstance.
2. Between you and (I, me), I think she's lying.
3. You've thanked everyone but (he, him) and his father.
4. We're never going to speak to the principal or (she, her) again.
5. No one is here except (we, us) and the servants.

6. Would you like to take a walk with Adelaide and (I, me)?
7. Let him sit near Mary and (we, us).
8. Take a place in line after the boys and (she, her).
9. This is a special arrangement between Charlie and (we, us).
10. I have nothing against Herb and (she, her); I do, however, wish to see justice done.

CHECK YOUR LEARNING—*answers to test 20*

As each of the required choices in the sentences on which you have just worked functioned as one of the objects in a prepositional phrase, the objective case of the personal pronoun should have been checked throughout. This was the second choice in each sentence.

as easy as A B C

A. What is the difference between *ingenious* and *ingenuous?*

B. Is it correct to say, "It's a *nice* day"?

C. Which is preferable: "Now you're talking like *I*," or "Now you're talking like *me*"?

A. *The Grammar of Meanings*

Ingenious, Ingenuous

Thomas Alva Edison was *ingenious.*

One must be *ingenious* to keep a jump ahead of the High Cost of Living.

One can be an *ingenious* liar, an *ingenious* inventor.

Young children, on the other hand, are *ingenuous.* They are (usually) frank, unsophisticated, aboveboard. (Some kids, of course, are quite the opposite—they are precocious as all hell.)

Thus, these two words, which are spelled and pronounced so similarly, are very different in meaning.

Ingenious (pronounced *in-JEEN-yus*) means clever, shrewd, inventive, resourceful. The noun is *ingenuity.*

Ingenuous (pronounced *in-JEN-yoo-us*) means open, frank, candid, free from reserve or dissimulation.

DO YOU GET THE POINT?—*test 21*

1. He (ingeniously, ingenuously) parried every question the opposing lawyer asked him.

104

2. He is too (ingenious, ingenuous) to try to deceive you.
3. Such (ingenuity, ingenuousness) in a grown woman is unusual.
4. If you are (ingenious, ingenuous) you'll be able to figure some means of escape.
5. He made a completely (ingenious, ingenuous) admission of his purposes.

CHECK YOUR LEARNING—*answers to test 21*

1. ingeniously   3. ingenuousness   5. ingenuous
2. ingenuous   4. ingenious

B. *The Grammar of Allowable "Errors"*

It's a *nice* day.

"Reprehensible!"
"Illiterate grammar."
"Vulgar, slang!"
"Never used by respectable people."
These are some of the reactions which purists have toward the idiomatic use of *nice* with the meaning of *pleasant* or *agreeable*. Yet the Merriam-Webster dictionary gives, among others, the following definitions of *nice:* "pleasing, agreeable, properly modest, well-mannered."

The judges who answered Leonard's questionnaire [1] almost unanimously approved the use of *nice* in the expression, "There are some *nice* people here," as established, correct English. And your own experience doubtless attests that cultivated people generally, frequently, and unashamedly use *nice* in the sense of *pleasant*. If you are normal, you use it yourself—without apologizing for your grammar.

(*Nice* formerly had only one meaning: *exact, precise;* and purists are sufficiently reactionary to try to restrict the word to that meaning.)

[1] See chapter 25.

Perfectly allowable and completely current are expressions like the following:

Be *nice* to him.
We've had a *nice* time.
We'll go if it's a *nice* day.
We had a *nice* dinner.

(Chief valid objection to the word is that it can be used to the point of monotony—everything that is not downright intolerable is often called *nice* by people whose vocabularies need a little freshening up. Such objection, of course, can be made to any word which is overused.)

PRO AND CON

Q. Many modern grammarians maintain that "We had a *nice* time at her party" is correct, idiomatic English, established by common usage among educated people. Do you agree? Would you use the expression in your everyday speech?

Con (but apparently not seriously)

A. I'd prefer "good" or "merry" or "fine." It's not nice to use *nice* that way.

—Walter Winchell

Walter Winchell is the well-known newspaper and radio columnist.

C. The Grammar of Correct Usage

Now you're talking like *I*, or Now you're talking like *me*?

Like is a preposition and is followed by the objective case of the pronoun.

PREFERABLE FORMS:

Now you're talking like *me* (not *I*).
He dresses just like *me* (not *I*).

Why do you act like *her* (not *she*)?
You talk just like *him* (not *he*).
They look like *us* (not *we*).
We look like *them* (not *they*).

chapter 10 HOW TO SHOW EMOTION

There are times in life when words are a superfluity—under the influence of a tremendous emotion the most expressive language seems inadequate. Great pain, or fear, or sorrow, or ecstasy, or wonder does not usually tend to loosen the tongue.

Human beings often relieve a deep feeling with single word exclamations like *alas! oh! ah! fie! pshaw! gosh! damn! wow!* or similar conventional syllables. Such words, if they may be called words, are unlike nouns, pronouns, verbs, adjectives, adverbs, conjunctions, or prepositions in that they do not function within the framework of a sentence nor in direct relation to other parts of speech.

These exclamations, and others like them, are called *interjections,* and are the last of the eight great categories into which English words are divided.

as easy as A B C

A. What is the difference between *rob* and *steal*?

B. Is it correct to say, *"Can* I have another piece of cake?"

C. Which is preferable: *"This* data *is* interesting," *or "These* data *are interesting"*?

A. The Grammar of Meanings

Rob, Steal

You *rob* a person, a house, a safe, an apartment, a desk.

You *steal* a person's wallet, his clothes from the house, his jewels from the safe, his valuables from the apartment, his love letters from the desk.

To *rob* is to take (illegally, of course) the contents of something or the possessions of someone.

To *steal* is to take (again, illegally) the thing itself, or to kidnap the person.

To *steal* a desk is to remove it physically (and illegally).

To *rob* a desk is to open the drawers of the desk and take therefrom what suits your fancy. The desk remains where you found it.

DO YOU GET THE POINT?—*test 22*

1. When we returned, we found the front door ajar and the house (robbed, stolen).

2. They (robbed, stole) Mrs. Van Sweringen's house, (robbing, stealing) her furs, jewels, and valuable paintings.

3. To (rob, steal) a bank is no mean task; to (rob, steal) it is probably quite impossible.
4. The thieves (robbed, stole) all my money.
5. I don't worry about anyone (robbing, stealing) my money; I'm insured against theft.

B. The Grammar of Allowable "Errors"

Can I have another piece of cake?

There is, at best, questionable wisdom in "correcting" the English of children who ask permission by means of the word *can*.

Psychologically, it is perhaps most unwise.

If it is your purpose to inculcate in your youngsters conventional habits of politeness, and if you believe that *may* (in place of *can*) is on a par with *please* and *thank you*, you will be interested to know that child psychologists generally agree (see *The Child from Five to Ten*, by Dr. Arnold Gesell) that politeness in speech is most effectively taught by example, not by precept.

If you wish your child to say "please" and "thank you" (say the psychologists), you have only to be quite sure that you yourself always do so, when the occasion warrants the use of such words.

If you wish your child to say "May I" when seeking permission and "Can I" only when questioning a physical or mental ability, you had best be quite certain that you yourself consistently follow the rigid rule that *may* refers to *permission, can* only to ability.

But there you will have trouble.

Suppose another child requests the pleasure of your youngster's company outdoors. (The other child will doubtless say, "*Can* Johnnie come out to play?" even if his mother is as polite as you are, for that is the natural, idiomatic way to phrase the request.)

Are you absolutely sure that you do not answer—and in your own child's hearing—"No, he *can't*—he's going to have a bath"?

Unquestionably you are talking about permission, for Johnnie has all the physical ability and mental competence he needs to go outdoors. However, what he lacks—and this is of course crucial—is your permission to leave the house.

If your child hears you using *can't* for a denial of permission, he may reflect darkly that the rules you set up are rather arbitrary and discriminatory (he'll phrase this thought in his own words of course, or the reaction may even be wordless) since you yourself do not always observe them.

The psychological effect of such a situation may be greater (especially on a sensitive child whose patience has been tried to the snapping point by continual corrections of *may* or *can*) than you realize.

The linguistic facts are as follows:

1. *Can't I* is used almost universally, by people of education, in preference to the somewhat stilted *mayn't I* or *may I not*. This refers to the other personal pronouns as well. ("Why *can't* we have this apartment, if the present tenant is moving out?" "Why *can't* he speak? Isn't this a free country?")

2. Similarly, *you can't* or *you cannot* is more generally used than *you may not*. ("No, you *can't* have your dessert until you finish your string beans!")

3. *Can* and *may* are often used interchangeably in reference to permission. (*"Can* I use your coat tomorrow?" "John *can* go if he wants to, but I'm staying home." *"Can* I speak to Mr. Sack, please?")

4. *May* is perhaps the somewhat politer form of asking permission—but *can* is perfectly correct English. An over-stressing of the niceties of distinction between *can* and *may* (that is, using *may* whenever any type of permission

111

is involved) is likely to make your speech sound a bit on the prissy side.

Webster's *New World Dictionary* gives as one of the definitions of the word *can:* "[Colloq.], to be permitted; may"—and adds, ". . . in informal and colloquial usage, *can* is most frequently used to express permission, especially in interrogative and negative statements (*can't* I go?, you *cannot!*)."

Professor Porter Perrin[1] states: "In informal and colloquial speech, *can* is used for both permission and ability."

Professor Sterling Andrus Leonard[2] remarks, in reference to the sentence *"Can I be excused from this class?"*: "Probably the fitness of this expression is a matter of taste, rather than usage. But it cannot be listed as vulgar or uncultivated in the face of the large number of judges who recognize its frequent use by cultivated people."

PRO AND CON

Q. Many modern grammarians maintain that "Why *can't* I run out and play, Mother?" is correct, idiomatic English, established by common usage among educated people. Do you agree? Would you use similar expressions in your everyday speech?

Pro

A. I'm afraid I have used similar expressions in my everyday speech and it pleases me to think that they may be legitimatized.

—Mary Margaret McBride

Mary Margaret McBride is a famous radio personality and newspaper columnist.

[1] *Writer's Guide and Index to English* (Scott, Foresman).
[2] *Facts about Current English Usage* (National Council of Teachers of English).

112

A. Yes, I'd vote for Johnny saying it to mother; anything else might sound stilted and upholstered. Quant à moi, I suppose I've used similar expressions in speech without feeling like a grammatical leper; but in print, I'm not so sure.

—Norman Cousins

Norman Cousins is the editor of the *Saturday Review*, and author of a number of books, including *Modern Man Is Obsolete*.

Q. Do you ever use the word "can" in an expression like *"Can* I see Mr. Brown if he is not busy?" Do you hear this use from your friends or associates?

Con

A. I look up sometimes when I am addressing a golf ball, and I assume that I am also inattentive in the matter of speech.

In answer to your question, however, I don't remember hearing myself use "can" when I am seeking a permission. So I would report that I don't use the expression, *"Can* I see Mr. Brown if he is not busy?" Nor do I hear friends or associates make such requests.

When an oculist is testing my eyes, however, I frequently hear the question, "Can you read that chart?" I also hear the expression, "Can you see by the dawn's early light?" and the answer is generally "Yes."

—William Chenery

Mr. Chenery was formerly publisher of *Collier's*.

Q. Many modern grammarians maintain that *"Can* I have another piece of cake?" (asking permission) is cor-

113

rect, idiomatic English, established by common usage among educated people. Do you agree? Would you use the expression in your everyday spech?

Noncommittal

A. At our house I neither *can* nor *may* have a piece of cake, because it's fattening.

—Leonard Lyons

Mr. Lyons is the conductor of the internationally famous "Lyons Den" in the New York *Post* and other newspapers.

Con

A. I guess I'm not a modern grammarian. I still hold to the old rules of grammar and syntax. Woolley taught that *can* and *may* have entirely different meanings—one suggests ability to do something; the other permission to do something. What's the point of eliminating that very important distinction?

—William I. Nichols

Mr. Nichols is editor of *This Week*.

Pro

A. Personally, I think we all are prone to misunderstand the function and use of language. Being mentally too lazy to think a thing out to its logical conclusion, we say, "Words convey ideas," and then let it go at that.

How do words convey ideas?

From the beginning of time when language grew from sounds into words, the human mind has associated certain ideas with spoken or written word combinations. Therefore, word combinations have individualized meanings, predicated solely on association.

The point I am making may seem elemental and trite,

114

but its significance is largely missed by all students of composition and grammar.

I have repeatedly found that many beginning writers have a basic idea for a good story. They tell it in inept language, but, because that is the language they have chosen in which to convey the idea, the same idea is brought back to their minds whenever they read what they have written. Therefore, a beginning writer will frequently have a good story and *think* he has placed it on paper so that other readers will get the atmosphere, characterization and action of the story. Other readers fail to do so because the writer has been inept in his choice of word combinations. The author, however, cannot detect this fault, because every time he reads the story, the story image is again formed in his own mind.

For this reason, there are actually many different languages spoken under the heading of the "English language." There are the sweat-covered, rugged word combinations that stand for power and virility, and there is the sterile, academic, superaccurate speech of the intellectuals.

In my own instance, I never care a hang about whether the things I say or the things I write are grammatically correct. I am trying to transmit an idea and convey an impression; and as long as I can do that, I will leave it to more erudite authorities to quarrel over whether a certain word usage has been sufficiently established to be considered correct grammar.

The fallacy of such arbitrary choosing lies in the fact that if such a position is carried to its logical conclusion, it is the mere repetition of error which eventually establishes authenticity.

So far as I am concerned, I'd say, "*Can* I have another piece of cake?"

—Erle Stanley Gardner

Mr. Gardner is the world famous author of *The D.A. Calls a Turn, Case of the Black-Eyed Blonde,* and *The Case of the Half-Awakened Wife.* He is perhaps the most prolific writer of mystery novels of our times.

C. *The Grammar of Correct Usage*

This data *is* interesting, *or*
These data *are* interesting?

Data is generally considered a plural noun, the singular of which is *datum. Datum* is rarely, if ever, used in everyday speech, and it is only natural, therefore, that many people look upon *data* as a singular, considering it to mean "a piece of information." However, in best usage, *data* means "a number of pieces of information" and takes a plural adjective (*these* or *those*) and a plural verb.

This is a list of the most common words which look like singulars but are in truth plurals. (They are all of Latin or Greek origin, and have the classical plural endings; hence, the lack of an *s* at the end of each word.)

data (sing.: *datum*)
phenomena (sing.: *phenomenon*)
criteria (sing.: *criterion*)
candelabra (sing.: *candelabrum*)
media (sing.: *medium*)

automata (sing.: *automaton*)
foci (sing.: *focus*)
formulae (sing.: *formula*)
memoranda (sing.: *memorandum*)
vertebrae (sing.: *vertebra*)

PREFERABLE FORMS:

These data *are* interesting.
These phenomena *are* worth noting.
Your criteria *are* not valid.
The candelabra *are* tarnished.
New media *are* necessary.
They act like automata.
Wounds present foci of infection.
The formulae *have* to be changed.
The memoranda on the Lillienthal case *are* on your desk.
Three vertebrae *were* broken.

116

chapter 11 HOW TO MEASURE YOUR
PROGRESS—YOUR FIRST
ACHIEVEMENT TEST

You have just finished a period of intensive training in the art of analyzing the functions of words.

The ability to identify parts of speech is not so sterile nor useless as it may at first sound. It is true that you are not going to be a happier person because you know the difference between adjectives and adverbs. Nor, certainly, will you materially increase your chances of commercial, social, professional, or amorous success by becoming an expert in distinguishing between, say, nouns and verbs.

But you have taken the first, and perhaps the most important, step in becoming grammatically sophisticated. If, by inspection, you can identify, with reasonable accuracy, the name of each word in a sentence, you have mastered the first principle of the interrelationship of words.

That, basically, is what grammar is—the interdependent functioning of the parts of a sentence. There is, of course, much more to grammar than the parts of speech—but the parts of speech are the foundation on which we will build your complete understanding of English grammar. From here on up, we can discuss subjects and predicates; simple, complex and compound sentences; transitive and intransitive verbs; active and passive voice; participles, infinitives, and gerunds; phrases and clauses; and other such fascinating mysteries of grammar. We can discuss them much more intelligently than we would otherwise have been able to do, now that you can tell one part of speech from another.

I cannot, therefore, stress too emphatically the importance of your feeling quite self-assured about parts of speech. And so let me ask you to make a rapid review of some of the main points we've covered—and then to take a quick test of your learning before we go on to more complex aspects of the subject.

The Main Points

IN GRAMMATICAL TERMINOLOGY AND FUNCTION

1. There are eight parts of speech: verb, noun, pronoun, adjective, adverb, preposition, conjunction, and interjection.

2. The verb is a word of action which carries the thought of a sentence. A few verbs, most commonly the forms of *to be*, show state of being rather than action. Such are copulative verbs. A verb may occur in two or more parts, in which case it is called a verb phrase.

3. A noun is the name of a person, place, thing, idea, concept, or activity.

4. An adjective describes, limits, or in some way modifies a noun or pronoun.

5. An adverb modifies a verb, adjective, or other adverb.

6. A preposition links a noun or pronoun to the rest of the sentence; and with such a noun or pronoun (plus any modifiers) forms a prepositional phrase.

7. The preposition *to* may introduce a verb, and with it forms an infinitive.

8. A gerund is an *-ing* form of a verb which, however, functions as a noun within the framework of the sentence.

9. A pronoun substitutes for a noun. The commonest types of pronouns are personal, interrogative, relative, demonstrative, and indefinite pronouns.

10. A personal pronoun has various forms, dependent on its case—nominative, objective, or possessive.

11. A pronoun used as object of a preposition is in the objective case form.

12. A conjunction joins parallel elements, such as noun and pronoun, adverb and adverb, idea and idea, etc.

13. A word may be any one of several parts of speech, according to its function in a sentence.

14. An interjection is a particle which is unrelated to the other words in a sentence, and which generally is indicative of emotion.

IN USAGE

1. *Effect* is usually a noun, *affect* usually a verb. *Effect* may also be a verb, with the specialized meaning of *bring about* or *cause to happen.*

2. *Principal* is an adjective, except when it refers to a person or sum of money, in which instance it may be a noun. *Principle* is only a noun.

3. *Slow* may be, and usually is, used adverbially in certain idiomatic patterns.

4. A sentence may end with a preposition.

5. Only the objective forms of personal pronouns may be used as objects of prepositions.

IN THE GRAMMAR OF MEANINGS

1. *Continual* means successive; *continuous* means uninterrupted.

2. *Let* means permit; *leave* means depart.

3. *Hung* means suspended; *hanged* means executed.

4. *Incredible* means unbelievable; *incredulous* means unbelieving.

5. *Imply* means to say indirectly; *infer* means to draw a conclusion.

6. *Stationary* means motionless; *stationery* means paper, etc.

7. *Ingenious* means clever, shrewd, inventive; *ingenuous* means frank, open, honest.

8. *Rob* means to remove the contents; *steal* means to take completely.

IN THE GRAMMAR OF ALLOWABLE "ERRORS"

Permissible usages:

1. He *got* sick.
2. Don't get *mad*.
3. I would like to speak *to* Mr. Sack.
4. I'll come *providing* you invite me.
5. The reason I love you is *because* you are so pretty.
6. That dress is different *than* mine.
7. It's a *nice* day.
8. *Can* I have another piece of cake?

IN THE GRAMMAR OF CORRECT USAGE

1. *Sense* is followed by *in*.
2. *Kind of day* not *kind of a day*.
3. The plural of *mother-in-law* is *mothers-in-law*. Other hyphenated or multiple nouns generally pluralize similarly.
4. *Spoonfuls, cupfuls,* etc., not *spoonsful, cupsful,* etc.
5. *It's* means *it is;* possession is indicated by *its*.
6. *Preventive* is probably preferable to *preventative*.
7. *Like,* the preposition, is followed by the objective form of the personal pronoun.
8. *Data, criteria, phenomena,* and certain other nouns are plurals and should be treated as plurals.

That's the whole story, so far.

If you feel weak in any of the points listed, now is the time to go back to the text and review, in order to be prepared to make a high score on the achievement test which follows.

Achievement Test 1

I. Indicate the part of speech of each word in the following sentence:

Our tragic failure in this war—one which may well cause us to lose the eventual peace—was our failure in what the Army calls orientation.
    —David L. Cohn, "Should Fighting Men Think?"
    Saturday Review, January 18, 1947

1. Our	....	14. lose	....
2. tragic	....	15. the	....
3. failure	....	16. eventual	....
4. in	....	17. peace	....
5. this	....	18. was	....
6. war	....	19. our	....
7. one	....	20. failure	....
8. which	....	21. in	....
9. may	....	22. what	....
10. well	....	23. the	....
11. cause	....	24. Army	....
12. us	....	25. calls	....
13. to	....	26. orientation	....

II. Indicate the part of speech of each word in the following sentence:

The Army meaning of this unfortunate word is instruction to our soldiers as to what the war was about.
—*Ibid.*

1. The	....	11. our	....
2. Army	....	12. soldiers	....
3. meaning	....	13. as	....
4. of	....	14. to	....
5. this	....	15. what	....
6. unfortunate	....	16. the	....
7. word	....	17. war	....
8. is	....	18. was	....
9. instruction	....	19. about	....
10. to	....		

III. Find in the first sentence by David L. Cohn:

1. Two prepositional phrases: ...., ...
2. One infinitive: ....
3. A copulative verb: ....
4. A verb phrase: ....

IV. Check the correct word in each sentence:

1. What (effect, affect) do handsome men have upon unmarried women?
2. Do doting mothers have a bad (effect, affect) on their children?
3. Can government action (effect, affect) the course of a business recession?
4. All during the war, the O.P.A. tried to (effect, affect) a stabilization of the price structure.
5. Thyroid extract (effects, affects) the body very quickly.
6. When sound (effects, affects) are needed, they can often be dubbed into any motion picture.
7. Harsh sound (effects, affects) the nerves.
8. Why does he (effect, affect) a British accent when he has lived in The Bronx all his life?
9. Charlie Jerome is the short order cook of Colonial Diner, one of the (principal, principle) eating places in New Rochelle.
10. Charlie is a man of (principal, principle); he never serves a dish that is not perfect in taste and appearance.
11. The People's Savings Bank pays 3½ per cent interest on your (principal, principle).
12. When we sell our house we will deal with (principals, principles) only.
13. We cannot do that; it would violate one of our most cherished (principals, principles).
14. This is just between you and (I, me); can you keep it under your hat?

15. We spoke to Herbert and (she, her) only yesterday.
16. Everyone seems well satisfied with the arrangement except (he, him).
17. I'm surprised that no one but (I, me) raised any objections.
18. That's a personal matter between Jules and (we, us); why don't you keep out of it?
19. Why do you give (he, him) and (I, me) so much work?
20. You can't talk that way to (we, us) girls!

V. Check the preferable word:

1. There is not a moment of quiet in that house—nothing but (continual, continuous) din.
2. (Let, Leave) me go.
3. The spy will be (hung, hanged).
4. Don't look so (incredible, incredulous) when I tell you these things. They're true!
5. It seems to me that you are (inferring, implying) that I took the necklace.
6. I think you can buy that paper in a (stationary, stationery) store.
7. That is an (ingenious, ingenuous) attitude for a grownup person to take.
8. His money was (robbed, stolen).
9. What's the sense (in, of) doing it that way?
10. What (sort of, sort of a) chap is he?
11. Are there any (notaries public, notary publics) in your town?
12. Use several (handfuls, handsful) of sand when you mix the cement.
13. Has that kitten found (it's, its) mother?
14. Is there any (preventative, preventive) for tuberculosis?
15. You look just like (he, him).
16. The data on the case (seem, seems) inconclusive.

I.

1. pronoun (This is the possessive case of the personal pronoun.)
2. adjective, modifies the noun failure
3. noun
4. preposition
5. adjective, modifies the noun war (When *this* is used as a substitute for a noun, rather than a noun modifier, it is a demonstrative pronoun, as in: "Why do you do this to me?" In the test sentence, however, it is a demonstrative adjective.)
6. noun
7. pronoun (*This* is a numerical pronoun, substituting for a noun. *One* would be a numerical adjective in a sentence like "One wife should be enough for any man." Do you see the difference?)
8. relative pronoun, referring to the pronoun *one*
9. verb, first part of the verb phrase *may cause*
10. adverb, modifying the verb phrase *may cause*
11. verb, second part of the verb phrase
12. personal pronoun
13. preposition, sign of the infinitive
14. verb, part of the infinitive
15. adjective, modifying the noun *peace* (*The, an,* and *a* are also called *articles,* which are a type of adjective.)
16. adjective, modifying the noun *peace*
17. noun
18. copulative verb
19. possessive personal pronoun
20. noun
21. preposition
22. interrogative pronoun
23. adjective (or article), modifying the noun *Army*
24. noun
25. verb
26. noun

II.

1. adjective
2. adjective, modifying noun *meaning*
3. noun
4. preposition
5. demonstrative adjective
6. adjective
7. noun
8. copulative verb
9. noun
10. preposition
11. possessive pronoun
12. noun
13. conjunction
14. preposition
15. interrogative pronoun
16. adjective
17. noun
18. copulative verb
19. preposition (ending a sentence!)

III.

1. in this war, in what
2. to lose
3. was
4. may . . . cause

IV.

1. effect	8. affect	15. her
2. effect	9. principal	16. him
3. affect	10. principle	17. me
4. effect	11. principal	18. us
5. affects	12. principals	19. him, me
6. effects	13. principles	20. us
7. affects	14. me	

V.

1. continuous	7. ingenuous	13. its
2. let	8. stolen	14. preventive
3. hanged	9. in	15. him
4. incredulous	10. sort of	16. seem
5. implying	11. notaries public	
6. stationery	12. handfuls	

SCORING

There were 85 different questions for you to ponder over in the achievement test. If you have studied your lessons honestly and intelligently, your score on the test should be at least 63—approximately 75 per cent success. Consider 63 correct answers a passing grade—you are then competent to proceed with your study of English grammar. Any score between 64 and 75 is good, between 76 and 85 excellent. If your grade is 62 or lower, further review of chapters 3 to 10, plus the interchapter sections, is indicated.

YOUR SCORE ON ACHIEVEMENT TEST I: .... (Record the result on page 13.)

as easy as A B C

A. What is the difference between *practicable* and *practical?*
B. Is it correct to say, "New York cannot boast a particularly *healthy* climate"?
C. Which is preferable: "None of the men *were* arrested," or "None of the men *was* arrested"?

A. *The Grammar of Meanings*

Practicable, Practical

If your plan is *practicable,* it will work, it can be put into effect, it is capable of being put to practice.

If you call an invention, an idea, or a suggestion *practicable,* you are voicing the opinion that said invention, idea, or suggestion can be translated from theory into actuality.

On the other hand, if you label something *practical,* you probably mean that it is useful, sensible, or worth while.

People who are not dreamy, who keep their two feet firmly planted on the ground, who are realistic, competent, and sensible, may be called *practical.*

Someone says to you: "Let's do it this way: We'll hook up an auxiliary boiler to the main boiler, draw the hot water out from the bottom and pipe cold water back through the top." You answer: "That's not *practicable*. Hot water *rises*. How can you draw it off from the *bottom?*" By using the words *not practicable*, you imply that the process just won't work as planned. If you had called the plan

127

impractical, you would have meant that it might possibly have worked, but still would not have been very useful or helpful. Perhaps the cost would have been too high for the benefits received.

Chiefly, then, *practicable* is used in preference to *practical* when special emphasis is placed on the future workability of what is being described. Similarly, *impracticable* emphasizes the unworkability of something.

The nouns are:

from *practicable* and *impracticable—practicability* and *impracticability;*

from *practical* and *impractical—practicality* and *impracticality.*

B. The Grammar of Allowable "Errors"

New York cannot boast a particularly *healthy* climate.

The distinction that *healthy* means *possessing health* (a *healthy* child) and *healthful* means *giving health* (*healthful* climate) is still subscribed to by some English teachers. However, just as *will* is displacing *shall, would* taking over the function of *should,* and *further* substituting for *farther,*[1] so also *healthy* seems, in cultivated, colloquial, usage, to be taking over the added meaning once reserved to *healthful.* One of the sentences in Sterling Andrus Leonard's questionnaire[2] was: "The New York climate is *healthiest* in the fall." This use of *healthiest* was considered established English by the experts, and Leonard comments: "No linguist disapproved the expression; about one third of the English teachers, probably influenced by the condemnation visited on this construction by most handbooks and rhetorics, condemned it. The preponderance of opinion is clearly in favor of its approval as cultivated colloquial English, the handbooks to the contrary notwithstanding."

[1] These points will be covered in later sections.
[2] *Facts About Current English Usage* (Appleton-Century).

128

Q. Many modern grammarians maintain that "He has lived in a *healthy* climate all his life" is correct, idiomatic English, established by common usage among educated people. Do you agree? Would you use the expression in your everyday speech?

Pro

A. Yes, I would use the expression in my everyday speech.

—William Rose Benét

Mr. Benét was a well-known author, poet, and columnist. He was an associate editor of *The Saturday Review of Literature.*

Pro (*with reservations*)

A. I always use *healthful* myself, both in writing and conversation, for I am inclined to pedantry. But I believe that *healthy* is a perfectly good American idiom, and that it will survive.

—H. L. Mencken

Mr. Mencken was the noted lexicographer, critic, and editor, and author of *The American Language.*

Q. Modern grammarians maintain that "Carrots are *healthy* for you" (in place of *healthful*) is correct, idiomatic English, established by common usage among educated people. Do you agree? Would you use the expression in your everyday speech?

Con

A. Both words wrong—"Carrots are good for you"; "Carrots build health"; "There's health in carrots." *Healthy*

129

is a state of being, not to be induced (by carrots). *Health-ful* nearer, because it refers to a quality of subject noun.

In fact, name me one "modern grammarian" who likes that *healthy* use of the predicate adjective.

—William D. Geer

Mr. Geer was associated with *Fortune*.

Con (*with reservations*)

A. Before giving you an answer that will settle forever the question, "Is it right to say, 'Carrots are healthy for you'?" I should like to consult Mr. Fowler's *Modern English Usage,* which is my final authority in these matters, if not everybody's. Unfortunately, when I came up here in the woods expecting to be safe from questions like yours, I left Fowler in New Jersey.

My answer therefore will have to be mere personal opinion. Long ago a professor of English hooted so scornfully at *healthy* as a substitute for *healthful* that I've been strongly prejudiced against it ever since. In this maybe I'm dead wrong. Since boyhood's happy day at Teacher's knee I've had to unlearn a lot of things.

P.S. Anyway, I won't eat carrots, no matter how *healthy* they are.

—Leonard H. Robbins

Mr. Robbins conducted the column "About——" in *The New York Times Magazine* up to his sudden death in June, 1947.

C. The Grammar of Correct Usage

None of the men *were* arrested, *or*
None of the men *was* arrested?

Newspapers generally use a singular verb with *none* (arguing from etymology, since *none* is a contraction of *not one*) even if the word is followed by a prepositional phrase containing a plural noun, but such usage in speech is both rare and stilted.

PREFERABLE FORMS:

None of the men *were* arrested.
None of the clothes *are* dry.
None of your answers *are* correct.
None of the applicants *seem* to be satisfactory.

Of course, if *none* is followed by a prepositional phrase containing a singular noun, it governs a singular verb:

None of your work *is* satisfactory.
None of the Jello *has* set yet.

When *none* is used without a limiting prepositional phrase, use either a singular or plural verb, depending on whether the meaning of *none* is singular or plural.

None *are* here.
None *are* ready.
None *were* used.
None *was* used. (Meaning, none of the food, the money, etc.)

1. The Problem

Which is correct: "The cost of new cars *is* dropping," or
"The cost of new cars *are* dropping"?[1]

2. The Solution

To determine whether to use *is* or *are* in such a sentence,
you must realize that you are dealing with the *number* of
a verb.

There are two numbers in grammar—*singular* and
plural.

Is is singular.

Are is plural.

That is easy enough to understand. We would say:

One is . . .

Two are . . .

We would also say:

One was . . .

Two were . . .

One has . . .

Two have . . .

One goes . . .

Two go . . .

Or, to put it in chart form:

SINGULAR VERBS		PLURAL VERBS	
is	sees	are	see
was	knows	were	know

[1] This is of course a joke, as of publication date. Someday the sentence
may have some truth in it.

132

SINGULAR VERBS		PLURAL VERBS	
has	takes	have	take
goes		go	

A singular verb is used with a singular subject.

A plural verb is used with a plural subject.

But what is a subject?

A subject is one of the two main parts into which every sentence may be divided.

The other part is the *predicate*.

The subject of a sentence is what (or whom) we are talking about.

The predicate of a sentence is what we are saying about the subject.

Consider these examples:

The housing shortage in America was once most acute.

What are we talking about? *The housing shortage in America.*

What about it? (It) *was once most acute*.

Thus the sentence divides up in this way: "The housing shortage in America" [subject] "was once most acute" [predicate].

Harry S. Truman was elected Vice-President of the United States in 1944.

Whom are we talking about? *Harry S. Truman* [subject].

What about him? (He) *was elected Vice-President of the United States in 1944* [predicate].

The subject of a sentence may consist of a single noun or pronoun, as in:

Gentlemen prefer blondes.

Wilson wrote a fascinating book entitled *Memoirs of Hecate County*.

Bilbo was operated on for cancer.

Houses could once be built in eight weeks.

Sex is here to stay.

This single noun or pronoun is called the *subject of the verb*. *It is this single word which directly, and exclusively, influences the number of the verb.*

The subject of a sentence (not to be confused with the subject of the verb, though they are frequently identical) may contain not only the subject of the verb, but also one or more adjectives, conjunctions, adverbs, prepositional phrases, or other assorted parts of speech.

Notice how we can start with a single-word subject (which in such a case would be both the subject of the sentence and the subject of the verb) and build around it.

Women are fascinating creatures.

Subject of the verb and subject of the sentence: *women.*

Let us add a prepositional phrase:

Women of beauty are fascinating creatures.

Subject of the sentence: *women of beauty.*
Subject of the verb: *women.*

Let us add some adjectives, an adverb, a conjunction, and a 2nd prepositional phrase:

Healthy young women of great beauty and delightfully curvaceous lines are fascinating creatures.

Subject of the sentence: *Healthy young women of great beauty and delightfully curvaceous lines.*
Subject of the verb: *women.*

The subject of the verb need not precede the verb, although it has done so in all the examples with which we have been working. In a question, the verb, or part of the verb, generally precedes its subject. In the following sentences the subject is printed in italics and the verb (or verb phrase) is underlined:

<u>Are</u> *women* fascinating creatures?

The subject may split a verb phrase:

How <u>do</u> *women* <u>improve</u> their figures? [verb phrase]

A verb may precede its subject in other common patterns:

There <u>are</u> many *reasons* for admiring the female sex.
Beyond the Alps <u>lies</u> *Italy.*

Finding the subject of a sentence is child's play. Finding the subject of the verb—that is, the single noun or pronoun which regulates the number of the verb—is somewhat more difficult.

This important point will help you: While the subject of a sentence may, and often does, contain one or more prepositional phrases, the single noun or pronoun subject of the verb is never found *within* or *as part* of the prepositional phrase.

With that rule to guide you, see how expert you can become at finding subjects of the verb.

DO YOU GET THE POINT?—*test 23*

Underline the subject of the verb in each sentence.

1. In China's Civil War, Nanking claimed further gains.
2. Premier de Gasperi's government won an overwhelming vote of confidence from the Italian Assembly.
3. Jugoslavia denied the existence of an anti-Catholic persecution plan.
4. Business and industrial leaders in New York predicted a rush of applications for price adjustments.
5. The President returned the functions of the Office of Economic Stabilization to the Office of War Mobilization and Reconversion under Director Steelman.

6. The cost of automobiles has just risen 25 per cent.
7. There go my brothers.
8. One of my best friends was killed yesterday.
9. The captain, with all his sisters, aunts, and cousins by the dozens, is coming aboard.
10. Nellie's beauty, as well as her versatility and charm, has made her a very popular girl.
11. Sam, like his mother and father, has red hair.
12. Has either of your parents married since the divorce?
13. Was each of the criminals tried separately?
14. His principal income is the checks he receives from his oil-wells.
15. The greater size of these houses accounts for their staggering cost.
16. Strange, weird, and frightening was the sound.
17. Your blood pressure, as well as your temperature, is up today.
18. His income, like that of many small businessmen, has taken a terrific drop this year.
19. That lot of houses was sold at a very steep price.
20. The aim of all countries today is for a lasting peace.

CHECK YOUR LEARNING—*answers to test 23*

1. Nanking. This was an easy one, to encourage you to go on. The verb is *claimed* and it is hard to see how you could have picked any other word in the sentence as the subject.
2. Government. Although the first four words in the sentence form the *subject of the sentence*, the single word *government* is subject of the verb *won*.
3. Jugoslavia. This is both subject of the sentence and subject of the verb *denied*.
4. Leaders. Here we have a rather long subject of the sentence (all the words up to the verb *predicted*), but the usual one-word subject of the verb.
5. President.
6. Cost. Now for the first time you were offered a sentence in which you might have been tempted to find

your subject within a prepositional phrase. Remember that a noun within a prepositional phrase is the object of the preposition, and never the subject of the verb. Note that *cost* is singular and that the verb *has risen* is also singular.

7. Brothers. This is an instance in which the subject of the verb follows the verb (*go*). *There* is an adverb.

8. One. *Of my best friends* is a prepositional phrase. *One* is the pronoun subject of the verb *was killed*. Note that both the subject and the verb are singular.

9. Captain. All the other nouns preceding the verb are contained within the prepositional phrase introduced by the preposition *with* (*dozens* is in a prepositional phrase of its own, introduced by the preposition *by*). Although the subject of the *sentence* is made up of all the words up to *is,* the subject of the *verb* is the single word *captain*. Since *captain* is singular, *is coming* is singular.

10. Beauty. This sentence is similar to the preceding. *As well as her versatility and charm* is a prepositional phrase introduced by the triple-ply preposition *as well as*. The subject is never found after a preposition.

11. Sam. *Like* is a preposition, and so the nouns *mother* and *father* have no influence on the number of the verb. *Sam* is singular and the verb *has* is singular.

12. Either. *Of your parents* is a prepositional phrase. *Either* in this sentence means *either one;* it is therefore singular and takes the singular verb *has married*.

13. Each. Like *either,* each means *each one*. It is a singular pronoun and takes the singular verb *was tried*.

14. Income.

15. Size.

16. Sound. The subject follows the verb. *Strange, weird,* and *frightening* are adjectives modifying the noun *sound*.

17. Pressure. Compare this sentence with number 9.

18. Income. Compare with number 11.

19. Lot.
20. Aim.

The drill you have just finished should have materially sharpened your instinct for discovering subjects of verbs. Note these important principles:

The subject of the verb is usually a single-word noun or pronoun.

Such noun or pronoun is not found within a prepositional phrase.

The subject generally precedes the verb but in certain sentence patterns may follow the verb.

The number of the verb depends on the number of the single-word subject. (There are minor exceptions, which we will discuss later.)

Singular subjects take singular verbs—plural subjects take plural verbs. (Again, minor exceptions will be discussed later.)

These facts make the solution of the problem which opened this chapter fairly simple. Consider the question once again:

The cost of new cars *is* dropping, *or* The cost of new cars *are* dropping?

SUBJECT OF THE SENTENCE: *The cost of new cars*

SUBJECT OF THE VERB: *cost*

PREPOSITIONAL PHRASE (which has no influence on the number of the verb): *of new cars*

Cost is a singular noun.

The verb must be singular

Hence, the correct form: "The cost of new cars *is* dropping."

3. The Rule

A verb agrees in number with its single-word subject.

4. The Test

Determine the subject of each verb, and then check the correct verb form.

1. A beautiful vase, filled with tall flowers of many kinds, (was, were) standing on his desk.
2. There (is, are) many ways of skinning a cat.
3. The number of absentees (is, are) larger on rainy days than in fair weather.
4. A new round of strikes (is, are) exactly what we do not want.
5. The conclusions reached by this report (is, are) very interesting.
6. The price of foodstuffs (has, have) gone up fantastically since 1940.
7. One of my brothers (is, are) coming in to help me.
8. The queen, with her complete retinue of servants, (is, are) waiting for you.
9. He, as well as his parents, (believes, believe) that you have treated him unfairly.
10. Truman, like some of his predecessors, (is, are) faced with an unfriendly Congress.
11. (Was, Were) either of your suggestions accepted?
12. Each of these problems (is, are) to be solved separately.
13. The appearance of these houses (is, are) most dubious.
14. The costs in your new estimate (is, are) altogether too high.
15. The attempts on his life (has, have) finally ceased.
16. The offerings of the new firm (is, are) explained in their prospectus.
17. Neither of your remarks (is, are) particularly polite.
18. If either of these subjects (is, are) too difficult, let us know.

19. Every one of his answers (is, are) wrong.
20. Lucy, unlike her sisters, (is, are) beautiful.

1. *was* (subject—vase)
2. *are* (subject—ways)
3. *is* (subject—number)
4. *is* (subject—round)
5. *are* (subject—conclusions)
6. *has* (subject—price)
7. *is* (subject—one)
8. *is* (subject—queen)
9. *believes* (subject—he)
10. *is* (subject—Truman)
11. *was* (subject—either [one])
12. *is* (subject—each [one])
13. *is* (subject—appearance)
14. *are* (subject—costs)
15. *have* (subject—attempts)
16. *are* (subject—offerings)
17. *is* (subject—neither [one])
18. *is* (subject—either [one])
19. *is* (subject—one)
20. *is* (subject—Lucy)

as easy as A B C

A. What is the difference between *alumnus* and *alumna*?

B. Is it correct to say, "He is not *as* tall as he looks"?

C. Which is preferable: "Measles *is* a bad disease" or "Measles *are* a bad disease"?

A. The Grammar of Meanings

Alumnus, Alumna

Bernard Baruch is an *alumnus* of the College of the City of New York.

There are thousands of *alumni* of City College, which was, until recently, an all-male institution.

When some years back City College began to admit women to its halls of learning, a female graduate became an *alumna* of the college.

City College has produced a small number of *alumnae* (female graduates) and a large number of *alumni* (male graduates) in the last five years.

Alumnus—male, singular.
Alumni—(pronounced a-lum'-nye) male, plural.
Alumna—female, singular.
Alumnae—(pronounced a-lum'-nee) female, plural.

DO YOU GET THE POINT?—*test 25*

Complete each sentence by correctly inserting one of the four following words: *alumnus, alumni, alumna, alumnae.*

1. He is an .... of West Point.
2. The .... of Yale University will hold their annual meeting next week.
3. She is an .... of The College of New Rochelle.
4. The .... of The College of New Rochelle are bright young women with good educations.

CHECK YOUR LEARNING—*answers to test 25*

1. alumnus   2. alumni   3. alumna   4. alumnae

B. The Grammar of Allowable "Errors"

He is not *as* tall as he looks.

Literature abounds in examples in which the word *as* follows a negative verb.

In the everyday speech of cultivated citizens, the popularity of *as* following a negative is even more pronounced.

There is not, and actually never has been, a grammatical rule in English to the effect that *so* must follow a negative, but many handbooks of rhetoric have claimed that *only* the following versions are "correct" English:

He is not *so* tall as you think.
We are not *so* stupid as you imagine.
She is not *so* old as her brother nor *so* pretty as her sister.

In comparisons, *as* may and frequently does follow a negative verb, if the speaker or writer so chooses. The following are perfectly correct literary and colloquial English:

He is not *as* tall as you think.
We are not *as* stupid as you imagine.
She is not *as* old as her brother nor *as* pretty as her sister.

142

A couple of Tasmanian devils showed up at the Bronx Zoo yesterday, much to the discomfiture of other animals who had never read the zoological report that the creatures were not *as* terrifying as they sounded, nor *as* mean as they looked.

—*The New York Times*

C. The Grammar of Correct Usage

Measles *is* a bad disease, *or*
Measles *are* a bad disease?

Just as certain plurals look like singulars (see page 116), so certain singulars, ending in *s*, look like plurals. For example:

measles	molasses	politics
rickets	news	athletics
mumps	acoustics	economics
shingles	mathematics	ethics

PREFERABLE FORMS:

Measles *is* a bad disease.
Mumps *is* catching.
Is rickets painful?
His shingles *is* very bad today.
That molasses *isn't* very sweet, is it?
The news from Europe *is* disturbing, as usual.
Acoustics *is* studied in Schools of Engineering.
Mathematics *is* an interesting subject.
Politics *makes* strange bedfellows.
Athletics *is* important in a boy's development.
Economics *is* studied in most colleges.
Ethics *is* also studied in most colleges.

143

But:

The economics of your budget *are* all wrong.
What *are* the ethics of the situation?
The acoustics of that auditorium *are* wonderful.
His politics *are* wrong.

Thus:

Diseases which end in *s* are singular.

Acoustics, economics, ethics, mathematics, politics, and *athletics* are singular when the words are used to denote subjects of study; otherwise they are plural.

News is singular.

(There is the famous story of the newspaper publisher who insisted that *news* was a plural word, and that his reporters use it as a plural in their dispatches. One belligerent reporter, on receiving a telegram from the publisher inquiring: "Are there any news?" wired back: "Not a single new.")

chapter 13 HOW TO GET THE
RIGHT NUMBER

1. The Problem

Which is it: "Your mother and father *are* proud of you,"
or "Your mother and father *is* proud of you"? and then,
how about: "Your mother or father *have* to come and see
me," or "Your mother or father *has* to come and see me"?

2. The Solution

"Your father and mother *is* proud of you" doubtless
sounds somewhat illiterate to you, and of course it is a violation of the rule we discovered in chapter 12. The verb
agrees with its subject in number—and the subject of the
verb is patently plural. Two people are involved—your
mother and your father. This is a sentence in which the
verb is governed by a *compound* subject, *mother* and
father. A compound subject with its individual parts combined by the conjunction *and* is plural, and therefore takes
a plural verb, thus:

Jules Perlmutter *and* Herbert Jaffe *are* practicing in New
Rochelle.
City College *and* Columbia University *are* in New York.
Pencil *and* paper *are* not all you need to become a writer.
Fear *and* horror *were* written on her face.

The logic is irrefutable—in each instance the compound
subject is made up of two single elements. It's as clear as
145

one and *one* are *two*.[1] In grammar, one and one *are* two, provided, however, that one *one* is joined to the other *one* by the conjunction *and*.

There is, of course, an obvious exception. Sometimes one and one are *one*, as when the two parts of the compound subject refer to the selfsame person or thing. For instance:

My severest critic and best friend *is* my wife.

To keep this from getting too involved, let us say that my wife's name is Mary (which, by an odd coincidence, it actually is). When I say *my severest critic*, I mean *Mary*. When I say *my best friend*, I still mean *Mary*. I am not referring to two people by the words *critic* and *friend*, but only one, *Mary*. Thus I have a compound subject relating to a single person. Such a compound subject is singular, and takes a singular verb.

I would also say: "My best friend and severest critic *is* here," for the subjects *friend* and *critic* still both refer to one person, my wife.

Another example along the same lines:

The president of the First National Bank and leader of the scout troop *has* just started to speak.

A compound subject, surely—*president* and *leader*. But both words refer to the same man, who, as it happens, holds two positions—bank president and scout leader.

[1] This might be a good place to make a relevant digression. Which is correct: "One and one *are* two" or "One and one *is* two?" "Six plus six (*is, are*) twelve?" "Five times five (*is, are*) twenty-five?" The answer is very simple—both forms of each sentence are correct. You may use either a singular or a plural verb in any mathematical equation. It is reasonable to consider *one and one* as a single and individual mathematical concept —hence *is*. It is equally reasonable to consider *one* and *one* as a compound subject connected by *and*—hence *are*. Similarly, *five times five* may be viewed as a single concept; therefore, "Five times five *is* twenty-five." Or *five* (units) may be considered the plural subject; therefore: "Five times five *are* twenty-five." You have a completely free choice in such usages, no matter what your arithmetic teacher's idiosyncrasy in this regard may have been.

146

There is, nevertheless, just one person involved—the subject, therefore, is singular (and so is the verb).

Another example:

Ham and eggs *is* a tasty dish.

Another compound subject, but again a single idea, an inseparable combination, as any devotee of this characteristically American breakfast will testify.

A third example:

The scourge of old age and the mystery of all medicine —cancer—*is* still ravaging the earth.

A singular verb, because the compound subject, *scourge* and *mystery,* is a single disease—cancer.

Although one *and* one are two, one *or* one is *not* two, but one. This may not appeal to your sense of logic nor your concept of mathematics, but the grammatical rule is pretty definite; one *or* one is one. In other words, a compound subject made up of singular elements joined by the conjunction *or* is singular, not, as in the case of *and,* plural.

This rule applies with equal force to the correlative conjunctions *either . . . or* and *neither . . . nor.*

Therefore:

Your mother or your father *has* to come and see me.

And also:

Either your mother or your father *has* to come and see me.

Neither your father nor your mother *has* been in to see me yet.

Neither America nor Russia *wants* war.

Either Congress or the President *has* to assume leadership.

Was a psychiatrist or a neurologist called in on the case?

An oculist or an optometrist *has* the right to prescribe glasses for a person with imperfect vision, but not an optician, who may only work from a prescription.

3. The Rule

Does your sentence have two or more singular subjects, connected by *and?* Use a *plural* verb.

However, if these two singular subjects refer to the same person or thing, use a *singular* verb.

Does your sentence have two (or more) singular subjects connected by *or, either . . . or,* or *neither . . . nor?* Use a *singular* verb.

4. The Test

DO YOU GET THE POINT?—*test 26*

Choose the correct verb in each sentence.

1. Claudia and her sister (has, have) already left.
2. Either Claudia or Nina (is, are) still here.
3. There (is, are) a package or a letter for you, I forget which.
4. There (was, were) a porterhouse steak and a leg of lamb in the tray just five minutes ago; what happened to them?
5. The brown hat and the blue hat (is, are) the same price; which color do you prefer?
6. The brown hat or the blue hat (is, are) the same price; which color do you want?
7. The number or the value of your bond (is, are) not what we're concerned with; the important question is where you got the money to pay for it.
8. Neither Jugoslavia nor Italy (seems, seem) entirely satisfied with the peace treaty.
9. Either Russia or Britain (is, are) certain to suggest a compromise before the actual voting takes place.

10. There (was, were) a student and a teacher in the room, going over some final term papers.
11. A chair or a couch (is, are) the only piece of furniture that will look good in this corner.
12. Either the drive shaft or the flywheel (is, are) broken.

CHECK YOUR LEARNING—*answers to test 26*

1. have	4. were	7. is	10. were
2. is	5. are	8. seems	11. is
3. is	6. is	9. is	12. is

PRO AND CON

Q. Do you ever countenance a plural verb with the pronoun subject *either*, as in the sentence "Either of the books *are* useful"?

Pro

A. Certainly not. The real subject is *one* understood.
                                        —Henry Seidel Canby

Mr. Canby was formerly chairman of the editorial board of the *Saturday Review*.

as easy as A B C

A. What is the difference between *childish* and *child-like?*

B. Is it correct to say, "She was most *aggravated* by what happened"?

C. Which is preferable: "One or two books *is* enough," or "One or two books *are* enough"?

A. The Grammar of Meanings

Childish, Childlike

Some women act like children. They pout when they don't get their own way. They use baby talk to cajole favors from the trusting male. They allow themselves to be guided exclusively by instinct and emotion, never by rational common sense. (*Some* women, not *all* women.) Such women we may call *childish.*

On the other hand, some women possess certain different qualities common to children. They may have the unspoiled beauty, the trustfulness, the innocence, the charm of young children. Such qualities would aptly be characterized as *childlike.*

We describe qualities or attitudes or people as *childish* if we are speaking in derogation—that is, if we are consciously referring to what we consider the less pleasing qualities of childhood: *childish* temper, *childish* meanness, *childish* ignorance, and the like.

However, we call those qualities *childlike* with which we are in sympathy, qualities we consider pleasant: *childlike*

150

innocence, *childlike* frankness, *childlike* simplicity, and so on.

The two words are synonymous: the distinction is one of atmosphere. Is something agreeable? It is *childlike*. Is it disagreeable? It is *childish*.

DO YOU GET THE POINT?—*test 27*

1. The (childish, childlike) directness of her questions left him nonplussed.
2. She was (childish, childlike) in her trust and belief.
3. Such (childish, childlike) naïveté in a grown-up person is most irritating.
4. May's (childish, childlike) charm has always captivated her husband.
5. That's a (childish, childlike) attitude for you to take —why don't you try to act more grown-up?
6. She burst into a (childish, childlike) fit of temper when her husband rebuked her.
7. Your constant petulance is most (childish, childlike).

CHECK YOUR LEARNING—*answers to test 27*

1. childlike   3. childish   5. childish   7. childish
2. childlike   4. childlike   6. childish

B. The Grammar of Allowable "Errors"

She was most *aggravated* by what happened.

Aggravated had, as its original meaning, "made worse, itensified." In recent years, the word has been used with the added meaning of "provoked, annoyed, exasperated, irritated." Academic textbooks and speech manuals have never sanctioned the new meaning of "aggravated," but educated people go on using the word to express the idea of "exasperated" notwithstanding. Everything considered, it would be pedantic and narrow-minded to consider the following expressions incorrect:

151

What an *aggravating* child!
I was never so *aggravated* in all my life!
She *aggravates* me with her prissy affectation.
This is an *aggravating* situation.

C. The Grammar of Correct Usage

One or two books *is* enough, *or*
One or two books *are* enough?

The plural verb is used with the phrase "one or two . . . ," thus: "One or two of my friends *have* already received checks" "Here *are* one or two things you've omitted" and "At least one or two of your answers *were* satisfactory."

PREFERABLE FORM:

One or two books *are* enough.

chapter 14 HOW TO TEST A VERB

1. The Problem

"Doctor, my child and *I* would like to visit you tomorrow" is correct English. Is it also correct to say: "Doctor, can you see my child and *I* tomorrow?"

2. The Solution

When I was a child, mothers used to spend time (which might preferably have been devoted to more important things) on warning their young to show politeness by putting themselves last. Unless the war has had an even more devastating effect on women than the sociologists are admitting, mothers still admonish their offspring, as they did thirty years ago: "Don't say: 'Me and John want some bread and jelly.' Say: 'John and I want some bread and jelly.'"

The child of my day (I have checked this observation with a number of honest adults who had childhoods contemporaneous with mine) soon developed the notion that *me* was not quite as elegant a term as *I*, although (or so it seemed in juvenile logic) both words meant exactly the same thing—*me* was not as elegant as *I*, nor anywhere nearly as acceptable to grown-up ears. As children, we learned that we could get things quicker, and with a lot less wrangling, if we substituted *I* for *me* whenever such a substitution was even remotely plausible. So we substituted. With the result that a lot of us grew up with the habit of phrasing our thoughts in such patterns as:

There isn't enough food for both *he* and *I*.
Why don't you let Mary and *I* try it?
Between you and *I*, I don't believe a word she is saying.
Doctor, can you see my child and *I* today?

The problem, however, is not one of politeness, but of
case.

Our experience with case has thus far been somewhat
limited. In chapter 8, we discovered that personal pronouns
had different forms for different cases. Let me refresh your
memory:

NOMINATIVE FORMS OF THE PERSONAL PRONOUN	OBJECTIVE FORMS OF OF THE PERSONAL PRONOUN
I	me
you	you
he	him
she	her
we	us
you	you
they	them

We have learned also that the objective forms of these
pronouns are used as objects of prepositions.

We wish now to begin to round out our knowledge of
case by considering two other uses:

USE 1: THE NOMINATIVE CASE OF THE PRONOUN IS USED
AS SUBJECT OF THE VERB

My child and *I* would like to visit you.
My wife and *I* are happy to see you.
She and *I* simply do not get along.
We and *they* have been friends for years.

USE 2: THE OBJECTIVE CASE OF THE PERSONAL PRONOUN
IS USED AS OBJECT OF THE VERB

But what is an *object*?

154

To answer this question, let us first recall what we have learned about subjects.

The subject of the verb is the person or thing we are talking about:

1. *He* works.
2. *He* sees.
3. *He* is seen.

In some instances, the subject initiates the action of the verb, as in illustrations 1 and 2. When this happens, the verb is said to be in the *active voice*.

We talk about a subject, say *Harry Truman*.

What does *Harry Truman* do—what action does he initiate?

Harry Truman outsmarts congress.

Outsmarts is a verb in the active voice.

On the other hand, the subject of a verb may in some instances *receive* the action of that verb, as in illustration 3 (*He* is seen).

When this happens, the verb is said to be in the *passive voice*.

We talk about a subject, say (not to become monotonous) *Herbert Hoover*.

What happens to *Herbert Hoover*—what action does he receive?

Herbert Hoover is sent to Europe to study food problems.

Is sent is a verb in the passive voice.

Verbs in the passive voice are always in phrase form (that is, made up of two or more parts) and are composed of some form of the verb *to be* plus the *perfect participle*.

Passive verb forms:
was *sent*

will be *recognized*
has been *used*
is *found*

(The italicized parts of the verb phrases are perfect participles.)

If the *subject* receives the action of the verb, frequently the *initiator* of that action is also found within the sentence. Such initiator occurs within a prepositional phrase introduced by the preposition *by.*

1. ACTIVE: Benny sent me.
   PASSIVE: I was sent *by Benny.*
2. ACTIVE: He will recognize you.
   PASSIVE: You will be recognized *by him.*
3. ACTIVE: Women have used cosmetics for centuries.
   PASSIVE: Cosmetics have been used *by women* for centuries.
4. ACTIVE: Diligent hunters find a house to live in.
   PASSIVE: A house to live in is found *by diligent hunters.*

To get back to objects:

The subject of an *active* verb *initiates* the action of that verb.

The object of an active verb *receives* the action of that verb.

Each of the *active* verbs illustrated above (1 to 4) has an object.

VERB	OBJECT
1. sent	me
2. will recognize	you
3. have used	cosmetics
4. find	house

The subject of a *passive* verb receives the action.
(A *passive* verb never has an object.)

The object of an *active* verb receives the action.

So now you know what an object is.

For the present let us work with this temporary definition of an object: *An object of the verb is a noun or pronoun which receives the action of that verb—provided the verb is active.*

Only active verbs have objects.

When an active verb has an object, such a verb is called *transitive*. (The term *transitive* is made up of two Latin roots, *trans,* across; and *it,* goes. The action of a transitive verb goes across to an object.)

However, not all active verbs have objects, as witness:

Truman *runs* for office.
Trains never *arrive* on time.
Can we *come* into your house?

An active verb which has no object is called, logically enough, *intransitive*.

Every active verb in a sentence is either transitive or intransitive.

Transitive verbs have objects.

Intransitive verbs do not have objects.

It's as simple as that.

But can you rely on your ability to determine whether or not a verb has an object? Can you see the difference, furthermore, between an active and a passive verb? Let's put it to a test.

DO YOU GET THE POINT?—*test 28*

Decide whether the verb in each sentence is transitive, intransitive, or passive. Underline the object if there is one.

1. He found his wife in the arms of another man. TRANSITIVE? INTRANSITIVE? PASSIVE?
2. He was found drunk on the corner of Hollywood and Vine. TRANSITIVE? INTRANSITIVE? PASSIVE?

3. The judge found for the defendant. TRANSITIVE? IN-TRANSITIVE? PASSIVE?

4. He ran faster than ever. TRANSITIVE? INTRANSITIVE? PASSIVE?

5. The meal was eaten in silence. TRANSITIVE? INTRANSITIVE? PASSIVE?

6. They ate in gloomy silence. TRANSITIVE? INTRANSITIVE? PASSIVE?

7. They ate all the leftovers. TRANSITIVE? INTRANSITIVE? PASSIVE?

8. The enemy attacked in force. TRANSITIVE? INTRANSITIVE? PASSIVE?

9. The enemy attacked our position at dawn. TRANSITIVE? INTRANSITIVE? PASSIVE?

10. Who last saw Hitler alive? TRANSITIVE? INTRANSITIVE? PASSIVE?

11. By whom was Hitler last seen alive? TRANSITIVE? INTRANSITIVE? PASSIVE?

12. We arrived on time. TRANSITIVE? INTRANSITIVE? PASSIVE?

13. Lay that pistol down. TRANSITIVE? INTRANSITIVE? PASSIVE?

14. Lie down for a nap. TRANSITIVE? INTRANSITIVE? PASSIVE?

15. The body was laid in the grave. TRANSITIVE? INTRANSITIVE? PASSIVE?

CHECK YOUR LEARNING—*answers to test 28*

1. transitive
   (object—wife)
2. passive
3. intransitive
4. intransitive
5. passive
6. intransitive
7. transitive
   (object—leftovers)
8. intransitive
9. transitive
   (object—position)
10. transitive
    (object—Hitler)
11. passive
12. intransitive
13. transitive
    (object—pistol)
14. intransitive
15. passive

Personal pronouns which function as objects of a verb are in the objective case.

I see *him*.
He sees *me*.
We see *them*.
They see *us*.

If two pronouns function as object of the verb, they are both in the objective case.

This pleases *him* and *me*.
Can you see *her* and *him?*

If a noun and pronoun form the compound object of the verb, the pronoun is in the objective case.

Can you see John and *me* now?
We heard Paul and *her* crying.
Why do you keep Ben and *us* waiting?
You can't treat *us* girls that way.

With this information, you can easily solve the problem which opened this chapter.

Doctor, can you see my child and (I, me) tomorrow?

The pronoun is part of the compound object of the verb phrase *can see*.
Hence the objective case is required.

CORRECT FORM:

Doctor, can you see my child and *me* tomorrow?

3. The Rule

As object of the verb, the personal pronoun is always in the objective case.

4. The Test

Check the correct pronoun in each sentence.

1. Harriet Dorn and (I, me) will attend the dance together.
2. (She, Her) and Ira certainly make a cute couple, don't they?
3. You and (we, us) had better go together, I think.
4. Send Mr. Sack and (I, me) separate bills, if you will.
5. Take her father and (she, her) into the next room, please.
6. This matter can best be settled, I believe, between (he, him) and his lawyer.
7. How was the letter addressed? Was it addressed to his father and (he, him) or to his mother and (he, him)?
8. That's something you can decide yourself, or else you and (she, her) can decide it between you.
9. We'll leave the decision up to you and (they, them).
10. Everyone is willing to play along with us but (she, her) and Bob.
11. Will you serve (he, him) and (I, me) now?
12. Women treat (we, us) men in a rather unsportsmanlike manner, don't you think?
13. Will you watch Ira and (she, her) so they don't get into trouble?
14. Please write your mother and (I, me) at least once a week.
15. Please call your father and (I, me) whenever you're in town.
16. Did you invite (we, us) and the Harrisons to your party?
17. He considers Margie and (I, me) his best friends.
18. We saw Sam and (she, her) together last night.

19. (They, Them) and (we, us) are not friends.
20. Do you consider (they, them) and (we, us) friends?

1. I	6. him	11. him, me	16. us
2. she	7. him, him	12. us	17. me
3. we	8. she	13. her	18. her
4. me	9. them	14. me	19. they, we
5. her	10. her	15. me	20. them, us

(The pronouns in test 29 were offered to you as subjects [nominative case], objects [objective case] and objects of prepositions [objective case]. Can you tell which is which?)

as easy as A B C

A. What is the difference between *uninterested* and *disinterested?*

B. Is it correct to say, "It's *liable* to rain," or "It's *apt* to rain"?

C. Which is preferable: "A number of men *are* here," or "A number of men *is* here"?

A. The Grammar of Meanings

Uninterested, Disinterested

The child sits in a classroom on a spring day, his mind far away. The subject bores him, the teacher bores him; he is totally indifferent to every activity in the classroom. He would like to be out fishing, playing baseball, swimming. . . . His inattentiveness is perfect. He is *uninterested*.

A judge sits on the bench, listening carefully to the evidence, pro and con, which the opposing sides present to him. He is far from being bored. His interest is most keen. His attentiveness to all that is going on is tremendous. The questions he asks of defendant and plaintiff, of counsel for both litigants, of one witness after another, attest to his alertness. Yet he is (since justice is to be served) *disinterested*.

A person is *uninterested* if he is bored and indifferent.

A person is *disinterested* if he is impartial, unbiased, neutral, not personally concerned or involved in a dispute.

1. As you are an (a) (uninterested, disinterested) party, we will let you settle our dispute.
2. Don't look so (uninterested, disinterested); the play is not as boring as you seem to think.
3. Try to arrive at an (a) (uninterested, disinterested) conclusion.
4. The war proved that we could not afford to maintain an (a) (uninterested, disinterested) attitude toward events in Europe.
5. She is (uninterested, disinterested) in her neighbors' personal affairs.

CHECK YOUR LEARNING—*answers to test 30*

1. disinterested   3. disinterested   5. uninterested
2. uninterested.   4. disinterested

B. The Grammar of Allowable "Errors"

> It's *liable* to rain, *or*
> It's *apt* to rain.

To denote probability, *likely* is the safe adjective to use. Strictly speaking, *liable* is restricted to the probability of an unpleasant or injurious occurrence, as:

You are *liable* to die if you drink cyanide of potassium.
You are *liable* to be fined if you spit on the sidewalk.

Still strictly speaking, *apt* is supposed to show a general tendency, as:

Little children are *apt* to be disobedient at times.
A college graduate is *apt* to be a well-read person.

However, many educated speakers do not conscientiously observe these narrow distinctions, and frequently

163

use *apt* and *liable* as interchangeable synonyms of *likely*, to show ordinary probability. Such use of *apt* and *liable* cannot reasonably be called incorrect English.

PRO AND CON

Q. What is your opinion of the acceptability of the statement: "It's *liable* to rain tomorrow"?

Noncommittal

A. I think the statement "It's liable to rain tomorrow" should concern only a weatherman—not a grammarian like me.

—Robert Ripley

Mr. Ripley was the creator of "Believe It or Not."

Pro (*with reservations*)

A. I should not write, and I think I should never say, *liable* in such a sentence as you quote. However, in the writing and certainly in the speech of any but excellent users of English in school I should probably not suggest the substitution of *likely*. The majority of young people in our high schools would better give attention to more important matters of usage.

P.S. I note that I unconsciously used the puristic *should* rather than *would*. It has here no flavor of *ought*.

—W. Wilbur Hatfield

Dr. Hatfield was formerly editor of *The English Journal*.

Q. What is your opinion of "It's *apt* to rain tomorrow" as correct, idiomatic English? Would you use the expression in your everyday speech?

Pro

A. In answer to your query about *apt*, for whatever it is worth my opinion is as follows:

164

I would normally use *apt* in the sense of "It's *apt* to rain tomorrow" as correct and idiomatic enough for all practical purposes, both in conversation and in print.

Perhaps, in extremely formal writing, I would make a slight distinction that *apt* should be reserved for the sense of having a habitual tendency, or especially fitted for. If intended to express probability that some event might happen in the nature of inanimate things, like weather, I believe the adjective *likely* would be more accurate. But the distinction is so tenuous that only a purist would probably observe it.

—Kenneth M. Gould

Mr. Gould was editor-in-chief of *Scholastic* magazines.

C. The Grammar of Correct Usage

A number of men *are* here, *or*
A number of men *is* here?

This is an instance in which the subject (*number*) is singular in form but so strongly plural in meaning that it takes a plural verb.

PREFERABLE FORMS:

A number of men *are* here.
A number of children *are* absent today.
A large number of your questions *do* not admit of answers.
A small number of houses *are* still unsold.

Also:

A lot of criminals *get* away with their crimes.
A lot of my friends *like* you, even though I don't.

But:

The number of workers in the industry *has* dropped.
The greatest number of errors *was* made on Part II.

165

The number of prisoners *has* decreased.
This lot of books *was* sold for a song.

In other words:

A number and *a lot* take *plural* verbs.
The number, this number, that number and *the lot, this lot, that lot* take *singular* verbs.

chapter 15 HOW TO KEEP YOUR SANITY WITH "LAY" AND "LIE"

1. The Problem

If it is correct to say, "*Lay* that pistol down, Mama," why can't we, with equal justification, say, "*Lay* down for a nap, Mama"?

2. The Solution

Pronouns cause the greatest *number of errors* among literate adults.

The verbs *lay* and *lie* cause the greatest *number of headaches*.

More errors are made with pronouns than with any other part of speech, perhaps because there is such a variety of ways for a speaker to go wrong. The eleven different forms of personal pronouns, including nominative and objective cases, form a healthy percentage of the average day's conversation, so the statistics I gathered in my classes, which show pronouns as the leading cause of error, are not exactly surprising.

Although errors in *lay* and *lie* run second, numerically speaking, to errors in pronouns, the results of the investigation I have described showed this curious twist:

1. The greatest number of *errors* was made in the use of pronouns.
2. However, the greatest number of *people* made errors in the use of *lay* and *lie*.

Of the 856 adults whose grammatical speech habits were charted, only seven showed a perfect knowledge of the ramifications of these perplexing verbs!

In the test given to these adults, nine of the one hundred sentences required the checking of the correct form of one of these verbs. These were the results:

7 made a perfect score on all 9 sentences.
   (These same seven had an over-all score of between 90 and 100.)
22 made 1 error.
162 made 2 or 3 errors.
534 made 4 errors.
131 made 5 or more errors.
None made more than 7 errors.

Of the 856 adults tested, roughly 12 per cent were college graduates, 20 per cent had had one or two years of college training, 55 per cent were high-school graduates but had gone no further, and all the rest, or about 13 per cent, were primary-school graduates. In other words, every one of these people had had some kind of training in grammar, either primary school, secondary school, or college, or all three. Yet 849 out of 856 made one to seven errors out of nine attempts to use *lay* and *lie* correctly.

Obviously these two verbs are a particularly common and troublesome problem in English grammar, and one well worth devoting some time and thought to.

The key to the entire problem lies in your complete understanding of the difference between transitive, intransitive, and passive verbs.

You recall, from the work we have just finished (chapter 14), that:

A verb is passive if its subject receives its action:

The gamblers were run out of town.
Gambling has been stopped in the city.

An active verb is transitive if it has an object:

He runs two gambling casinos in Florida.
Her face would stop a clock.

An active verb is intransitive if it does not have an object:

We ran all the way home.
The clock has stopped.

Since the rest of this chapter will be practically meaningless to you unless you have become a past master in the fine art of distinguishing transitive from intransitive verbs, let me impose upon your patience by asking you to submit to a quick test of your ability before we go any further.

DO YOU GET THE POINT?—*test 31*

Each sentence contains an italicized verb. Check the symbol TR if that verb is transitive, INT if the verb is intransitive.

1. Charles Jackson, author of *The Lost Weekend, has* also *written* a book called *The Fall of Valor*. TR INT
2. Bernard Baruch *accused* Henry Wallace of making false statements about the atomic-energy proposals. TR INT
3. When you *lie* down on that bed, be careful. TR INT
4. He *walked* upstairs, slowly, methodically, one step at a time. TR INT
5. He *has walked* his dog several times around the block, but with no success. TR INT
6. Do not *eat* so quickly. TR INT
7. Do not *eat* so much. TR INT

8. Landlords *have* no sympathy for the plight of their tenants.   TR   INT
9. The teacher *spoke* fluently about her troubles.   TR   INT
10. She *spoke* her piece and sat down.   TR   INT

CHECK YOUR LEARNING—*answers to test 31*

1. TR 2. TR 3. INT 4. INT 5. TR 6. INT 7. TR 8. TR 9. INT 10. TR

Here, now, are the three keys that will unlock for you all the puzzling secrets of *lay* and *lie:*

KEY 1: *Lie* (or one of its forms) is exclusively an *intransitive* verb.

KEY 2: *Lay* (or one of its forms) is, on the other hand, a *transitive* verb.

KEY 3: Only *lay* (in its passive form) may be used in the *passive* voice. *Lie* is never passive.

When you are confronted with the necessity for making a choice between the forms of *lie* and *lay*, these are the three points to remember:

POINT 1: If an intransitive verb is required (because there is *no* object), use some form of *lie*.

POINT 2: If a transitive verb is required (because there *is* an object), use some form of *lay*.

POINT 3: If a passive verb is required (because the subject receives the action), use the passive form of *lay*. In the passive voice, the perfect participle of a verb is used. In the case of *lay*, the perfect participle is *laid*.

For example:

Lie—intransitive

1. The hope of democracy lies in the economic security of the common man.
2. Lie down for an hour before dinner.
3. Why do you lie asleep all morning when there is so much work to be done?

170

4. Whenever she lies down, the phone rings.
5. His interests lie in the fields of science and technology.

Lay—transitive

1. The hen lays an *egg*.
2. That show will lay an *egg*.
3. Please lay the *baby* on its back.
4. Peace is here; shall we lay down our *arms*?
5. They will lay the *body* to rest in Woodlawn Cemetery.

(The object in each sentence is in italics.)

Laid (the perfect participle of *lay*)—passive

1. The keel of the ship was laid on Friday.
2. When will the cornerstone of the building be laid?
3. The rug was laid in the wrong room.
4. The body was laid to rest in Woodlawn.
5. The groundwork for our understanding of *lay* and *lie* is now laid.

Do the distinctions seem fairly easy and clear-cut? Then try a test of your learning.

DO YOU GET THE POINT?—*test 32*

1. When we (lie, lay) on this bed, we can feel the springs coming through the mattress.
2. If you will (lie, lay) away a few dollars every week, you will soon learn the painful habit of thrift.
3. (Lie, Lay) still for a few minutes.
4. Don't (lie, lay) the books on that shelf; it's too high up.
5. (Lie, Lay) the patient on the sofa so the doctor can examine him.
6. We found the wounded man (lying, laying) on the floor.

7. She has become accustomed to (lying, laying) down for a short nap before dinner.
8. (Lie, Lay) the baby in its crib, and perhaps it will go to sleep.
9. We saw a penny (lying, laying) in the mud.
10. If you (lie, lay) in a stock of coal now, you may save some money next winter.

1. lie	3. lie	5. lay	7. lying	9. lying
2. lay	4. lay	6. lying	8. lay	10. lay

Every verb has a past tense—and *lie* and *lay* are no exceptions.

This is where our trouble really starts.

The past tense of *lay* is *laid*—reasonable enough so far.

But the past tense of *lie* is *lay!*

No, this is not a misprint.

Lay is the past tense of the verb *lie.*

It is not of course the same *lay* as the transitive verb with which we have been dealing. *Lay,* as a verb in the past tense (that is, the past tense of *lie*), is an *intransitive* verb.

Before you become too confused to be of any further use to society, let us make a table:

VERB	PRESENT	PAST
lay (transitive)	lay	laid
lie (intransitive)	lie	lay

For example:

Lay

Today I *lay* the baby in the crib.
Yesterday I *laid* the baby in the crib.

172

Today I *lie* down.
Yesterday I *lay* down.

With that as a starter, try a short problem:

DO YOU GET THE POINT?—*test 33*

Complete each sentence with the correct past tense of the required verb.

1. She .... down for a nap this morning.
2. Yesterday, when she .... down for a nap, her dinner burned.
3. She .... the work aside for a few days.
4. The nurse .... the patient on her back and then called the doctor in.
5. We .... the foundation of your understanding of *lay* and *lie* by presenting 3 clear-cut principles.
6. He .... quietly for a moment, then finally arose and began to dress.

CHECK YOUR LEARNING—*answers to test 33*

1. lay   2. lay   3. laid   4. laid   5. laid   6. lay

If success crowned your attempts in test 33, you are ready for further troubles.
To wit:
Lay and *lie* have a third tense which often proves troublesome, namely the *perfect*.
The perfect tense of the transitive verb *lay* is *have laid*.

We have laid rugs in all the rooms.

The perfect tense of the intransitive verb *lie* is *have lain*.

Have you lain awake all night?

173

The perfect tense of any verb is that form which combines *has, have, having,* or *had* with the past participle. Here are further examples of the use of the perfect tenses of *lay* and *lie:*

She *has laid* her winter garments away.

The lawyers *had* already *laid* the groundwork for an appeal, so there were only a few papers to prepare and sign.

Having laid his business cares away for the day, he went to the Stork Club to meet Gypsy Rose Lee.

The baby *has lain* asleep for two hours.

She *had lain* down for a short nap when her husband came home.

Having lain on the shelves all year, the books had gathered a considerable layer of dust.

The perfect tense is a *verb phrase* made up of two parts:

(*a*) the auxiliary *has, have, had,* or *having;*

(*b*) the *past participle* (in the case of the two verbs under discussion, *laid* and *lain*).

Has, had, have, or *having* is called an *auxiliary* since it *helps* the main verb.

The *past* participle of any verb is that form used in the perfect tenses: has *worked,* had *lain,* have *known,* and so on.

The italicized forms are the past participles of *work, lie,* and *know.*

There is still another *participle*—the *present participle,* which is the *-ing* form of the verb: *working, laying, lying, knowing, seeing,* and so on.

We can now considerably amplify the table we made earlier:

VERB	PRESENT	PAST	PAST PARTICIPLE	PRESENT PARTICIPLE
lay (transitive)	lay	laid	laid	laying
lie (intransitive)	lie	lay	lain	lying

Now, if you could somehow manage to memorize this diagram, you would be well on your way toward conquering any difficulties you might ever happen to have with *lay* and *lie*. And performing this feat of memory will take you no longer than 2½ minutes. Students in my classes do it every term in that time or less.

To test your memory, fill the proper forms into the blanks below:

VERB	PRESENT	PAST	PAST PARTICIPLE	PRESENT PARTICIPLE
lay (transitive)				
lie (intransitive)				

One final thought: you may possibly run into a little confusion on this minor point.

The past of lie is *lay:* "He *lay* asleep all morning."

However, in the negative and interrogative forms of this sentence, we allow the auxiliary to carry the burden of expressing past time, and keep the main verb, *lie,* unchanged.

INTERROGATIVE: *Did* he lie asleep all morning?
NEGATIVE: He *did* not lie asleep all morning.

The negative and interrogative forms of *lay* follow the same rule, as do all negative and interrogative verbs in English.

AFFIRMATIVE: We *laid* the child in its crib.
NEGATIVE: We *did* not lay the child in its crib.
INTERROGATIVE: *Did* we lay the child in its crib?

And that is the full story on *lay* and *lie*.
There are only three simple principles to keep in mind:

1. *Lie* is intransitive.
2. *Lay* is transitive.
3. Only *lay* has a passive voice.

Once you have mastered these principles, the rest is a matter of forming good habits—forming them so well that they become reflexive. There is no sanction whatever for any misuse of either verb. There is no trend whatever among educated speakers to substitute forms of *lay* for forms of *lie*—though the tendency is very much pronounced among speakers whose grammar is generally incorrect.

If you study the history of English words, you will observe many instances in which one word displaces another of closely allied meaning. Today, in educated speech, *further* is displacing *farther*, *will* is displacing *shall*, and *prone* is displacing *supine*.[1] There were, at one time, certain distinctions between *shall* and *will*, *further* and *farther*, and *prone* and *supine*. But *farther*, *shall*, and *supine* are today practically obsolete words. The displacement which I have described is one of the factors making for the fine economy of the English language.

However, *lay* and *lie* are apparently impervious to this common trend. In educated speech, *lay* does not show any promise or portent of ever displacing *lie*, though it has already completely done so in uneducated speech!

In the problem at the beginning of this chapter, *lay* in the first sentence is correct because a transitive verb is required—the verb has an object, namely *pistol*. In the sec-

[1] Prone, strictly speaking, means lying *face downward*. Supine, on the other hand, means lying *face upward*. Most people today use *prone* for both positions, especially the latter.

ond sentence, there is no object, the verb is intransitive, and so *lie* is the only acceptable form.

3. The Rule

Lie is intransitive. *Lay* is transitive. *Lie* has only an active voice. *Lay* may be either active or passive.

How to remember the rule: The *i* in *lie* will remind you of *intransitive*, which begins with the letter *i*. The *a* in *lay* will remind you of *transitive* and *passive;* in both these terms the first vowel is *a*.

4. The Test

DO YOU GET THE POINT?—*test 34*

Check the correct form of each verb:

1. The patient is (laying, lying) on the couch.
2. (Lie, Lay) the baby down so the doctor can examine him.
3. Estelle has (lain, laid) down for a nap.
4. Allan picked up the sticks and (lied, laid, lay) them straight.
5. We (laid, lay, lied) in the sun all yesterday morning.
6. He (laid, lay) his hands on the controls, waiting for the signal to start the train.
7. Have you (lain, laid) away your summer clothes yet?
8. The bill has (laid, lain) on the President's desk all week, waiting for his signature.
9. Which shelf did you (lay, lie) the curtains on?
10. Did you (lay, lie) on your back all night?
11. Why don't you (lie, lay) down for a short rest before supper?
12. There the diamond (lay, laid) in the gutter, and the hundreds of people passing by never noticed it.
13. Let sleeping dogs (lay, lie).

14. There he was, (lying, laying) on the hard floor.
15. The work has been carefully (laid, lain) out for you; you should have very little difficulty.
16. Certain principles of government were (laid, lain) down by the Founding Fathers in the United States Constitution.
17. If she had only (laid, lain) quietly, this would not have happened.
18. (Laid, Lain) on its side the child was able to breathe better.
19. (Laying, Lying) on its side, the child was able to breathe better.
20. Let us (lay, lie) our plans carefully and nothing will go wrong.

CHECK YOUR LEARNING—*answers to test 34*

1. lying	6. laid	11. lie	16. laid
2. lay	7. laid	12. lay	17. lain
3. lain	8. lain	13. lie	18. laid
4. laid	9. lay	14. lying	19. lying
5. lay	10. lie	15. laid	20. lay

as easy as A B C

A. The Grammar of Meanings

Fiancé, Fiancée

Sex is one of the most delightful phenomena of human living; it is sometimes one of the most confusing. This confusion occasionally spills over into grammar.

We are all of us more or less adjusted to the unavoidable fact that there are two sexes—male and female. (This being a book on grammar rather than one on abnormal psychology, we'll ignore any other possibilities.)

Though little confusion exists as to the differences between these two sexes, some bewilderment attaches at times to the grammar of sex. We have already learned that a male is an *alumnus*, a female an *alumna*. A man is an *aviator*, an *excutor*, a *masseur*, a *waiter*, an *actor;* a woman is an *aviatrix*, an *executrix*, a *masseuse*, a *waitress*, an *actress*.

The democratization of sex has gone further in English than in most foreign languages. In French, for example,

179

everything, animate or inanimate, animal, vegetable or mineral, is either masculine or feminine, sometimes with ridiculous results, as in the case of *la barbe,* the beard, which is feminine. In Latin, every word is either masculine, feminine, or neuter, not according to strict logic, but more likely in accordance with the spelling of the word.

But in English, both grammatically and logically, a doctor, a lawyer, a teacher, a worker, a thief, a genius may be either male or female, either masculine or feminine.

The difference between *fiancé* and *fiancée* is entirely one of sex, as you would logically expect. With the one *e,* *fiancé* is a man; with two *e*'s, *fiancée* is a woman. Both words are pronounced identically: fee-ahn-*say*. The French accent (*é*) may or need not be used in spelling—either *fiancé* or *fiance;* either *fiancée* or *fiancee.*

DO YOU GET THE POINT?—*test 35*

1. His (fiancé, fiancée) is a beautiful blonde.
2. Her newest (fiancé, fiancée) has just jilted her.
3. "Your (fiancé, fiancée)," said John to his sister, "is handsome enough. But has he any brains?"
4. A king of England gave up a throne for his (fiancé, fiancée).

CHECK YOUR LEARNING—*answers to test 35*

1. fiancée   2. fiancé   3. fiancé   4. fiancée

B. *The Grammar of Allowable "Errors"*

The *above* remarks are not intended to imply . . .
The *above* is a verbatim report of . . .

"The remarks quoted *above*" (adverbial function, modifying the participial adjective *quoted*) is the only use sanctioned in pedantic circles, but "the *above* remarks" (adjective) and "the *above* is true" (noun) are uses which have always been so current in educated speech and writing that it is ridiculous to condemn such constructions. Pooley [2] notes the adjective and noun use in a number of reputable authors, and adds: "Any writer may feel free at any time to use 'the *above* statement,' and with only slightly less assurance, 'the *above* will prove.' In either case, he has the authority of scholars and standard literature."

PRO AND CON

Q. Modern grammarians maintain that "The *above* remarks are not to be taken at face value" is correct, idiomatic English established by common usage among educated people. Do you agree? Would you use the expression in your everyday speech?

Pro

A. I agree that the expression, "The above remarks," is correct, idiomatic English, established by common usage among educated people. For myself, I tend to use the expression, "The foregoing remarks," or "The preceding remarks," because of a prejudice acquired in years of teaching English in high school and college. However, I never criticize students for using the expression you inquire about, and have the impression that it is probably less stilted and therefore more effective than the expressions which my purist teachers induced me to adopt.

—John J. De Boer

Dr. De Boer is editor of *Elementary English* and professor of education at Roosevelt College, Chicago.

Q. Many modern grammarians maintain that "The *above* is a verbatim report of the proceedings" is correct, idiomatic English, established by common usage among

[2] Robert C. Pooley, professor of English at the University of Wisconsin, in *Teaching English Usage: A Guide for English Teachers in High School.* (Appleton-Century).

educated people. Do you agree? Would you use the expression in your everyday speech?

Pro

A. Yes, I'd use it just as above.

—Ed Sullivan

Mr. Sullivan is the well-known television personality.

C. *The Grammar of Correct Usage*

> Three-quarters of the work *is* done, *or*
> Three-quarters of the work *are* done?

A unit of measure, when it has a collective meaning, is generally treated as a singular, even if it is in a plural form. Thus:

Two-thirds of the population *is* illiterate.
Four-fifths of the book *is* sheer pornography.
Three-quarters of the day *was* spent in idleness.
Two thousand dollars a year *is* a lot of money.
Twenty cents *is* too much for that candy.
Six yards *is* too long.
Five bushels per acre *is* a good yield.
Two pounds *is* all I need.

On the other hand, consider these:

Two-thirds of the pupils *were* sick.
Four-fifths of the books *were* damaged.
Two-thirds of the population *are* farmers.
Three-quarters of the soldiers *were* killed.
Half of the students *were* ill.
The majority of men *prefer* blondes.

When a fraction or a measuring word, like *majority*, indicates a single idea or a collective unity (*two-thirds of the*
182

work), a singular verb is required: "Two-thirds of the work *is* done." However, when the fraction or measuring word is followed by a prepositional phrase containing a plural noun (*three-quarters of the soldiers*) or in some other way shows strong plurality, a plural verb is required: "Two-thirds of the men *are* farmers"; "Three-fourths of the population *are* farmers."

PREFERABLE FORM:

Three-quarters of the work *is* done.

chapter 16 HOW TO LET
CIRCUMSTANCES ALTER CASES

1. The Problem

Which is correct, "It is *I*," or "It is *me*"?

2. The Solution

You have become adjusted to the fact that personal pronouns change form according to case—

And to the added fact that case depends on circumstances.

You know that the objective case (namely, *me, him, her, us, them*) is used when the pronoun is object of the verb or object of the preposition. ("He called John and *me*"; "This letter is addressed to *me* and *him*.")

And you know that the nominative case (namely, *I, he, she, we, they*) is used when the pronoun is subject of the verb. (*"He* and *I* will do it.")

The nominative case is also used as the *complement of a copulative verb.*

What's a complement? And what's a copulative verb?

A complement (note the spelling) is a word which completes the meaning of the verb. The object is one form of complement. *I take* is relatively incomplete in meaning. Add an object, *book,* and the meaning of your sentence becomes relatively complete: *I take the book.*

A copulative verb is one which expresses, not action, but state of being.

To be, or any one of its forms, is a copulative verb.

To be has a large family, and every member is a copulative verb:

am	shall be	has been	will have been
are	will be	had been	would have been
is	would be	have been	should have been
	should be		
was			may have been
were	could be		might have been
	may be		could have been
	might be		

A transitive verb in the active voice transmits action from the subject to the complement, as in "I *know* a doctor," in which action is transmitted from the subject *I* to the object, or complement, *doctor*. But a copulative verb does not transmit action; instead, it establishes an identity. When we say "I *am* a doctor," we are expressing the fact that *I* and *doctor* are the same person; we are establishing the identity of subject and complement.

The complement of a copulative verb is identical to the subject not only in meaning, but also in case.

The subject of a verb, as you know, is in the nominative case.

Therefore, the complement of a copulative verb is also in the nominative case.

In the sentence, "I am a doctor," *I* is the subject, *am a doctor* is the predicate. The complement *doctor,* then, is in the predicate of the sentence. And it is in the nominative case. Such a complement, therefore, is called, not an object, but a *predicate nominative.*

In the problem under consideration ("It is *I,*" or "It is *me,*"), the pronoun in question is the predicate nominative of the sentence. Now, if we consider the expression from the point of view of grammatical rule, *It is I* is the only allowable form. The rule is clear and to the point: *the complement of a copulative verb is in the nominative case.*

But correct English is not always entirely predicated on grammatical rules.

Rules are sometimes violated. The rule about using the nominative *I* as the complement of the copulative verb *to be* is violated rather consistently by a large number of educated speakers. According to a survey made by the National Council of Teachers of English among several hundreds of high school and college teachers of English and Speech; editors; established authors; linguists and grammarians; and business executives, "It is *me*" is considered established, acceptable English, even though a rule is being violated. Most of the experts questioned admitted that they use "It is *me*" in their own speech and hear it from their contemporaries; and some of them went so far as to label "It is *I*" pedantic and stilted.

Should you be confronted with a choice between *I* and *me* as the complement of a copulative verb on, say, a civil service test or a high school or college English examination, you would, of course, select the nominative form, for obviously you are being tested on your knowledge of grammatical rules. However, in informal conversation and writing, you should feel perfectly free to use "It is *me*," which is accepted in common usage, in place of "It is *I*," which conforms to grammatical rule.

In all consistency, it would seem that the objective forms of the other personal pronouns, that is, *him, her, us,* and *them,* should also be acceptable as complements of a copulative verb. However—such is the illogicality of language —that is not so. Educated speakers who unconscionably say "It is *me*" generally shy away from "It is *him*," "It is *her*," "It is *us*," and the like. We may possibly account for this anomaly by reasoning that "It is *me*," or a variant form, is more likely to crop up with some frequency in everyday conversation than are the other forms ("Who's there? It's *me*"; "That's *me* all over"; "Which picture is *me?*" "Is that picture supposed to be *me?* No, sir, not on your life, that's not *me* in a hundred years").

In informal speech and writing (friendly letters, scribbled interoffice memos, and the like), you may certainly feel free to say "It is *me*" or "It's *me*," or "That's *me*," or "It wasn't *me*" without any acute feelings of guilt.

The answer to our problem, then, is that both forms, "It is *I*" and "It is *me*," are correct—one by virtue of grammatical rule, the other by virtue of common educated usage.

3. The Rule

The nominative pronoun is used as the complement of a copulative verb. However, the expression "It is *me*" (or any variant) is acceptable in informal speech and writing.

CORRECT	EQUALLY ACCEPTABLE
It is I.	It is me.
It's I.	It's me.
It will be I.	It will be me.
It has always been I.	It has always been me.
Did you think it was I?	Did you think it was me?

CORRECT	NOT UNIVERSALLY ACCEPTABLE
It is he.	It is him.
It was she.	It was her.
It will be they.	It will be them.
It wasn't we.	It wasn't us.
I thought you were they.	I thought you were them.
This is he.	This is him.

4. The Test

DO YOU GET THE POINT?—*test 36*

Applying grammatical principles *strictly*, check the proper form of the pronoun in each sentence. Choose a nominative pronoun as subject of the verb or as complement of a copulative verb; choose an objective pronoun as object of the verb or as object of the preposition.

1. Was it (she, her) you were talking about?
2. It is (we, us) you will have to answer to if anything goes wrong.

3. (He, Him) and Frank are our best workers.
4. Let's keep this information strictly between (we, us) men.
5. Why, he spoke to you and (I, me) as if we were babies.
6. He sent Charlie Jerome and (I, me) over to the main office.
7. Now it is (I, me) who am at a loss for words.
8. Was it (they, them) who gave you all that misinformation?
9. An American is (he, him) who loves America.
10. That picture doesn't look a bit like (I, me).
11. That picture surely isn't (I, me), is it?
12. It won't be (he, him) who will suffer, it will be (I, me).
13. Why don't you invite (she, her) and her brother to go with you?
14. Everyone seems more than satisfied, except (she, her).
15. No one but (he, him) would take your offer seriously.

CHECK YOUR LEARNING—*answers to test 36*

1. she	4. us	7. I	10. me	13. her
2. we	5. me	8. they	11. I	14. her
3. he	6. me	9. he	12. he, I	15. him

Some added information about pronouns that will prove useful in later work:
Personal pronouns have number:
I, you, he, and *she* are singular.
We, you, and *they* are plural.
I and *we* are considered *first-person* pronouns—an arbitrary distinction referring to the fact that *I* and *we* describe the person speaking.
You is considered a *second-person* pronoun—the person spoken to.
He, she, and *they* are considered *third-person* pronouns —the person spoken about.

We can now combine our knowledge of person, number, and case into the following table:

Singular		Plural	
First Person:	nominative—I objective—me	nominative—we objective—us	
Second Person:	nominative objective } —you	nominative objective } —you	
Third Person:	nominative—he, she objective—him, her	nominative—they objective—them	

That *you* has two identifying numbers (singular and plural) is due of course to the fact that whether we address *one* person or *many*, we use the word *you* interchangeably. This lack of distinction between singular and plural seems to cause a certain amount of instinctive annoyance to many ungrammatical speakers—hence you will hear them addressing a number of people as *youse* or perhaps *yez* or *yiz*. Many educated Southerners prefer the expression *you-all* to indicate plurality. I have it on good authority that Southerners say *you-all* only when speaking to more than one person.

PRO AND CON

Q. Do you ever use the expression "It is me"? Or do you prefer to say "It is I"? What do you hear from your friends or associates? What is your opinion of the usage "It is I"?

Pro

A. The expression "It is *me*" has justification through convenience and very common usage; in French the usage has long been accepted as classic.

—Louis Bromfield

189

Mr. Bromfield was the famous novelist and writer on agricultural problems.

Pro (with reservations)

A. It seems that I am one of those people who always say "It is I," but I must admit that the trend seems to be toward "It's me"! However, be consoled. I make other errors and split infinitives hither and yon.

—Alma Dettinger

Miss Dettinger conducts "Other People's Business" daily over radio station WQXR.

Con

A. In spite of the fact that a Harvard professor (I've forgotten his name) recently exploded the idea that "It is me" is ungrammatical I prefer to use "It is I." And canvassing my associates I find that only one prefers the more colloquial form, "It is me" and that he invariably contracts it to "It's me."

—Sumner Blossom

Mr. Blossom is editor of *American Magazine.*

Pro

A. In reply to your inquiry, we assure you that "It is me" has long been established as good colloquial speech. The following are a few of the many quotations in our files in support of the construction. Raymond Paton, *Autobiography of a Blackguard* (Houghton Mifflin Co.), 1924, page 42, ". . . not more than four people know that *it is me . . .*" R. L. Stevenson, *Treasure Island,* "But Silver . . . called out to know if *that were* me."

—Edward A. H. Fuchs

Dr. Fuchs was a member of the editorial staff of G. &

C. Merriam Co., publishers of the Merriam-Webster *New International Dictionary* and the Merriam-Webster *Collegiate Dictionary*.

Confused

"Ah, it's me," said Mr. Squeers, "and *me's* the first person singular, nominative case, agreeing with the verb *it's* and governed by *Squeers* understood, as a acorn, a hour."

—Charles Dickens, *Nicholas Nickleby*

as easy as A B C

XIV

A. What is the difference between *allude* and *refer?*

B. Is it correct to say, "Everyone stood up and shouted at the top of *their* lungs"?

C. Which is preferable: "Neither the President nor the members of the cabinet *is* behind the bill," or "Neither the President nor the members of the cabinet *are* behind the bill"?

A. The Grammar of Meanings

Allude, Refer

Allude is not, as some people seem to think, the more literary, or more elegant, term for *refer*. There is a definite distinction in meaning. For example:

Your fiancée is a divorcee, a fact which makes her unacceptable to your parents.

One day, as if in general conversation, your father talks about the sanctity and permanence of marriage. Nobody in his family, he says pointedly, has ever been in the divorce courts.

You might then correctly ask: "Are you *alluding* to Jane?"

Your father has not specifically mentioned Jane by name, so he is making an *allusion,* which is an indirect and unspecific *reference,* a reference by suggestion or implication.

A *reference,* unlike an *allusion,* leaves nothing to the imagination, is distinct, specific, to the point.

Thus, you make a *reference*, not an *allusion*, to Shakespeare when you name one of his plays, or quote a line from him.

You make an *allusion* to your need for money when you talk generally about the high cost of living or about your added financial burdens since you got married, or in fact when you say anything but the direct, "I need more money."

B. The Grammar of Allowable "Errors"

Everyone stood up and shouted at the top of *their* lungs.

The revised form, "Everyone stood up and shouted at the top of *his* lungs," is a typical instance of pedantic English when used in ordinary conversation.

It is true that a certain grammatical "rule" requires a singular possessive pronoun with the antecedent *everyone* —but this is a rule as often violated as observed in educated usage. And if violations of a so-called rule are prevalent in cultivated speech, the rule may be considered virtually nonexistent. Bear in mind, now that you are well immersed in your study of grammar, that "correctness" is determined by common usage, not by ukase, not by demands made in outmoded or puristic textbooks.

Indefinite pronouns like *everyone, everybody, no one, nobody, someone, somebody, anyone,* and *anybody* are indeed often treated as singulars, as in the following patterns:

Everyone *is* here.
Everybody *has* arrived.
No one *was* missing.
Nobody *has* returned.
Someone *is* going to get hell for this.
Somebody *has* made a mistake.
Anyone *is* willing to admit the truth of that statement.
Anybody who *comes* late will be punished.

No one who speaks English as a native language would ever think of using plural verbs with these pronouns. Nevertheless, there is, you will have to admit, both logic and sanity in the feeling of plurality that many people get from these words. Hence, sentences like:

If anyone is waiting, ask *them* to come in.
Since everybody understood French, I spoke to *them* in that language.
Everyone was waiting when I arrived, and so I greeted *them* all happily.

may not be excessively "pure" English; but they are a lot more natural, more sensible, and more common among educated speakers than the forms which the precisionists would ask us to use:

If anyone is waiting, ask *him* to come in.
Since everybody understood French, I spoke to *him* in that language.
Everyone was waiting when I arrived, and so I greeted *him* happily.

(To me, the last two sentences, while indubitably "correct," sound slightly insane, as if uttered by some poor soul who had just had himself a nervous breakdown caused by studying too much grammar.)

When you say: "Everyone decided to go home," you are certainly implying the existence of more than one person. You are therefore speaking logical, correct English if you change the sentence to: "Everyone put on *their* coats and went home." Such a construction is part of the idiom of the language—it is acceptable in informal conversation; it is used by educated speakers; it is, in short, not a sin.

PRO AND CON

Q. Modern grammarians maintain that "As soon as everyone had arrived, we started to speak to *them*" is cor-

194

rect, idiomatic English, established by common usage among educated people. Do you agree? Would you use the expression in your everyday speech?

Pro

A. That's the way I'd talk.

—Lewis Gannett

Mr. Gannett was formerly a literary critic of the New York *Herald Tribune*.

Pro

A. I am very much afraid that my opinion in respect to the grammatical question posed in your letter wouldn't be very helpful to anyone. I happen to use a great number of idiomatic expressions in my conversation, which would lead me to uphold those who favor the expression you quote.

I guess I believe in a double standard of grammar, for where we try to be as proper as possible in editing articles for *Coronet*, nothing peeves me more than the person who quibbles over grammar in everyday speech. To me it has always been most important to convey a meaning, and when an ungrammatical expression can better get across a point, I am all for it.

—Harris Shevelson

Mr. Shevelson was formerly an editor of *Coronet* and of *Pageant*.

Q. Modern grammarians maintain that "Everyone was here, but *they all* left early" is correct, idiomatic English, established by common usage among educated people and completely acceptable in informal conversation. Do you agree? Would you use the expression in your everyday speech?

Pro

A. Not being a grammarian I don't know the wrongs and rights of the expression of "Everyone was here, but they all left early." I am afraid it would be rather awkward to say "Everyone was here, but he left early." That might imply that the party was rather dull because only one person came or the party involved was pretty important because the one person meant all the world to the person giving it. Or am I getting too involved?

At any rate, I would be inclined to accept the expression without getting too excited about what the purists might say. It would be difficult to substitute another phrasing that would be as succinct and one that would carry the same meaning. You might perhaps say "All were here but all left early," but that does not give the same meaning.

—Benjamin Fine

Dr. Fine was education editor of *The New York Times*. He is the author of *A Giant of the Press; College Publicity in the U.S.; Educational Publicity; Democratic Education;* and a series of articles on the teaching of American history. At present, he is Dean of the Graduate School of Education at Yeshiva University.

Q. Many modern grammarians maintain that "If anyone is waiting, let *them* come in" is correct, idiomatic English, established by common usage among educated people. Do you agree? Would you use the expression in your everyday speech?

Con

A. I am sorry but I think it is incorrect, confusing, irritating, and certainly not idiomatic. In the first place, I doubt if "anyone" is ever idiomatic. It sounds like an intellectual pronoun. The English for it is "anybody." However, if you say "any one," thus making it hopelessly singular, why try to use it as an antecedent for a plural

196

pronoun? I know people say that kind of thing, but it is a boner.

If you are "writing" a grammar, I think part of your responsibility is to try to help to keep the language as accurate as possible, because it is very difficult to say anything in English or any language accurately, and the plea to introduce confusing, "idiomatic" antecedents and pronouns "as correct" is a specious one.

—Hervey Allen

Hervey Allen, who died in 1952, was the author of *Anthony Adverse, Bedford Village,* and other well-known books.

Con

A. I'm a helluva one to ask about grammar—the way I kick the language around for a living—but that ("If anyone is waiting, let *them* come in") happens to be one of my pet hates! I think it's wrong—and sounds terrible!

—Arthur Godfrey

Mr. Godfrey is the famous radio and television personality.

Con

A. Understandable, and therefore inevitable and "acceptable" among the peasantry of speech—but obviously illogical and incorrect. Among precisians, abominable!

—Christopher Morley

Mr. Morley, who died in 1957, was the author of *Kitty Foyle; Thorofare; The Middle Kingdom;* and numerous other books.

Q. Modern grammarians maintain that "Everyone arose and took off *their* hats" is correct, idiomatic English, established by common usage among educated people and completely acceptable in informal conversation. Do you agree? Would you use the expression in your everyday speech?

Pro (*with reservations*)

A. In reference to your question, was I not taught that the correct sentence should be "Everyone arose and took off *his* hat"? My Oxford dictionary assures me that everyone and everybody (formerly two words) are "often erroneously used with plural verb or pronoun."

I recognize and rejoice in the induction of idiomatic common usage into our language. Some time ago, if you recall, *ain't* was proper and the English still use *mayn't*. However, I think this ("Everyone took off *their* hats") is awkward in sound, and "Everyone took off *his* hat" less so, but still a bit stiff. Well, it must be a masculine uprising, as women rarely remove *their* hats; certainly they don't have to, in the presence of the flag or the dead and never (unless browbeaten) in the cinema or theater!

But that's beside the point. If ever I used the expression correctly or otherwise, I shall henceforward avoid it. I doubt if I ever did use it; it sounds so *very* unconversational. I would probably say, "Off came the hats"!

—Faith Baldwin

Faith Baldwin is a famous novelist, author of *Change of Heart* and *You Can't Escape*.

Con (*with reservations*)

A. Perhaps I am not a good person from whom to get an example of idiomatic English in everyday use, for a long career of writing has given me a habit of mind which tends to translate precision in writing into precision in common talk. However, I doubt if I should use the phrase you mention; I think that instead of "everyone" I should probably say "everybody." I have some distaste for too much stickling for grammatical precision. If a phrase or word comes

198

to be in common use, then it is part of the English language, regardless of grammarians.

—Mark Sullivan

Mr. Sullivan, before his death in 1952, was the well-known Washington columnist of the New York *Herald Tribune.*

Pro

It's the same story with *them* and *their* after indefinite pronouns. If possible, the so-called incorrect usage is even firmer established. "In older English the plural was common here," says Curme. And why not? As long as English does not do away with gender, like Hungarian, why not use *their* as a practical makeshift device where neither *his* nor *her* fits? What's wrong with this sentence from Fielding's *Tom Jones?*

Everyone in the house were in their beds.

Or with this one from a speech by Franklin D. Roosevelt:

There have always been cheerful idiots in this country who believed that there would be no more war for us, if everybody in America would only return to *their* homes and lock *their* front doors behind them.

Or this from a speech by Winston Churchill (on the British Policy toward Spain):

Everyone can have *their* opinion about that . . .

Even one of our leading literary critics, Edmund Wilson, uses this construction:

For years I have been hearing about detective stories. Almost everybody I know seems to read them, and *they* have long conversations about them in which I am unable to take part.

And speaking of detective stories, what would a mystery-story writer do if he had to use *his* or *her*, giving away the murderer's sex for the sake of correct grammar? Or would you rewrite this sentence from a mystery story by Ngaio Marsh?

> Someone came this way between 4:30 and 6 on Monday evening. I hope to learn something of *their* identity.
> —Rudolph Flesch, *The Art of Plain Talk* (Harper)

Pro

Recommended to anyone who ever played high-stake bridge, doubled *their* poker stakes after 12:30 A.M., joined a baseball pool at the office, matched a companion for a dinner check, flipped a coin to make a decision, played the eighteenth hole for double or nothing, or went broke trying to beat the slot machine in Joe's bar.
> —From a Simon and Schuster advertisement for *Hazard,* by Roy Chanslor

C. The Grammar of Correct Usage

Neither the President nor the members of the cabinet *is* behind the bill, *or* Neither the President nor the members of the cabinet *are* behind the bill?

If you find yourself in the awkward position of having both a singular (*President*) and a plural (*members*) noun in a compound subject connected by the conjunction *or* or *nor*, be guided by this rule:

The verb agrees with the subject which is geographically nearer to it.

Thus, in the sentence under discussion, *members* is nearer the verb than *President,* and so the verb is plural, agreeing with *members.*

PREFERABLE FORMS:

Neither the President nor the members of the cabinet *are* behind the bill.

However, we might turn the subject around, and the sentence would then correctly read:

Neither the members of the cabinet nor the President *is* behind the bill.

Contrast these sentences:

Either a man or two women *are* required for that job.
Either two women or one man *is* required for that job.
Either John or his parents *have* to see me.
Either John's parents or his sister *has* to see me.
Neither you nor I *am* responsible for that error.
Neither I nor you *are* responsible for that error.
Neither he nor they *are* coming tonight.
Neither they nor he *is* coming tonight.

Most preferably, such double subjects, when they require different verbs, should be avoided by some such circumlocution as the following:

The President is not behind the bill and neither are the members of his cabinet.
Either a man is required for that job or two women.
I have to see either John or his parents.
I have to see either John's sister or his parents.
You are not responsible for that error and neither am I.
He is not coming tonight and neither are they.

chapter 17 HOW TO KEEP ON GOOD TERMS WITH YOUR RELATIVES

1. The Problem

Is *"Whom* do you see?" correct English? How about *"Whom* do you think you are?" or "This is the man *whom* I believe can help you"? How can one know when to use *who* for *whom* and vice versa?"

2. The Solution

The problems which start this chapter are quoted almost verbatim from a letter I received recently. I say *almost* verbatim because I have omitted, out of deference to the postal authorities, several items of profanity which graced my correspondent's language.

The writer started out gently enough to explain how he seriously desires to use correct English. Nothing would please him more, he declared, than to be able to employ the right word in the right place. However, he went on, becoming by now a little highstrung, the harder he tried the more confused he got. When he used *I,* it always turned out that *me* was the proper word. If he used *is,* it almost certainly developed that *are* was correct; on the other hand, if he chose *are, is* would inevitably be the grammatically preferable form.

As he continued, his wrath got hotter. "As for *who* and *whom,* only a genius or a fool can apparently get them straight! I used to say *who* most of the time—it seemed to me to be a good, respectable, expressive word—it said just what I intended it to say. But it seems that whenever I said *who,* I should have said *whom!* So I started using *whom*—and that never pleased my teachers either, because where I used *whom* only *who* seemed to fit! What the profanity kind of language is this anyway?

"For example, is '*Whom* do you see?' correct English? I have been told that it is. Well, then, how about '*Whom* do you think you are?' This seems to be the same kind of sentence, yet I've been told that I'm using bad grammar in it. And then how about 'This is the man *whom* I believe can help you'? This is wrong also, I've been informed. It still seems to me to be the same kind of sentence as my first one. How the profanity profanity can I tell when to use *who* for *whom* and vice versa?"

That my correspondent should have reached the end of his patience is understandable enough. That he should as a logical next step have descended to profanity is equally understandable. *Who* and *whom* can have that effect on someone who seriously tries to unravel their mysteries.

Unless—

Unless one approaches the problem with a working knowledge of the architecture of the sentence.

Then confusion vanishes, and the whole subject becomes so simple that a child of ten can easily understand it (in fact, a few children of ten do!).

If *who* and *whom* have been a source of constant annoyance to you, your worries are now practically over—provided you have become thoroughly familiar with the interrelationships of the words in a sentence.

Provided you clearly understand the function of the subject of a verb.

And the function of the complement of a copulative verb.

And the function of the object of a verb.

And, finally, the function of the object of a preposition.

As with personal pronouns, the choice of the proper form of the relative or interrogative pronoun depends on the rules for *case*.

The nominative form of the relative or interrogative pronoun is *who*.

The objective form is *whom*.
Here are the keys:

KEY 1: As subject of the verb, the nominative case—*who*—is used.

Who spoke?
It was John *who* spoke.

In each sentence *who* is subject of the verb *spoke*.

KEY 2: As complement of a copulative verb, the nominative case—*who*—is used.

Who are you?
I know *who* you are.

In each sentence *who* is the complement of the copulative verb *are;* the subject of *are* is *you*.

KEY 3: As object of the verb, the objective case—*whom*—is used.

Whom do you see?
Is this the man *whom* you saw?

In each sentence, *whom* is object of the verb (*do see* or *saw*); the subject of the verb in each instance is *you*.

KEY 4: As object of a preposition, the objective case—*whom*—is used.

Whom are you talking to?
Is this the man *whom* you were talking to?

In each sentence, *whom* is object of the preposition *to*, and forms with the preposition a standard prepositional phrase, except that pronoun and preposition are geographically separated by the other words in the sentence. If the sentence were couched in somewhat more formal language, namely:

To whom are you talking?
Is this the man *to whom* you were talking?

the prepositional phrase would take on the more normal aspect to which you have perhaps become accustomed. The preposition and its object *whom* are frequently split up in informal speech and writing.

That's all there is to *who* and *whom* (for the present, anyway).

Four keys, corresponding to the four rules for case with which we are familiar, tell the entire story:

1. SUBJECT—*who*
2. PREDICATE NOMINATIVE—*who*
3. OBJECT—*whom*
4. OBJECT OF A PREPOSITION—*whom*

With these four rules to guide us, the three problems presented by my truculent correspondent are practically self-solving:

PROBLEM 1: *Who* or *whom* do you see?
The pronoun is object of the verb *see*. Correct form: *whom*.

PROBLEM 2: *Who* or *whom* do you think you are?
The pronoun is the complement of the copulative verb *are* ("You do think you are *who*"). Correct form: *who*.

PROBLEM 3: This is the man *who* or *whom* I believe can help you.
The pronoun is subject of the verb *can help*. The words *I believe* are parenthetical in function, and as such do not affect the relationship of the other words in the sentence.

This will be clearer if you place *I believe* at the end of the sentence, thus: "This is the man who can help you, I believe."

My correspondent's fourth problem can now also be answered:

PROBLEM 4: How the profanity profanity can I tell when to use *who* for *whom* and vice versa?

Answer: By learning and applying the four rules for pronoun case.

3. The Rules

Who is used in constructions which require a nominative pronoun, namely as subject of the verb and as predicate nominative.

Whom is used in constructions which require an objective pronoun, namely as object of the verb and as object of the preposition.

We have rather loosely spoken about *who* and *whom* as interrogative and relative pronouns. The distinction is quite simple:

When a direct or implied question is asked, the pronoun is interrogative, as in:

Who are you?
I know who you are (that is, I know the answer to the
    question: Who are you?)

When the pronoun refers (or relates) to some previously expressed noun or pronoun in the sentence, it is a relative pronoun, as in:

The girl whom I see
    ⟵
The man who came to dinner
    ⟵

Whether the pronoun is interrogative or relative, the rules for its use are the same.

The pronouns *whoever* and *whomever,* variant forms of the interrogative and relative, also follow the same rules. It is often necessary to supply understood words in order to see the proper relationship between *whoever* or *whomever* and its verb. Consider:

Invite (whoever, whomever) you meet to the party.

This sentence in its complete form would be: "Invite (the one) whomever you meet to the party." *Whomever* is the object of the verb *meet* (not of the verb *invite*) and is therefore in the objective form.

Ask (whoever, whomever) is here to come in.

This sentence in its complete form would be: "Ask (the one) whoever is here to come in." *Whoever* is thus seen to be the subject of *is,* not, as might at first appear to be the case, the object of *ask.* The nominative form is required.

4. The Test

DO YOU GET THE POINT?—*test 37*

In determining whether to use *who* or *whom* in the following sentences, be guided by case. Ask yourself what relationship the pronoun in question bears to its verb or perhaps to a preposition. When you have made your decision check the proper form and then note in the space following each sentence whether the pronoun is functioning as a subject, predicate nominative, object of a verb, or object of a preposition.

1. Mike Quill (who, whom) is the leader of the Transport Workers' Union, has been conferring with Mayor O'Dwyer for several days. ....

2. J. A. Krug, (who, whom) Truman appointed Secretary of the Interior after the resignation of Harold Ickes, has also been conferring—with John L. Lewis, of the United Mine Workers. ....

3. Alfred E. Driscoll, (who, whom) you no doubt recall was elected Governor of New Jersey in 1946, has promised to eliminate government interference with industry. ....

4. Dr. Joseph R. Sizoo, (who, whom) many people consider is one of the ablest speakers of his day, has been upheld by his congregation in his resignation from the Reformed Dutch Protestant Church of New York. ....

5. An executive of a large soap company (who, whom) we understand did not wish to be quoted, announced a 50 per cent rise in soap prices after the demise of the O.P.A. ....

6. (Who, Whom) do you think you are anyway? ....

7. (Who, Whom) would you like to be? ....

8. (Who, Whom) do you think he is? ....

9. (Who, Whom) did you think he spoke to? ....

10. (Who, Whom) are you waiting for? ....

11. (Who, Whom) do you love best in all the world? ....

12. (Who, Whom) do you imagine will be the next President of the United States? ....

13. (Who, Whom) was responsible for Truman's original veto of the Case Bill? ....

14. (Who, Whom) do you think was responsible for Truman's original veto of the Case Bill? ....

15. It is hard to say (who, whom) we will vote for in the next elections. ....

16. It is hard to say (who, whom) the country will decide is to be considered responsible for the misfortunes that befell the Democrats in the 1946 elections. ....

17. It is hard to say (who, whom) the country will hold responsible for this election debacle. ....

18. (Who, Whom) do you wish to speak to? ....

19. (Who, Whom) do you wish to see? ....
20. (Who, Whom) do you wish to visit today? ....
21. (Who, Whom) do you believe is best qualified to take care of you? ....
22. Let me speak to (whoever, whomever) is waiting for the General. ....
23. To (who, whom) this may concern . . . .
24. (Who, Whom) you've chosen for this task is your own business. ....
25. He's the man (who, whom) I believe robbed the First National Bank. ....

CHECK YOUR LEARNING—*answers to test 37*

1. *who* (subject of the verb *is*)
2. *whom* (object of the verb *appointed*)
3. *who* (subject of the verb *was elected* [The parenthetical clause *you no doubt recall* has no effect on the case of the relative pronoun. This type of usage will be more fully treated on page 239.])
4. *who* (subject of the verb *is* [This type is similar to that in sentence 3. See page 239.])
5. *who* (subject of the verb *did wish* [see page 239.])
6. *who* (complement of the copulative verb *are;* hence, predicate nominative)
7. *who* (complement of the copulative verb *to be;* predicate nominative)
8. *who* (complement of the copulative verb *is;* predicate nominative)
9. *whom* (object of the preposition *to*)
10. *whom* (object of the preposition *for*)
11. *whom* (object of the verb *love*)
12. *who* (subject of the verb *will be*)
13. *who* (subject of the verb *was*)
14. *who* (subject of the verb *was*)
15. *whom* (object of the preposition *for*)
16. *who* (subject of the verb *is* [Compare sentences 3 and 4.])
17. *whom* (object of the verb *hold*)

18. *whom* (object of the preposition *to*)
19. *whom* (object of the verb *see*)
20. *whom* (object of the verb *visit*)
21. *who* (subject of the verb *is*)
22. *whoever* (subject of the verb *is waiting* [*To* governs the understood pronoun *one*.])
23. *whom* (object of the preposition *to*)
24. *whom* (object of the verb *have chosen*)
25. *who* (subject of the verb *robbed* [Compare sentences 3, 4, 5.])

Colloquial Patterns
—A Word to the Overcautious

This is probably a good place in the book to make another important digression on the subject of pedantic grammar.

As you proceed with these pages, bear in mind that you are gradually becoming an expert in formal grammar. You are learning the rules that govern the choice of the absolutely correct word in a sentence pattern. You are becoming master of the basic principles, the fundamentals on which English grammar is built.

This type of training presents a certain hazard, however. You may begin, in your everyday speech, to apply the rules too rigorously.

The language of everyday life, the pattern of informal conversation, is usually described by the adjective *colloquial*. Colloquial grammar is that used by educated speakers on informal occasions. It is less strict than formal, literary grammar; it allows violations of rules which formal grammar darkly frowns upon. But—and this is the point to remember—colloquial grammar bears no stigma; it is not incorrect; it is not uneducated, let alone illiterate; it is not to be avoided. Note that we are talking about colloquial grammar—the grammar you use in your day-to-day speech. In your formal writing, in public addresses, on grammar

210

tests and other dignified occasions, you should, I believe, adhere rather strictly to the essential rules set forth in these chapters. In writing friendly letters, on informal speech occasions, you may—perhaps you should—allow yourself greater latitude.

For example, we have already spoken of the preferability of the expression "It is *me*" for ordinary occasions, despite the violation of a grammatical rule. Similarly, the use of *whom* should not, in your mind, take on the aspect of a rigid requirement—in everyday speech. If you feel that *whom* sounds a little schoolteacherish—a little pedantic—a little stiff—then by all means avoid the word. If you feel that a question is preferably, though ungrammatically, phrased in the form *"Who* are you referring to?" instead of *"Whom* are you referring to?" then by all means substitute *who* for *whom.* And if you see lifted eyebrows as a result, you can be pretty sure that the owner of those eyebrows is well on the way to becoming a linguistic snob. If you find the expression *"Who* do you love?" less awkward or stiff than *"Whom* do you love?" then use the nominative case of the interrogative pronoun as object of the verb —in your everyday speech. Use it and suffer no conscience pangs—for you are, take my word for it, in the numerous company of well-educated, expressive speakers.

To violate a grammatical rule through sheer ignorance is one thing. It is perhaps not reprehensible, but on the other hand it is not exactly praiseworthy. However, to violate a rule of grammar through choice, because of a conscious desire to attain greater effectiveness, greater simplicity, greater clarity, is quite another thing. It is not only permissible; in many instances it is admirable and desirable.

Especially should you be warned not to lean over backward, on informal occasions. As a result of your work with this book, do not let your speech become pedantic and prissy. Once you know the rules, do not hesitate, where you believe necessity dictates, to violate them.

The New York *News* recently ran an editorial on grammar which makes essentially the same point:

The question on the *News* mayorality poll ballot is worded—"Who Do You Want for Mayor?"—and some sticklers for pure English have written in to ask don't we know it ought to be "Whom," etc. Abstractly, yes, we do. But if our canvassers were to go around asking people; "Whom Do You Want for Mayor?" a lot of people would get the impression that the *News* was being pretty high-hat.

This "who" and "whom" business is only one of numerous cases where the popular tongue is out of tune with the grammarians' rules.

There is, for another example, the difference between "shall" and "will"—"shall" denoting simple futurity, "will" determination. The difference is illustrated by the story of the Frenchman who didn't know quite enough English, fell in a river, and after some wild struggles shouted in despair: "I will drown, and no one shall save me!" when drowning actually was farthest from his hopes. "Will," however, is rapidly driving out "shall" in popular usage. . . .

The same goes for "It is I" as against "It's me." The former may be grammatically correct; but when you knock on the door of your wife, mother or anyone else near and dear to you, and she calls, "Who is it?" the natural reply is: "It's me."

The written word follows the spoken word, though sometimes quite a distance behind; which is one reason for these popular violations of the rules of grammar.

Another reason is that 100 or 150 years ago few people could read and fewer could write, whereas nowadays in civilized countries most people learn at least to read. The oldtimers could grasp the niceties and nuances of language, and had time to study them, and to apply the rules in their writings. Most people these days have neither the time nor the ear for language to be so precise.

PRO AND CON

Q. Do you ever use the word *whom* in your general

informal conversation, and do you usually hear that word from your associates?

Pro

A. I do try to use the word *whom* in its proper place, in my informal conversation, but, like most Americans, I am afraid I forget frequently. Most of my friends in the writing and publishing business seem to have the same trouble.
—Ben Hibbs

Mr. Hibbs is editor of *The Saturday Evening Post.*

Pro

Who do labor leaders associate with in their leisure hours? Never mind the grammar—*who* do they associate with?

—Howard Lindsay, coauthor of the Broadway stage hit *State of the Union*, writing a guest column for the New York *Post.*

as easy as A B C

A. What is the difference between *credible* and *creditable*?

B. Is it correct to say, "Have you *got* my book"?

C. Which is preferable: "Was it *he* you were talking to?" or "Was it *him* you were talking to?"

A. The Grammar of Meanings

Credible, Creditable

A story is *credible*—it can be believed.

A performance is *creditable*—it is worthy of esteem, it is deserving of praise.

Though both words come from the same Latin root, *credo,* to trust, *creditable* has suffered a change in meaning.

DO YOU GET THE POINT?—*test 38*

1. Your story is far from (credible, creditable).
2. He gave a (credible, creditable) account of his actions.
3. His actions are not very (credible, creditable); though I suppose a person like him cannot resist temptation very well.
4. The book is a (credible, creditable) attempt to make science understandable to the man in the street.
5. He conducted the defense in a (credible, creditable) manner, and the judge praised him highly.

1. credible   2. credible   3–5. creditable

B. The Grammar of Allowable "Errors"

Have you *got* my book?

Though some authorities call "got," in a construction like this, redundant (which means unnecessarily repetitious), the fact remains that the word is part of current English usage.

"I've got a cold"; "He's got a good idea"; "Have you got your winter underwear on?" and similar sentences are correct English on both the colloquial and literary level.

The only serious violation of good usage occurs in a sentence like "I got a dollar" or "I got rhythm" or "I gotta go," in which *got* is used as a substitute for *have*. This is a serious violation not because of any arbitrary distinction, but because educated people rarely use *got* in this way. *Got* meaning *have* is, however, prevalent in illiterate speech patterns. In cultivated speech, on the other hand, "I've got a dollar," "I've got rhythm" and "I've got to go" are expressions which are current, accepted, correct English.

PRO AND CON

Pro

I agree with you that "Have you *got* . . . ?" is good idiomatic English—I use it in speech without thinking about it and would write it if colloquialism seemed appropriate to the passage. The phrase is certainly better in every way than "Do you have?" "Yes, I do" which has crept in from the Middle West and is now heard everywhere.

—Jacques Barzun

215

Dr. Barzun is the author of *Teacher in America,* and Provost and Dean of Faculties at Columbia University.

Q. Modern grammarians maintain that "I've *got* a bad cold" is correct, idiomatic English, established by common usage among educated people. Do you agree? Would you use the expression in your everyday speech?

Pro (with reservations)

A. To answer your query, I might say "I've *got* a cold," but I should suffer a twinge of usage conscience at the word *got.* Probably that is because I have perpetrated several books on the public inveighing against this common error. We must not strain at gnats. At the same time, I can't go along with all that Dr. Leonard [1] defended. The mores of the man in the street are constantly remaking the language.

—William Dodge Lewis

Dr. Lewis, now retired, was editor of the *Winston Dictionary.*

Pro (with reservations)

A. In reply to your question, I shall be very brief: "I do say—I've *got* a bad cold—but I don't think it is good usage." I guess that just about sums up my answer.

—Alma Kitchell

Miss Kitchell is a well-known radio personality and director of "The Women's Exchange," a daily radio program.

Pro

The phrase *have got,* for *have,* in the sense of *possess,*

[1] Sterling Andrus Leonard, in his *Current English Usage* (see chapter 25).

own, . . . is objected to by many grammarians, but is common in colloquial use.

—Merriam-Webster *New International Dictionary,* Second Edition

Pro (with reservations)

I regret to say that I have probably been guilty in everyday speech of using the expression, "Have you *got* any sisters?" I know that modern grammarians have accepted this usage as idiomatic; but to me it is still redundant. Certainly, I am sure that I would not use the expression in written English.

—C. P. Chadsey

Mr. Chadsey is editor-in-chief of *Words: The New Dictionary,* published by Grosset and Dunlap.

Pro

If radio can write better books than novelists and must necessarily write different ones, why bother with great books at all? How is it a service to education or culture to misrepresent a great book? How much privilege of corrupting literature *has radio got?*

—Bernard De Voto, in *Harper's Magazine,* September, 1947

C. The Grammar of Correct Usage

Was it *he* you were talking to? *or*
Was it *him* you were talking to?

In such a sentence, the personal pronoun *he* is *not* the object of the preposition *to,* but the predicate nominative governed by the copulative verb *was. To* governs the omit-

217

ted relative *whom*, and the complete sentence correctly reads: "Was it he to whom you were talking?"

PREFERABLE FORMS:

Was it *he* you were talking to?
It was *she* I was thinking about.

chapter 18 HOW TO FILL IN

1. The Problem

Why is the nominative pronoun required in the sentence "Harvey is taller than *I*"? And why, on the other hand, is the objective pronoun required in "Frank Fay loves Harvey more than *me*"?

2. The Solution

Than, as used in the two sentences under discussion, is a conjunction joining two *clauses.*

The case of the pronoun following *than* is determined by the function of that pronoun in the second clause of each sentence.

But what is a clause? And where are the two clauses of which we so glibly speak?

A clause is a portion of a sentence which contains a subject and predicate.

You will recall from our first discussion of the architecture of the sentence that every sentence is easily and naturally separable into its two basic elements—the subject and the predicate.

Some sentences contain a single subject and predicate; other sentences contain two or more subjects and predicates.

A few examples will make this abstract principle clear.

EXAMPLE 1: A sentence containing one subject and one predicate:
Harry S. Truman succeeded Roosevelt as President of the United States.
SUBJECT: Harry S. Truman

PREDICATE: succeeded Roosevelt as President of the United States.

A sentence which has but one subject and predicate (or we may say but one clause) is called a *simple sentence*.

EXAMPLE 2: A sentence containing two subjects and predicates:

Harry S. Truman succeeded Roosevelt as President of the United States and the office of Vice-President became vacant.

FIRST SUBJECT: Harry S. Truman
FIRST PREDICATE: succeeded Roosevelt as President of the United States
SECOND SUBJECT: the office of Vice-President
SECOND PREDICATE: became vacant

Thus we are dealing here with a sentence containing two clauses. The first clause is made up of the first subject and predicate; the second clause consists of the second subject and predicate.

The clauses of any sentence are joined by a conjunction, in this instance *and*.

When a sentence contains two or more clauses joined by the conjunction *and, or, but, nor,* or *for,* it is called a *compound sentence*.

EXAMPLE 3: Another sentence containing two clauses:

When James Byrnes resigned as Secretary of State, Truman appointed Marshall to fill the vacant post.

FIRST SUBJECT: James Byrnes
FIRST PREDICATE: resigned as Secretary of State
SECOND SUBJECT: Truman
SECOND PREDICATE: appointed Marshall to fill the vacant post

The two clauses of this sentence are joined by the conjunction *when*. A conjunction, as you see, need not come between the *clauses,* but may occur at the beginning of the first clause. When the conjunction is any other than *and, but, or, nor,* or *for,* the sentence is called *complex.*

(We shall deal more thoroughly with the various types of sentences as soon as we have arrived at a solution to our chapter problem.)

A clause, then, has all the attributes of a complete sentence:

It has a subject.

It has a predicate.

But, unlike a sentence, a clause is not separate and complete of itself, but instead is joined, by means of a conjunction, with other clauses to form a sentence.

Where are the two clauses we have spoken about in the sentences which illustrate the problem of this chapter?

Let us look at the first of these sentences.

Harvey is taller than I. [Harvey, you may recall, is the six-foot invisible rabbit of Mary Chase's delightful comedy of the same name.]

FIRST CLAUSE: Harvey is taller

THE SUBJECT: Harvey

THE PREDICATE: is taller

CONJUNCTION JOINING THE TWO CLAUSES: than

And all we have left for our second clause is the single word *I.*

Apparently something is missing.

If we examine the sentence for a moment, we can easily add the missing element.

"Harvey is taller than I . . . *am.*"

Where is the second clause? "*I am.*"

SUBJECT: I

PREDICATE: am

Why the nominative pronoun? We now know enough about grammatical case to answer that question without any hesitation.

The nominative form *I* is used because the pronoun is the subject of the understood verb *am* in the second clause of the sentence.

Now let us examine the second sentence in our problem.

Frank Fay loves Harvey more than me. [Fay first played
the role of Elwood P. Dowd, the only character in the
play who was able to see Harvey.]

Again two clauses, with part of the second clause missing.

FIRST CLAUSE: Frank Fay loves Harvey more
CONJUNCTION: than
SECOND CLAUSE: [he loves] me.
Our complete sentence is: "Frank Fay loves Harvey
more than he loves me."

The objective pronoun *me* is used as object of the understood verb *loves* in the second clause of the sentence.

In a complex sentence containing the conjunction *than*,
the second clause is almost always lacking in one or more
words—words which an imaginative citizen can easily
supply. The process of omitting words which are perfectly
obvious from the context of the sentence is known as
ellipsis—and a sentence from which such words have been
omitted is called an *elliptical* sentence.

For example:

ELLIPTICAL SENTENCE	COMPLETE SENTENCE
She is happier than I.	She is happier than I [am].
He obeys his mother quicker than me.	He obeys his mother quicker than [he obeys] me.
He obeys his mother quicker than I.	He obeys his mother quicker than I [do].
Are the Russians freer in their personal lives than we?	Are the Russians freer in their personal lives than we [are]?
Government regulations affect the Russians more than us.	Government regulations affect the Russians more than [they affect] us.

As is another conjunction that is generally found in an
elliptical sentence.

For example:

ELLIPTICAL SENTENCE	COMPLETE SENTENCE
Are the Russians as free as we?	Are the Russians as free as we [are]?
We are just as rich as they.	We are just as rich as they [are].
She loves her mother as much as I.	She loves her mother as much as I [do].
She loves her mother as much as me.	She loves her mother as much as [she loves] me.

From these examples it is easy to see that the proper case of the pronoun to use after the conjunctions *than* and *as* can be determined by removing the ellipsis—in other words, by completing the second clause of the sentence. And then, of course, we apply the basic rules for case.

Use the nominative pronoun as subject of the verb or as predicate nominative.
Use the objective pronoun as object of the verb or as object of the preposition.

3. The Rule

The pronoun following *than* and *as* derives its case from its use in the completed second clause of an elliptical sentence.

4. The Test

DO YOU GET THE POINT?—*test 39*

Check the correct form of the pronoun in the following elliptical sentences.

1. We are more truthful than (she, her).
2. No one else can drink a quart of Scotch as fast as (he, him).
3. I am always being blamed; they are never blamed,

223

no matter what they do. Why do you blame me more often than (they, them)?
4. They work much faster than (we, us).
5. You may be older than (I, me), but I'm a lot wiser than you.
6. We can fight just as hard as (they, them).
7. No wonder you're not hungry—you ate much more breakfast than (I, me).
8. He earned more than (I, me) and he worked less.
9. When you're as rich as (they, them), you'll vote Republican also.
10. You're just as much in error as (he, him).

CHECK YOUR LEARNING—*answers to test 39*

1. she	3. them	5. I	7. I	9. they
2. he	4. we	6. they	8. I	10. he

Before we leave the subject of clauses and types of sentences, you should become completely familiar with a number of basic concepts.

You can express your thoughts in four possible ways:

STATEMENT: The New York Police Department wants a 35 per cent increase in salary. (This is a *declarative* sentence.)

QUESTION: Is life worth living with the police of 13 states after you? (This is an *interrogative* sentence.)

COMMAND: Order your holiday wines and liquor now. (This is an *imperative* sentence.)

EXCLAMATION: Ladies! Useful gifts for "his" Christmas! (This is an *exclamatory* sentence.)

Every time you express a thought, whether in speech or writing, you phrase your words, with or without conscious planning, into one of these four patterns, *declarative, interrogative, imperative,* or *exclamatory*.

As a way to save time and unnecessary words, your sentences are often elliptical, especially in speech—you omit the words that your listener can supply for himself. Almost every imperative sentence omits the understood subject *you*. When you say "Stop," "Go," "Wait," "Run for your life," the listener understands that you mean him, that you are commanding him to stop or go or wait or run, and since you are speaking to him, you would address him as *you*, except that the word is unnecessary, and is therefore almost always omitted. When you are asked, "Are you happy?" you may answer with a single word, such as "Yes," or "No," or "Very," or "Hardly," and you have a complete, well-rounded, grammatically perfect, but elliptical sentence, namely:

Yes [I am happy].
No [I am not happy].
[I am] Very [happy].
[I am] Hardly [happy].

Exclamatory sentences are frequently elliptical, perhaps because in an excess of emotion (and all exclamatory sentences are indicative of emotion of one sort or another) we tend to be as sparing and economical of words as possible. In the example given, "Ladies! Useful gifts for 'his' Christmas!" we have two separate elliptical sentences, each one indicative of the speaker's excitement, and which, if they were written out completely, might look like this:

[You listen,] Ladies!
[Here are] Useful gifts for "his" Christmas!

In good writing, exclamatory sentences are avoided as much as possible. The choice of words, rather than the exclamation point, is used to indicate emotion.

Every sentence, as we have said, has two major, indispensable, parts, the *subject*, and the *predicate*. If we should wish to explain this without the use of grammatical terminology, we would say that every sentence divides precisely into two elements: *what (or whom) we are talking about;* and *what we are saying*. For instance: "Harry S. Truman succeeded Roosevelt as President of the United States."

225

Whom are we talking about? Harry S. Truman. What are we saying about him? He succeeded Roosevelt as President of the United States. Another instance: "The Republican Party promised a 20 per cent reduction in income taxes for 1947." What are we talking about? The Republican Party. What about the Republican Party? It promised a 20 per cent reduction in income taxes for 1947. *Harry S. Truman* and *The Republican Party* are the respective subjects of their sentences; *succeeded Roosevelt as President of the United States* and *promised a 20 per cent reduction in income taxes for 1947* are the respective predicates of their sentences.

A subject and its predicate combine to form a *clause.* If, as in the two preceding sentences used for illustrations, there is but one subject and one predicate, the sentence is *simple.*

If there are two or more clauses, the sentence is either *compound* or *complex.*

In a compound sentence, the clauses have a certain independent relationship, and are connected by a co-ordinate conjunction, of which, you will recall, there are only five: *and, or, nor, for,* and *but.* Note that each clause in the following compound sentences has its own subject and predicate:

1. Clifton Fadiman is the quiz-master of "Information, Please," *and* John Kieran is one of the "experts" on the same program.
2. Can a minority rule Congress *or* should control be entirely in the hands of the majority?
3. It doesn't take luck to make a million dollars, *nor* is hard work the only requisite.
4. She ran the show, *but* her husband wielded the power behind the scenes.

Occasionally a semicolon (;) acts as the co-ordinate conjunction separating the clauses of a compound sentence:

5. MacIntosh stood up; rage was written all over his face.

Divide each clause of the preceding five sentences into its component parts, the subject and the predicate. Fill in the necessary parts of the following chart:

IDENTIFICATION OF SUBJECT AND PREDICATE

Sentence	Clause	Subject	Predicate
1.	a		
	b		
2.	a		
	b		
3.	a		
	b		
4.	a		
	b		
5.	a		
	b		

Sentence	Clause	Subject	Predicate
1.	a	Clifton Fadiman	is the quiz-master of "Information, Please"
	b	John Kieran	is one of the experts on the same program
2.	a	a minority	can rule Congress
	b	control	should be entirely in the hands of the majority
3.	a	It	doesn't take luck to make a million dollars
	b	hard work	is [not] the only requisite [*nor* is equivalent to *and not*]
4.	a	She	ran the show
	b	her husband	wielded the power behind the scenes
5.	a	MacIntosh	stood up
	b	rage	was written all over his face

In a complex sentence, there is one main clause, which carries the burden of the idea; and one or more clauses which are subordinate to, and dependent on, the main clause.

Let us start with a central idea:

John L. Lewis called a coal strike.

For the American populace, this should be a sufficiently familiar concept. Let us play around with it a little.

The sentence as it now stands, "John L. Lewis called a coal strike," is, grammatically, a *simple* sentence, containing a single clause with one subject (*John L. Lewis*) and a single predicate (*called a coal strike*). Suppose we add another concept, combining our two clauses with a co-ordinate conjunction:

John L. Lewis called a coal strike and the nation froze.

We now have a compound sentence made up of two principal clauses, each with its own subject and predicate.

However, we might combine our concepts in a different way, so that there is a time, or *temporal*, relationship between the two clauses:

When Julius Krug, Secretary of the Interior, refused to re-open the miners' contract, John L. Lewis called a coal strike.

Logically, the second clause has a measure of dependence on the first; it is to be assumed, from the wording, that the strike was an aftermath of Secretary Krug's refusal, although people will be found who claim that John L. would have called the strike in any event. However, grammatically, we consider the first clause, the one introduced by the connective *when*, the subordinate clause. Logic and grammar are not, as you have doubtless already begun to suspect, always identical.

A sentence containing a main clause and one or more subordinate clauses, the latter introduced by any connective

229

other than *and, or, nor, for,* or *but* (the co-ordinate conjunctions) is called a *complex* sentence.

In Old English, direct off-shoot of our parent tongue, Anglo-Saxon, complex sentences were comparatively rare. But in modern writing, complex sentences form 50 per cent or more of the substance of any material on an adult level, with the exception, of course, of William Saroyan.

To get back to the coal strike, we can also show a temporal relationship between two concepts by the use of the connective *after.*

After Secretary Krug turned down the mine chief's request, John L. Lewis called a coal strike.

A swift inspection of the sentence will show two clearly defined clauses, each one with its subject and predicate. This too, then, is a complex sentence, with the subordinate clause *after Secretary Krug turned down the mine chief's request,* and the main clause, *John L. Lewis called a coal strike.*

A sentence is not complex unless the two clauses are complete (subject and predicate). Consider this sentence:

Upon Secretary Krug's rejection of the mine chief's request, John L. Lewis called a coal strike.

It was a matter of some dispute as to whether Lewis *called* the strike, or whether the strike happened by a kind of spontaneous combustion, so I do not wish to be held accountable for the factual accuracy of these sentences. The whole matter went to the United States Supreme Court to be threshed out.

This sentence has virtually the same meaning as the previous one, but it is not, please note, a complex sentence. There is but one subject—*John L. Lewis*—and one verb —*called.* The words *upon Secretary Krug's rejection of the mine chief's request* do not form a clause. Close examination will reveal a complete absence of verbs (*rejection* and *request* are nouns, although they may seem to have some verbal force) and no clause can exist without an expressed or implied verb. What we do have is a series of prepositional phrases. The words in italic are prepositions, the underlined words are nouns:

PHRASE 1: *Upon* Secretary Krug's <u>refusal</u>
PHRASE 2: *Of* the mine chief's <u>request</u>

The sentence is a simple sentence.

The following version also forms a simple sentence:

Acting after Krug's refusal, Lewis called a strike.

If you do not exercise extreme caution, you may be tempted to consider that portion of the sentence up to the comma as a clause. But there is no verb—*acting* is a *participle*, a grammatical element which we will cover more thoroughly at a later time. And there is no subject—*after Krug's refusal* is a prepositional phrase, and you will recall that a prepositional phrase never contains a subject.

As a third possibility, we might take our original idea (the calling of the coal strike) and elaborate upon it as follows:

John L. Lewis called a coal strike although the government contended that such action was a violation of the contract.

Analysis shows the following:

MAIN CLAUSE: John L. Lewis called a coal strike
CLAUSE SUBORDINATED TO THE MAIN CLAUSE: although the government contended
CLAUSE SUBORDINATE TO THE FIRST SUBORDINATE CLAUSE: that such action was a violation of the contract.

Each clause has its own subject and predicate:

MAIN CLAUSE—SUBJECT: John L. Lewis
  PREDICATE: called a coal strike
FIRST SUBORDINATE CLAUSE—SUBJECT: the government
  PREDICATE: contended
SECOND SUBORDINATE CLAUSE—SUBJECT: such action
  PREDICATE: was a violation of the contract

We have been dealing with a complex sentence made up of one principal clause and two subordinate clauses.

Subordinate clauses are introduced by connectives to which are given the general name of *subordinate conjunctions*. This is a partial list of the common subordinate conjunctions:

who, whom, whose	although	unless
which	where	whether
that	why	as
if	since	for
when	because	so

You have begun to learn how to distinguish between simple, compound, and complex sentences. How would you analyze the following sentence?

John L. Lewis called a coal strike and Justice T. Alan Goldsborough fined the mine leader $10,000 and the union $3,500,000 because Lewis violated the terms of the temporary injunction which had been issued.

Analysis shows four separate clauses:

1. John L. Lewis called a coal strike
2. (and) Justice T. Alan Goldsborough fined the mine leader $10,000 and the union $3,500,000

3. (because) Lewis violated the terms of the temporary injunction
4. (which) had been issued

The second clause, introduced by the co-ordinate conjunction *and,* makes the sentence *compound.* But the third and fourth clauses, introduced respectively by the adverbial conjunction *because* and the relative pronoun *which,* make the sentence *complex.* Which type of sentence is it? It is both. Correct name: a compound-complex sentence.

DO YOU GET THE POINT?—*test 41*

Decide whether each of the following sentences is declarative, interrogative, imperative, or exclamatory. Write the proper descriptive label in the space provided for that purpose.

1. What a man! ....
2. Who killed Cock Robin? ....
3. Love that soap. ....
4. Many people fear that a third World War is imminent. ....
5. Other people feel that the atom bomb makes another war impossible. ....
6. What is your opinion? ....
7. Don't sell America short. ....
8. Invest your surplus cash in Savings Bonds, and hold on to them. ....
9. Because prices have risen to their highest point in years, many a salaried worker is hard put to it to meet his ordinary financial obligations. ....
10. Hold that line! ....

CHECK YOUR LEARNING—*answers to test 41*

1. exclamatory
2. interrogative
3. imperative
4. declarative
5. declarative
6. interrogative
7. imperative
8. imperative
9. declarative
10. exclamatory

Decide whether each of the following sentences is *simple, compound, complex,* or *compound-complex,* and write your decision in the space following the sentence.

1. A man has bought a house. ....
2. It is a small, poorly built, unsatisfactory house, and it has cost too much money. ....
3. However, if our friend had not bought the house, he would have had to sleep in a tent in the park and his family would not have welcomed that possibility. ....
4. Because shelter is one of the basic needs of a normal human being, this unfortunate victim of the housing shortage used up most of his cash reserve as a down-payment. ....
5. In addition, he signed away the rest of his earning potential for the next twenty years in order to get a mortgage. ....
6. Now he has a house but no bank account. ....
7. He is not very happy. ....
8. He wonders if it would not have been better to have slept in the park after all. ....
9. None of his friends sleep in the park, however; and although he has no money he at least has a roof over his head. ....
10. He is pessimistically waiting for this roof to start leaking. ....
11. If it does not leak in the near future, he will probably be disappointed. ....
12. Some day prices on houses will come down; the average citizen will then be able to buy shelter without mortgaging away his entire future. ....

CHECK YOUR LEARNING—*answers to test 42*

1. simple	3. compound-	4. complex
2. compound	complex	5. simple

6. simple	9. compound-	11. complex
7. simple	complex	12. compound
8. complex	10. simple	

EXPLANATION OF THE ANSWERS

1. Single clause; subject: *a man;* predicate: *has bought a house.*
2. Two clauses, connected by the co-ordinate conjunction *and.*
3. Three clauses:

    MAIN CLAUSE: However, he would have had to sleep in a tent in the park

    CO-ORDINATE CLAUSE: (and) his family would not have welcomed that possibility

    SUBORDINATE CLAUSE: (if) our friend had not bought the house

4. Two clauses:

    MAIN CLAUSE: This unfortunate victim of the housing shortage used up most of his cash reserve as a down payment

    SUBORDINATE CLAUSE: (because) shelter is one of of the basic needs of a normal human being

5. Despite the length of the sentence, there is but one clause, one subject, one predicate.
6–7. Also simple sentences, containing one subject, one predicate each.
8. MAIN CLAUSE: He wonders

    SUBORDINATE CLAUSE: (if) it would not have been better to sleep in the park after all

9. Inspection will show a subordinate clause introduced by the adverbial conjunction *although,* and two co-ordinate clauses connected by the conjunction *and.*
10. There is but one true verb: *is waiting; to start* is an infinitive.
11. Conventional complex sentence, the clauses connected by the adverbial conjunction *if.*
12. The two co-ordinate clauses are connected by a semi-

colon. *Without mortgaging, etc.* is a prepositional phrase, with a *gerund, mortgaging,* acting as a noun and object of the preposition. A form of a verb which functions as a noun within the framework of the sentence is a *gerund;* it is not a true verb.

as easy as A B C

A. What is the difference between *ophthalmologist, oculist, optometrist,* and *optician*?

B. Is it correct to say, *"Due to* the telephone strike, only dial calls are going through"?

C. Which is preferable: "He has finally found a teacher *whom* he believes can handle the class," or "He has finally found a teacher *who* he believes can handle the class"?

A. The Grammar of Meanings

Ophthalmologist, Oculist, Optometrist, Optician

You have, let us suppose for the sake of argument, a visual defect. You could, if you liked, visit an *ophthalmologist,* who is a medical doctor, a specialist in diseases of the eye. (He is also called an *oculist,* the title preferred by those who cannot pronounce *ophthalmologist.*) This doctor may prescribe glasses, or may treat your eyes by drugs or surgery, depending on how badly off you are. If he does write out a prescription for glasses, you would repair to an *optician,* a man skilled in the grinding of lenses, the owner of a store whose business it is to fill prescriptions for eyeglasses. An *optician* is like a pharmacist; both fill doctors' prescriptions. Unlike a pharmacist, however, an *optician* does not hold a college degree.

On the other hand, you might decide to visit an *optometrist.* Not a medical doctor, this gentleman holds a degree from a college of optometry and is an expert in measuring refraction of the eyes and in providing lenses for proper correction. In New York at least, an *optometrist* may not administer drugs or perform surgery—he may only prescribe and fit glasses.

Some *optometrists* (and some *oculists* also) follow a recent theory of correction of visual defects without glasses, without drugs, without surgery. The treatment is eye-muscle exercise. I have heard this remedy praised by those whom it has helped (the novelist Aldous Huxley has written a glowing and laudatory book about this technic, called *The Art of Seeing*), and damned by those on whom it has had little or no effect. Eye training is probably still in the experimental stage.

The difference boils down to this:

ophthalmologist
or   } a medical doctor, specialist in the treatment of diseases of the eye.
oculist

optometrist: a specialist in prescribing and fitting glasses, not an M.D.

optician: a lens grinder, proprietor of, or mechanic in, a store; holds no college degree.

B. The Grammar of Allowable "Errors"

Due to the telephone strike, no calls are going through.

Due to as a preposition, substituting for the more formal *because of* or *owing to,* is acceptable on the informal level and is often seen today in newspapers and the popular magazines. *Due* should, theoretically, be used only as a predicate adjective, as in:

His failure is *due* to his stupidity.
His illness is *due* to neglect.
Your bill is *due* today.

However, *due to* as a preposition is being used more and more widely, and it would be unrealistic to condemn its use in constructions like:

238

Due to the weather, we have stayed indoors all day. ᒧ
Due to your remark, he feels insulted.
Due to poor circulation, the air was close.
The man died, *due to* over indulgence in narcotics.

PRO AND CON

Q. What is the standing of *due to* as a preposition?

Pro

A. The prepositional use of *due to* is encountered in such quality magazines as *Harper's* and *Scribner's* and sometimes even in the scholarly journal *Modern Language Notes*.

—Edward A. H. Fuchs

Dr. Fuchs was a member of the editorial staff of G. & C. Merriam Co., Publishers of the Merriam-Webster *New International Dictionary*.

Q. Many modern grammarians maintain that *"Due to* the telephone strike, only emergency calls are going through" is correct, idiomatic English, established by common usage among educated people. Do you agree? Would you use the expression in your everyday speech?

Pro

A. Yes, I would consider that expression correct. In fact I am sure I used it in one or more of my broadcasts.

—Lowell Thomas

Lowell Thomas is the former radio news analyst.

C. *The Grammar of Correct Usage*

He has finally found a teacher *whom* he believes can handle the class, *or* He has finally found a teacher *who* he believes can handle the class?

Clauses like *he believes, he thinks, I know, we expect, they consider* are parenthetical in sentences like the one above and have no grammatical effect on the case of the relative pronoun.

The case of the relative pronoun can correctly be arrived at by omitting such clauses. Complete sentence:

He said he met the countess in a hotel in Brussels and had been instructed to watch her by a fellow spy *whom* he said was known only as "The Mongolian." (From *PM*)

Revised sentence, with the parenthetical clause omitted:

He said he had met the countess in a hotel in Brussels and had been instructed to watch her by a fellow spy *whom* was known only as "The Mongolian."

This is of course ridiculous, idomatically, grammatically, and phonetically. The relative pronoun is seen, once the parenthetical clause is removed, to be subject of the verb phrase *was known*, and therefore should be in the nominative case, *who*, not in the objective case, *whom*.

The nominative case of the relative is preferred in sentences like the following, in each of which the relative is subject of the verb. The parenthetical clause will be italicized; get the feel for the correctness of *who* by reading the sentence without the parenthetical clause.

He met John P. Marquand who *many critics think* is the finest writer today.
He has at last discovered a woman who *he believes* can be trusted.
We have found a leader who *we feel* can lead us to our goal.
This is the man who *she said* stole her purse.

Now, on the other hand, the relative pronoun may precede a parenthetical clause and still function as *object* of the verb, as in:

He has at last discovered a woman whom *he believes* he can trust.
This is a leader whom *we feel* we can safely follow.
This is the man whom *she said* she saw last week.

PREFERABLE FORM:

He has finally found a teacher *who* he believes can handle the class.

Pro

As you may know, the customary procedure is to send out the first printed copies that come off the press to book editors for review. In addition we often send advance copies to prominent people *who* we think should have a particular interest in the particular book, authors, professors, radio commentators, and so on. In this way we receive interesting advance reactions which not only help us to tell the general public about the book, but also enable us to make our advertising and printing plans.

—Advertisement of a book publisher in
Saturday Review

chapter 19 HOW TO MEASURE YOUR
PROGRESS—A SECOND
ACHIEVEMENT TEST

Well, we're getting on. We've explored rather thoroughly some of the intricate problems in the architecture of the sentence: subject and predicate, objects, tense of verbs, predicate nominatives, transitive and intransitive verbs, active and passive voice, relative and interrogative pronouns, person, number, and case, ellipsis, simple, complex and compound sentences, declarative, imperative, interrogative and exclamatory sentences, and dozens of other fascinating facets of English grammar—all to the end that you will always know what word to use and how most effectively to use it.

Has your learning been successful? Are you straight on all the topics covered? Are you building up reflexive habits of good grammar? Are you developing healthy attitudes toward correct usage? I'll test your knowledge and ability shortly, but first let us spend a little time on a quick review.

Grammatical Terminology

1. A sentence or a clause is divisible into subject and predicate.
2. The single-word subject of the verb governs the number of the verb.
3. Singular subjects require singular verbs; plural subjects require plural verbs.
4. The subject of a verb is not found within a prepositional phrase.
5. The subject of an active verb initiates the action of the verb.

6. The object of an active verb receives the action of the verb.

7. The subject of a passive verb receives the action of the verb.

8. Active verbs are transitive when they have objects.

9. Active verbs are intransitive when they do not have objects.

10. The subject of a verb is in the nominative case.

11. The object of a verb is in the objective case.

12. The object of a preposition is in the objective case.

13. *Lay* is a transitive verb.

14. *Lie* is an intransitive verb.

15. Only *lay* has a passive voice.

16. The perfect tenses are used with the auxiliaries *has, have,* or *had.*

17. *To be,* or any one of its forms, is a copulative verb.

18. The complement of a copulative verb is in the nominative case.

19. Such a complement may be called a predicate nominative.

20. An elliptical sentence is one in which an understood word, or several understood words, are omitted.

21. A declarative sentence makes a statement.

22. An interrogative sentence asks a question.

23. An imperative sentence issues a command.

24. An exclamatory sentence makes an exclamation and is followed by an exclamation point (!).

25. A clause contains a subject and predicate.

26. A simple sentence contains one main clause.

27. A compound sentence contains two or more clauses connected by *and, or, but, nor, for,* or a semicolon (;).

28. A complex sentence contains two or more clauses connected by a subordinate conjunction.

29. A subordinate conjunction is any conjunction other than those listed in No. 27.

30. A compound-complex sentence contains clauses connected by both subordinate and co-ordinate conjunctions (the ones listed in No. 27).

Usage

1. Prepositional phrases like *filled with flowers, of strikes, with her servants, like his predecessors, of new cars, unlike her sisters, as well as his brothers* do not affect the number of the verb. If the one-word subject is singular, and is followed by a prepositional phrase containing a plural noun, the verb is still singular.
2. Compound subjects connected by *and* take a plural verb.
3. Singular subjects connected by *or, nor, either . . . or,* or *neither . . . nor* take a singular verb.
4. Compound subjects, connected by *and,* if both such subjects refer to the same person or thing, take a singular verb.
5. The pronoun in a compound object is in the objective form.
6. The pronoun in a compound object of a preposition is also in the objective form.
7. Use some form of *lie, lay, lain, lying* if the verb required is intransitive.
8. Use some form of *lay, laid, laid, laying* if the verb required is either transitive or passive.
9. Use the nominative personal pronouns (*I, he, she, we, they*) as predicate nominatives.
10. Use the nominative *who* as subject of the verb or predicate nominative.
11. Use the objective *whom* as object of the verb or as object of a preposition.
12. After *than* and *as,* fill in the ellipsis to determine what case of the personal pronoun to use.

The Grammar of Meanings

1. *Practicable* means able to be put into use; *practical* usually means common-sense, worthwhile, etc.

2. An *alumnus* is a male; an *alumna* is a female; *alumni* are males; *alumnae* are females.
3. *Childish* refers to the unpleasant qualities of childhood, *childlike* to the pleasant qualities of childhood.
4. *Uninterested* means bored; *disinterested* means impartial.
5. A *fiancé* is a male; a *fiancée* is a female.
6. To *allude* is to *refer* indirectly.
7. *Credible* means believable; *creditable* means worthy of praise.
8. An *ophthalmologist* and an *oculist* are medical doctors; an *optometrist* is a specialist in prescribing and fitting glasses; an *optician* is a lens-grinder or owner of a store specializing in optical equipment.

The Grammar of Allowable "Errors"

The following usages are permissible:

1. A *healthy* climate.
2. *As* after negative verbs in comparisons.
3. *Aggravated* meaning irritated. Likewise *aggravate, aggravating, aggravates*, etc., with the same meaning.
4. *Liable* or *apt* with the sense of probability.
5. *Above* as a noun or adjective.
6. *Everyone, no one*, etc. with plural pronouns.
7. Have you *got*.
8. *Due to* as a preposition.

The Grammar of Correct Usage

1. *None* is usually followed by a plural verb, unless its meaning is distinctly singular.
2. Names of diseases or of fields of study are singular even if they end in *s*.
3. *One or two* . . . is followed by a plural verb.

4. *A number of* . . . is followed by a plural verb. Similarly *A lot of.* . . .
5. A fraction or measure word, even if plural, is followed by a singular verb if a single unit is implied.
6. With *either* . . . *or* and *neither* . . . *nor,* the verb gets its number from the *nearer* subject.
7. In "Was it *he* you were talking to?" the preposition governs an understood relative, *whom*.
8. In "He has finally found a teacher *who* he believes can handle the class" the clause *he believes* is parenthetical, and therefore does not affect the case of the relative pronoun.

That was quite a stint, and if you feel fuzzy on any of the points mentioned now is the time to go back to the text and get a fresh view. As soon as you feel competent on all the points covered in chapters 12 through 18, take your

Achievement Test 2

Directions: Check the preferable word in each sentence.

1. He always takes a (practical, practicable) view of things.
2. None of the boys (was, were) absent today.
3. None of your work (is, are) satisfactory.
4. "British efforts to check at its various European sources the stream moving toward Palestine (has, have) aggravated conditions still further." (Adapted from *The Nation*)
5. "The revolt of the backbenchers led by Richard Crossman and Michael Foot (has, have) not subsided." (From *The Nation*)
6. "A natural reluctance to be bound to America's doubtful economic fortunes (has, have) been converted into a determination to separate Britian from involvement in what is generally interpreted as

America's imperialist adventure." (From *The Nation*)

7. How (is, are) your father and mother today?
8. One of my friends (has, have) promised to help me.
9. The teacher, with her forty pupils, (is, are) waiting to see you.
10. (Was, Were) either of your attempts successful?
11. Each of these reports (is, are) excellent.
12. Your attempts at comedy (fall, falls) flat.
13. Evan, unlike his wife, (has, have) a pleasant disposition.
14. Evan, like his wife, (has, have) a pleasant disposition.
15. Lucile as well as her husband (is, are) working on the magazine.
16. Neither of your brothers (is, are) very smart.
17. She is an (alumnus, alumna) of the New Rochelle College for Women.
18. Mumps (is, are) an awful thing to get right now.
19. (Is, Are) measles contagious?
20. Mathematics (is, are) a difficult study.
21. What (is, are) the ethics of the situation?
22. Your aunt and uncle (is, are) proud of you.
23. His health and intelligence (is, are) not in question.
24. The commander-in-chief of the armed forces and the highest executive officer of the government (is, are) the President.
25. Either Max or Ralph (is, are) willing to help you.
26. Neither Max nor Ralph (is, are) willing to help you.
27. The White House or the Supreme Court (is, are) his goal.
28. She has a (childish, childlike) temper.
29. One or two cars (has, have) already been sold.
30. Mary and (I, me) are your only friends.
31. Can you visit Mary and (I, me) tonight?
32. Can you have supper with Mary and (I, me) tonight?

33. She is most (uninterested, disinterested) in your problems. Why continue to bore her with them?
34. A lot of the pictures (is, are) excellent.
35. A number of the pictures (is, are) excellent.
36. Please (lie, lay) down.
37. Did you (lie, lay) down for a nap?
38. He (lay, laid) asleep all morning.
39. Have the clothes (laid, lain) in that filth all week?
40. (Lying, Laying) on his side, he was able to breathe better.
41. (Lie, Lay) the baby in its crib.
42. He (lay, laid) his books on top of mine.
43. Have his words (laid, lain) your fears to rest?
44. Her (fiancée, fiancé) is the most repulsive man I have ever met.
45. Four-fifths of Gertrude Stein (is, are) sheer gibberish.
46. Three pounds of meat (is, are) all I'll need for supper.
47. A majority of the voters (is, are) still for free enterprise.
48. Was it (he, him) who answered the phone?
49. It is (they, them) who have tricked you.
50. Without mentioning any names, he made an (a) (allusion, reference) to your wife; I'm sure of it.
51. Neither he nor I (am, is, are) sympathetic to your plans.
52. Neither the President nor the cabinet members (is, are) here today.
53. (Who, Whom) do you think you are?
54. (Who, Whom) do you see?
55. (Who, Whom) are they talking to?
56. This is the actress (who, whom) his father claims has seduced his son.
57. Was it (she, her) you were referring to?
58. He is taller than (I, me).
59. I can talk as fast as (he, him).
60. The (oculist, optometrist, optician) performed a very delicate surgical operation on his eyes.

ANSWERS

1. practical	17. alumna	33. un-	48. he
2. were	18. is	interested	49. they
3. is	19. is	34. are	50. allusion
4. have	20. is	35. are	51. am
5. has	21. are	36. lie	52. are
6. has	22. are	37. lie	53. who
7. are	23. are	38. lay	54. whom
8. has	24. is	39. lain	55. whom
9. is	25. is	40. lying	56. who
10. was	26. is	41. lay	57. she
11. is	27. is	42. laid	58. I
12. fall	28. childish	43. laid	59. he
13. has	29. have	44. fiancé	60. oculist
14. has	30. I	45. is	
15. is	31. me	46. is	
16. is	32. me	47. are	

SCORING

Each correct choice counts 1 point.

56–60................Excellent
50–55................Good
45–49................Passing
44 or less..........Indicates that further study of
chapters 12 through 18 is required.

YOUR SCORE ON ACHIEVEMENT TEST II: .... (Record the result on page 13.)

as easy as A B C

A. What is the difference between *prophecy* and *prophesy?*

B. Is it correct to say, "There are *less* people here than we expected"?

C. Which is preferable: "What we need in this country *is* more blondes," or "What we need in this country *are* more blondes"?

A. The Grammar of Meanings

Prophecy, Prophesy

You are making a prediction—you are looking into the future. You expect war with Russia by 1970? That is your *prophecy.*

You claim that a Republican will win the next presidential election? You *prophesy* that the next election will be won by a Republican.

The distinction between *prophecy* and *prophesy* is one of function: With the *c*, *prophecy* is a noun.

SINGULAR: prophecy
PLURAL: prophecies
PRONUNCIATION: *proff*-e-see, *proff*-e-sees

With the *s*, *prophesy* is a verb.

PRESENT TENSE: prophesy, prophesies
PAST TENSE: prophesied

250

PRESENT PARTICIPLE: prophesying
PRONUNCIATION: *proff*-e-sigh, *proff*-e-sighs,
                     proff-e-sighed, *proff*-e-sighing

DO YOU GET THE POINT?—*test 43*

1. He (prophecied, prophesized, prophesied) that the end of the world would come within two weeks.
2. They made many dire (prophecies, prophesies), none of which ever came true.
3. In a section called "The Clouded Crystal Ball," *The New Yorker* lists those (prophecies, prophesies) which never materialized.
4. Do you (prophecy, prophesy) a return to war-time prosperity?
5. He is an expert in (prophecy, prophesy).
6. He is an expert at (prophecying, prophesying).

CHECK YOUR LEARNING—*answers to test 43*

1. prophesied	3. prophecies	5. prophecy
2. prophecies	4. prophesy	6. prophesying

B. *The Grammar of Allowable "Errors"*

There are *less* people here than we expected.

Again, we have an instance in which formal grammar conflicts with popular usage. The strict rule is that *less* may be used only with singular nouns, that *fewer* is required with plural nouns. This is an eminently logical, and, as it happens, age-old rule which you can find in textbooks way back to 1850. Unfortunately (for the rule), modern writers and contemporary educated speakers often ignore the distinction between *less* and *fewer,* and you will find *less* frequently used with plural nouns in current magazines, newspapers, and books, and will hear it even more frequently from the lips of educated people. Such being the case, *less* cannot realistically or effectively be restricted to

251

singular nouns. The restriction operates, in other words, mainly in theory—that is, in rhetorics and in handbooks and in grammar lessons but not always in practice.

Fewer is joining the ranks of words like *farther, shall, should* and *supine*—words whose functions are gradually being taken over by their partial-synonyms: *less, further, will, would,* and *prone.*

However, as you will note from some of the opinions that follow, many people consciously prefer to use "fewer" with plural nouns. It is obvious that the question is still a controversial one.

PRO AND CON

Pro

Like anything else to do with Senator Taft, my story propelled itself soberly, methodically and carefully along scheduled lines; it encountered *less* pitfalls and booby traps than anything I have done. All this I attribute to the personality of the senator, who makes a virtue of predictability.

—Arthur M. Schlesinger, Jr.

Professor Schlesinger, author of *Age of Jackson*, describing an article he wrote for *Collier's*, as quoted in *Collier's.*

Pro

The publishers are facing up boldly to the situation, Mr. Streit says, by issuing many *less* titles . . .
—A. J. Leibling, in *Esquire* for September, 1947.

Pro

You'll see the first completely new car in 50 years . . . the first rear-engine car on American roads . . . the car with 800 *less* parts than conventional cars.
—Advertisement for the Tucker '48

Pro

Less nicotine, *less* throat irritants.
—Advertisement for Raleigh cigarettes

Q. Modern grammarians maintain that "We have *less* workers than we need" is correct, idiomatic English, established by common usage among educated people. Do you agree? Would you use the expression in your everyday speech?

Pro *(with reservations)*

A. Spare me from usage controversies! But I'll give you an honest answer for your file.

Since I was brought up on *fewer workers* I would say *fewer*—with no lack of respect for people who were brought up on *less workers* and stand by it.

I find the following in a well-written article just come to my desk: "By 1840, a decade after Brisbane's student days, less than a hundred American names had appeared on the rolls of all the German universities combined." What would be "correct" here?

The big question here is what we mean by correct. Socially correct? Approved by linguists? "According to the XXX Handbook?"

—Lennox Grey

Professor Grey is chairman of the Department of English, Teachers College, Columbia University.

Con *(with reservations)*

A. I have a pet prejudice against using this expression myself; can't explain it—just a case of "I do not like you, Dr. Fell; the reason why, I cannot tell; but this I know full very well: I do not like you, Dr. Fell." If anybody else wants to say it or write it, though, it's O.K. by me.

—Reuben Maury

Mr. Maury is chief editorial writer of the New York *News*.

Con

A. Thanks for your letter, and for asking my opinion concerning the use of the expression, "We have *less* workers than we need."

Here at the paper we use Webster's *New International* Second Edition, Unabridged, as a source for spelling; and Fowler's *Modern English Usage* for grammar. Therefore, we are in favor of using the word *fewer* in the above sentence, rather than *less*, when the word to which it is applied deals with actual numbers.

—John P. Lewis

Mr. Lewis was editor of *PM*.

Con

A. You had better count me out on this one. I would say, "We have *fewer* workers than we need," and would not use *less* in the sense indicated—either in writing or in everyday speech.

However, I cannot prove that I am right or wrong grammatically. *Less* has always meant smaller to me. I would not think of saying, "We ought to have *less* soldiers." Where numbers are concerned, I always use *fewer*.

—Lawrence E. Spivak

Mr. Spivak was formerly publisher of *The American Mercury*.

Q. Do you use the word *less* with a plural noun as in the sentence "We have *less* books in stock than we need"? Or do you prefer to use *fewer* in such sentences? Do you have a very strict attitude toward the distinction between these words?

Con

A. I must confess that I am puzzled by your question, which seems to me to deal with a usage not only obviously incorrect, but so clumsy that I don't see why even an illiterate should go out of his way to employ it. It seems to me that anybody familiar with the word *less* would be just as familiar with the word *fewer* and with the distinction between their meanings.

—Bruce Gould

Mr. Gould is editor of the *Ladies' Home Journal*.

Tolerant

I think that I would say *fewer* people, but I would not find *less people* objectionable.

—Jinx Falkenburg McCrary

Mrs. McCrary and her husband, Tex McCrary, conduct the popular program "Tex and Jinx" over WNBC. Under her maiden name of Jinx Falkenburg, Mrs. McCrary is the well-known movie star and model.

Q. Modern grammarians maintain that "There are *less* people here than we expected" is correct, idiomatic English, established by common usage among educated people and completely acceptable in informal conversation. Do you agree? Would you use the expression in your everyday speech?

Con

A. Having been the originator of the abbreviated words "natch," "def," etc., perhaps I'm not qualified to answer. However, I have a peculiar psychology regarding the spoken word. . . . I go in for slang expressions when they are not generally used . . . as soon as they become an accepted part of the language I drop them. On the other hand, I make no compromise with what is known as "good English." I think modern usage has undoubtedly given the seal of approval to a preposition ending a sentence, but somehow it doesn't sound right to me.

In the case of the sentence under discussion, I believe *fewer* would be my choice or "there aren't as many as we expected."

—Maggi McNellis

Maggi McNellis is the popular radio and television personality.

C. The Grammar of Correct Usage

What we need in this country *is* more blondes, *or*
What we need in this country *are* more blondes?

Blondes is a predicate noun and, though plural, does not attract the verb into the plural, since the verb is governed by its subject, which in such a sentence is the entire clause *what we need in this country;* and clauses are considered singular in number.

Similarly, in "All I need is pictures," the clause *all I need* is subject of *is* and since clauses are singular, requires a singular verb.

PREFERABLE FORMS:

What we need in this country *is* more blondes.
What I want *is* better tools.
All I see *is* six new houses.
What I need *is* five new workers.
All I want *is* friends and money.

256

chapter 20 HOW TO ANALYZE A VERB

A verb shows action; or, in the single exception of the copulative verb, denotes a state of being.

Action can happen at various times.

It can occur in the present time.

It can be described as having taken place in the past.

It can be described as being expected to occur in the future.

Thus we have three principal *tenses* (or times) of English verbs:

PRESENT TENSE: He *is* a young man.
PAST TENSE: He *was* a boy.
FUTURE TENSE: He *will be* an old man.

More subtle variations of time are indicated by other tenses:

CONDITIONAL TENSE: "He *would be* happy." As the name implies, such a tense is used to show a condition dependent on another idea. "He would be happy *if he had more money*." "He would be sad *if he had less money*."

PRESENT-PERFECT TENSE: "He *has been* ill." This tense indicates action that started in the past and continued into, or nearly into, the present. The implication of the illustration used is that he has just recently recovered, or is perhaps even now in the process of recovering. In the sentence, "He *has worked* hard all his life," the present-perfect tense implies either that he is still working hard or has just recently stopped.

PAST-PERFECT TENSE: "He *had* always *believed* in Santa Claus until his friends disabused him of that juvenile notion." This tense indicates action that started at some time in the past remoter than some other past time mentioned. This sounds more complicated than it is. In the illustration used, we have two verbs: *had believed,* a past-perfect tense; and *disabused,* a past tense. The action of believing in Santa Claus occurred prior to the action of being disabused. "He *had failed* to make many friends until he *read* Dale Carnegie's book." Both verbs (*had failed* and *read*) show action in the past time, but which happened first, the failure or the reading?

FUTURE-PERFECT TENSE: "She *will have earned* $15,000 by the end of the year." This tense is a paradoxical wedding of the apparently contradictory concepts of future and past. In the illustration used, the action will not be complete until the end of the year—a time in the future. But by the end of the year, the action will already have taken place, the deed will already have been consummated. So there is an added concept of the past in the idea.

CONDITIONAL-PERFECT TENSE: "We *would have done* the work if you had offered to pay us." This tense shows a condition occurring in the past.

If we take the verb *to see,* we can very easily form the four simple (present, past, future, conditional) and the four compound (present-perfect, past-perfect, future-perfect, and conditional-perfect) tenses:

SIMPLE TENSES		COMPOUND TENSES	
PRESENT:	I see	PRESENT PERFECT:	I have seen
PAST:	I saw	PAST PERFECT:	I had seen
FUTURE:	I will see	FUTURE PERFECT:	I will have seen
CONDITIONAL:	I would see	CONDITIONAL PERFECT:	I would have seen

Each of these eight tenses can be slightly changed to show action continuing over an extended period of time. Such continuity is indicated by the *progressive* tenses.

PRESENT PROGRESSIVE:	He *is working* on the railroad.
PAST PROGRESSIVE:	He *was working* on the railroad for a time.
FUTURE PROGRESSIVE:	He *will be working* on the railroad.
CONDITIONAL PROGRESSIVE:	He *would* now *be working* on the railroad if he had joined the union.
PRESENT-PERFECT PROGRESSIVE:	He *has been working* on the railroad for twenty years.
PAST-PERFECT PROGRESSIVE:	He *had been working* on the railroad for twenty years when he died.
FUTURE-PERFECT PROGRESSIVE:	He *will have been working* on the railroad for twenty years come Christmas.
CONDITIONAL-PERFECT PROGRESSIVE:	He *would have been working* on the railroad for twenty years if he had lived another week.

It can be seen, then, that the progressive tenses are formed by combining some form of the verb *to be* (is, was, will be, would be, has been, had been, will have been, would have been) with the *-ing* form of another verb (is playing, was playing, will be playing, etc.). Such an *-ing* form of a verb is known as the *present participle*.

Similarly, it can be seen that the compound tenses of a verb (present perfect, past perfect, future perfect, conditional perfect) are formed by combining the simple tenses of the verb *to have* (has, had, will have, would have) with another form of the main verb (has played, had played, etc.). The form of the main verb used in compound tenses is known as the *past participle*.

Every verb has two participles: the present participle, used in the progressive tenses, and the past participle, used in compound tenses. The present participle always ends in the letters *-ing*:

VERB	PRESENT PARTICIPLE
to know	knowing
to have	having
to feel	feeling
to see	seeing
to wish	wishing
to vote	voting
to lie	lying
to lay	laying

The past participle generally ends in *-ed:*

VERB	PAST PARTICIPLE
work	(have) worked
vote	(have) voted
use	(have) used
play	(have) played
wish	(have) wished

Occasionally, the past participle ends in *-n:*

VERB	PAST PARTICIPLE
know	(have) known
see	(have) seen
begin	(have) begun
lie	(have) lain
break	(have) broken
fall	(have) fallen
give	(have) given

Occasionally in *-d* or *-t:*

VERB	PAST PARTICIPLE
have	(have) had
feel	(have) felt
flee	(have) fled
pay	(have) paid
seek	(have) sought

Occasionally, in completely irregular, unclassifiable forms:

VERB	PAST PARTICIPLE
do	(have) done
drink	(have) drunk
swim	(have) swum
hang	(have) hung
shine	(have) shone

A verb may show tense by means of a single word:

PRESENT: He swims.
PAST: He swam.

Or a verb may show tense by combining with some special tense word, such as *will, is, have,* and so on:

PRESENT: He *is* working.
PAST: He *has* worked.
FUTURE: He *will* work.
PRESENT: He *does* not work.

In such combined forms, the verb is made up of two or more parts and is called a *verb phrase*. The tense word (will, shall, would, should, etc.) is called an *auxiliary*.

The auxiliary *do, does,* or *did* is used to form negative and interrogative present and past tenses.

AFFIRMATIVE	NEGATIVE	INTERROGATIVE
He works.	He does not work.	Does he work?
He worked.	He did not work.	Did he work?
They work.	They do not work.	Do they work?

In other tenses besides the present and past, negative forms are made by the simple addition of the adverb *not:* "He will work," "He will not work." Interrogative forms

261

in these tenses are made by a simple reversal of word order: "He has worked," "Has he worked?"

Tense is no great problem in English, except in the case of a few irregular verbs whose past tenses and past participles are not conventional forms ending in *-ed*. These are the most troublesome of the irregular verbs:

VERB	PAST TENSE	PAST PARTICIPLE
begin	began	has begun
break	broke	has broken
drink	drank	has drunk
eat	ate	has eaten
flee	fled	has fled
lay	laid	has laid
lie	lay	has lain
rise	rose	has risen
shrink	shrank *or* shrunk	has shrunk
spring	sprang *or* sprung	has sprung
strive	strove	has striven
swim	swam	has swum

In summary: verbs in English have the following functions:

1. *Transtive and Intransitive*
   TRANSITIVE: He *blew* a whistle.
   INTRANSITIVE: A whistle *blew*.
2. *Voice*
   ACTIVE: He saw.
   PASSIVE: He was seen.
3. *Tense*
   SIMPLE TENSES: present, past, future, conditional.
   COMPOUND TENSES: present perfect, past perfect, future perfect, conditional perfect.
   PROGRESSIVE TENSES: simple progressive and compound progressive tenses.
4. *Mood*

INDICATIVE: The tenses discussed in this chapter were all of the indicative mood.

INFINITIVE: Made up of the preposition *to* plus the verb: *to see, to wait, to lie,* etc. The infinitive is not truly a verb, but rather a verbal, and may function in a sentence as a noun, adjective, or adverb.

SUBJUNCTIVE: The subjunctive mood, which is used only under special circumstances, will be discussed in a later chapter.

IMPERATIVE: commands, like *Go, Stop,* and so forth.

5. *Form*

  FFIRMATIVE: He goes.

  ˉEGATIVE: He does not go.

  ˉNTERROGATIVE: Does he go?

6. *Person.* Person depends on the subject:

FIRST PERSON: *I* go, *we* go.

SECOND PERSON: *you* go.

THIRD PERSON: *he* goes, *she* goes, *they* go, *the man* goes, *the men* go.

7. *Number.* Number also depends on the subject:

SINGULAR: The cost *is* high.

PLURAL: The data *are* incomplete.

Verbs have:
  voice
  tense
  mood
  form
  person
  number

Verbs are either transitive or intransitive.

Verbs also have subjects and, at times, objects.

Some verbs are copulative; most verbs are verbs of action.

In a verb phrase, some verbs are auxiliary, some are main verbs.

A verb has two participles, the present participle and the past participle.

Problem 1. Consider the verb in the following sentence:

How long has he been speaking?

1. Identify the full verb: ....
2. Tense? ....
3. Voice? ....
4. Mood? ....
5. Person? ....
6. Number? ....
7. Form? ....
8. Transitive or intransitive? ....
9. Subject? ....
10. Is there an object? ....
11. Write the present participle ....;
    the past participle ....; the infinitive ....

Problem 2. Consider the verb in the following sentence:

Why did you break your promise?

Answer questions 1–11, as in problem 1:

1.	....	7.	....
2.	....	8.	....
3.	....	9.	....
4.	....	10.	....
5.	....	11.	....
6.	....		....
			....

CHECK YOUR LEARNING—*answers to test 44*

Problem 1:

1. has been speaking
2. present-perfect progressive
3. active
4. indicative
5. third person
6. singular
7. interrogative
8. intransitive
9. he
10. no
11. speaking, spoken, to speak

Problem 2:

1. did break
2. past
3. active
4. indicative
5. second person
6. singular or plural
7. interrogative
8. transitive
9. you
10. yes, *promise*
11. breaking, broken, to break

as easy as A B C

A. What is the difference between *sensuous* and *sensual?*
B. Is it correct to say, "I *will* write him a letter tomorrow"?
C. Which is preferable: "He should *of* gone," or "He should *have* gone"?

A. The Grammar of Meanings

Sensuous, Sensual

Perhaps you are a creature of the senses. You enjoy music, poetry, beautiful sunsets, delicious food. You react strongly to influences on your sense of hearing, seeing, tasting, touching, smelling. You are *sensuous.*

Sensuous music appeals to the ear, rather than to the intellect. Young children, largely dependent on their five senses for a comprehension of the phenomena of life, are more *sensuous* than older people, who rely on memory, experience, analogy, intellectual grasp. (Perhaps older people, however, are more *sensual* than children, though not according to Freud.)

Poetry has a more *sensuous* appeal than mathematical equations.

However, poetry, music, art can have a *sensual* as well as a *sensuous* appeal. If the appeal of a painting is chiefly *sensual,* it excites, shall we say, the *grosser* appetites of the viewer. If music is *sensual,* it titillates, shall we say, the *fleshly* desires.

What the distinction boils down to, of course, is that *sensuous* is a complimentary or, at worst, a neutral adjective, while *sensual* is in general derogatory. The senses implied by the word *sensuous* are, ethically speaking, the "higher" senses (biologically, anatomically, semantically, there is no such thing as a "higher" sense); those implied by *sensual* are the more animal-like, more lascivious, less "refined" senses. Thus, *sensual* is in some connotations synonymous with lewd, sexy, voluptuous, perhaps even immoral.

Your choice of terms will depend entirely on the moral implications you wish to give to your ideas.

Thus: "The *sensuous* delights of good food." You consider a delight in good food a worth-while attitude.

Thus: "A *sensual* approach to life." You imply that such an approach is excessively self-indulgent, not entirely moral, certainly not to be recommended or condoned.

Swinburne's poetry is sometimes called *sensual;* it seems to titillate the desire, to appeal to the animal emotions.

DO YOU GET THE POINT?—*test 45*

1. He spent his evenings in the (sensuous, sensual) delights of Bacchanalian revelry.
2. The bracing air and good, clean sea smells provide a (sensuous, sensual) enjoyment not found elsewhere.
3. The (sensuous, sensual) pleasures of Tchaikowsky's "Swan Lake Ballet" have made the piece popular throughout the world.
4. His thick (sensuous, sensual) lips give an indication of the type of enjoyment he prefers.

CHECK YOUR LEARNING—*answers to test 45*

1. sensual   2. sensuous   3. sensuous   4. sensual

B. The Grammar of Allowable "Errors"

I *will* write him a letter tomorrow.

The law of gravity will never change. It was in full and successful operation long before Newton—it will remain a factor to be dealt with as long as the earth as we know it exists.

So long as human nature remains the same, the law of supply and demand is likely to be similarly impervious to change.

But the laws of English grammar are far less resistant to alteration than the laws of physics or economics. Grammatical principles that were held in the greatest veneration by one generation may be entirely discarded by the next. One of the few certainties of language is that change will take place. If you compare the English used by writers and speakers several hundred years ago with the modern tongue used by educated people today, you will understand how constantly our patterns of grammar keep changing.

One specific instance is in the future tense of English verbs.

Futurity can be expressed by both *shall* and *will*. According to laws that are today pretty nearly outmoded, a painfully precise distinction was once made between these alternative tense words. At the risk of boring the reader, I shall summarize *some* of these rules very briefly:

1. *Shall* is used:
   To denote simple futurity with a subject of the first person.
   To denote promise or determination with a subject of the second or third person.
2. *Will* is used:
   To denote simple futurity with a second- and third-person subject.
   To denote promise or determination with a first-person subject.
3. *Shall* is used:
   In questions in which the answer is expected to employ *shall* according to the two rules elucidated above.
4. *Will* is used.
   In questions in which the answer is expected to employ *will* according to rules 1 and 2.

There is much more to the subject, equally confusing, equally unrealistic. The *facts* of everyday speech (which you can easily verify from your own listening) are:

1. *Will* is used almost universally to express futurity—no matter what person the subject is in, no matter what implication is intended by the phraseology of the sentence. (*Shall,* with the subject *I* or *we,* is fairly common in writing.)

2. *Shall* is almost exclusively restricted to interrogative sentences in which a form of permission is asked. For example:

Shall I open the box now? (Implying, "Do you give me permission to open the box?")

Shall my sister phone you tomorrow? (That is, "Do you wish my sister to phone you?")

But of course in questions asking for simple information, such as, "Will we have dinner on time?" *will* is used almost exclusively.

(Perhaps the most current use of *shall* is in legal and government documents: "The defendant *shall,* within five days of the date of this notice . . ."; "Each company commander *shall* immediately repair to . . ." In such language, *shall* has the force of a command.)

Modern teachers in high school no longer pay much attention to *shall-will* distinctions; most modern grammar textbooks used in high-school classrooms concentrate on the hard facts of actual usage.

If you have a vague recollection that your own high-school English teacher devoted a lot of time and pother to the topic, and wonder if there isn't something you should keep in mind about it if you wish to speak good English, let me suggest that you relax. In informal speech, *will* has almost completely superseded *shall* as the expression of futurity. With the exceptions noted, *will* is always correct, established, cultivated English.

Q. Modern grammarians maintain that "I *will* be happy to see him" is correct, idiomatic English, established by common usage among educated people and completely acceptable in informal conversation. Do you agree? Would you use the expression in your everyday speech?

Pro

A. Yes, of course.

—Hallett D. Smith

Dr. Smith is a professor of English at Williams College.

Pro

A. I'm for *will*, though not nearly so staunchly as I am for *ain't*.

—H. Allen Smith

Mr. Smith is the author of *Low Man on a Totem Pole; Life in a Putty Knife Factory*, and other best-sellers.

Pro

A. The artificial distinction between *shall* and *will* to designate futurity is a superstition that has neither a basis in historical grammar nor the sound sanction of universal usage. It is a nineteenth-century affectation which certain grammarians have tried hard to establish and perpetuate. That they have not succeeded is corroborative evidence of the fact that grammatical rules are not made by grammarians but that they grow out of the sound instincts of intelligent writers and speakers of a language.

—Gustave O. Arlt

Professor Arlt is editor of *Modern Language Forum,* University of California.

C. The Grammar of Correct Usage

He should *of* gone, *or* He should *have* gone?

Have is the correct form, making the conditional-perfect tense with the past participle, *gone*. *Should have* is the auxiliary verb, *gone* is the main verb.

In speech, *have* in such a construction sounds exactly like *of*, but it is still *have* and should be so written.

PREFERABLE FORMS:

He would *have* gone.
I would *have* done it.
You should *have* spoken up.
They would *have* taken you.

chapter 21 HOW TO EXPRESS A MOOD

1. The Problem

When may one say *"If I was"*? When is *"If I were"* preferable?

2. The Solution

This question involves an understanding of the *subjunctive mood* of the verb.

While the subjunctive is used far less today than in the past, there are still a number of important instances in which it is heard in English sentences. To wit:

1. I suggest he *keep* his ideas to himself.
2. I wish I *were* richer.
3. I insist that he *report* every day.
4. If I *were* you, I would not do that.
5. She acts as if she *were* his wife.
6. It is necessary that an employee *finish* his work on time.
7. God *forbid* that it should happen.
8. Heaven *help* the working girl.

It is apparent that these are special uses of the verb, since under normal circumstances we say:

1. He *keeps*.
2. I *was*.

3. He *reports*.
4. I *was*.
5. She *was*.
6. An employee *finishes*.
7. God *forbids*.
8. Heaven *helps*.

If we examine the meanings of the sentences involved, we see that they are not, strictly speaking, statements:

Sentence 1 is a suggestion.
Sentence 2 is a wish.
Sentence 3 is a demand.
Sentence 4 is a condition contrary to fact, since, of course, I am not you.
Sentence 5 is another condition contrary to fact. She is not his wife, in truth, but only acts as if she were.
Sentence 6 is an expression of necessity.
Sentence 7 is a wish.
Sentence 8 is a wish.

It follows then that the indicative mood, which we explored tense by tense in chapter 20, is used in statements; that the subjunctive mood is used in nonstatements (wishes, demands, conditions contrary to fact, and the like) such as those listed above.

In the active voice, the subjunctive is identical in appearance to one of two indicative tenses:

THE PRESENT INDICATIVE PLURAL, EVEN IF THE
SUBJECT IS SINGULAR:

We demand that he *fulfill* his contract.
Do you wish that my brother *return* the compliment?
Do you suggest that she *work* overtime?
It is essential that he *use* more care.

THE PAST PROGRESSIVE INDICATIVE, PLURAL, EVEN IF THE SUBJECT IS SINGULAR:

He wishes he *were going*.
He talks as if he *were spending* his own money.
How nice this would be if it *were happening* to you!

In the passive voice, the subjunctive of a verb is the auxiliary *be* plus the perfect participle: *be seen, be known, be used*, etc.:

We demand that the contract *be fulfilled*.
It is important that you *be seen* in the right places.
It is essential that this machine *be used* with greater care.

With the verb *to be*, the subjunctive is the form *were*, even with a singular subject.

He wishes he *were* stronger.
He acts as if he *were* rich.
How nice this would be if it *were* only true.

The subjunctive need cause no confusion, except when there is a possible choice between *was* and *were*. You will be faced with this choice only after the verb *wish* and after the conjunctions *if* and *as if*. In other instances, the subjunctive is so definitely part of the idiom of the language that no one ever uses the indicative where the subjunctive is required. However, care must be exercised after the verb *wish* and also after the conjunctions *if* and *as if*.

ITEM 1. Use the subjunctive after the verb *wish*:

PREFERABLE	OCCASIONALLY HEARD IN EDUCATED SPEECH, BUT NOT PREFERABLE
I wish I *were* going.	I wish I *was* going.
She wishes she *were* married.	She wishes she *was* married.
I wish I *were* braver.	I wish I *was* braver.

ITEM 2. Use the subjunctive after the conjunction *as if,* which always introduces a condition contrary to fact:

PREFERABLE	OCCASIONALLY HEARD IN EDUCATED SPEECH, BUT NOT PREFERABLE
Martin talks as if he *were* innocent.	Martin talks as if he *was* innocent.

(Actually, he is not innocent.)

Alice ran as if the devil *were* after her.	Alice ran as if the devil *was* after her.

(Actually, the devil was not after her.)

Alice screamed as if she *were* being murdered.	Alice screamed as if she *was* being murdered.

(Actually, she was not being murdered.)

ITEM 3. Use the subjunctive after the conjunction *if* in contrary-to-fact conditions:

PREFERABLE	OCCASIONALLY HEARD IN EDUCATED SPEECH, BUT NOT PREFERABLE
If he *were* less sarcastic, he would be more popular.	If he *was* less sarcastic, he would be more popular.

(But, as a fact, he is *not* less sarcastic.)

If she *were* not so stupid, she would understand how you feel about her.	If she *was* not so stupid, she would understand how you feel about her.

(But, as a fact, she *is* stupid.)

If he *were* acting out of sincerity, he would not do that.	If he *was* acting out of sincerity he would not do that.

(But, as a fact, he is not acting out of sincerity.)

ITEM 4. In conditions of fact, or possible fact, use the *indicative* after the conjunction *if:*

CORRECT

If Dr. Jaffe *was* in his office, why didn't he answer the phone?
> (Maybe he was in his office.)

If the builder *was* opposed to the plan, why didn't he say so?
> (Maybe he was opposed to the plan.)

If her husband *was* at home that night, he certainly did not take part in the festivities.
> (Maybe her husband was at home.)

ITEM 5. It is not necessary to make a lengthy analysis of the factuality or possible factuality of a condition, before deciding on the use of the subjunctive after the conjunction *if*. A condition contrary to fact is found only in a sentence in which the main clause is in the *conditional tense*. The conditional tense, you will recall from chapter 20, contains the auxiliary *would*. In other words, if the main clause contains *would*, the *if* clause requires the subjunctive. (*As if* clauses, however, always require the subjunctive.) It's as simple and mechanical as that. (*Should*, an alternate form of *would;* and *could*, which is the conditional tense of *be able*, also signify a condition contrary to fact.)

Notice how a change in the main clause of the sentences above removes the factuality of each sentence:

Dr. Jaffe would answer the phone if he *were* in his office. (Subjunctive)

If the builder *were* opposed to the plan, he would say so. (Subjunctive)

If her husband *were* at home that night, he would not have countenanced such shenanigans. (Subjunctive)

3. The Rule

The subjunctive is used in preference to the indicative:

after *as if*
after *if,* in conditions contrary to fact
after *wish*

This completes our discussion of *mood.*
A verb has four moods:

INDICATIVE: He *speaks.*
SUBJUNCTIVE: If Henry Wallace *were speaking,* more tickets would be sold.
INFINITIVE: *To speak* now would be a mistake.
IMPERATIVE: *Speak* now or forever hold your peace.

DO YOU GET THE POINT?—*test 46*

1. If it (was, were) a nice day, we could have a picnic.
2. That man, if he (was, were) really your father, should have treated you better.
3. If that man (was, were) your father, he would not have treated you so shamefully.
4. That man acts as if he (was, were) your father.
5. I wish he (was, were) your father.
6. If the boss (was, were) here, you would do more work.
7. If that (was, were) the reason for your refusal, why didn't you say so?
8. If that book (was, were) sold in Boston without police interference, then we won't run into any trouble with our book.
9. If he (was, were) the last man on earth, she wouldn't marry him.
10. Does she wish she (was, were) going to the party?

1. were	3. were	5. were	7. was	9. were
2. was	4. were	6. were	8. was	10. were

as easy as A B C

A. What is the difference between *desert* and *dessert?*

B. Is it correct to say, "I *would* like to see you to-night"?

C. Which is preferable: *"Those* kind of apples *are* too sour," or *"That* kind of apples *is* too sour"?

A. The Grammar of Meanings

Desert, Dessert

The Sahara is a *desert* (one *s;* accent on the first syllable). Chocolate pudding is a *dessert* (two *s's;* accent on the second syllable).

How can you remember which is which?

A *desert* is made up chiefly of sand—one *s* in *sand.*

Dessert is an added attraction in a meal—an added *s* in *dessert.*

DO YOU GET THE POINT?—*test 47*

1. People on diets are asked to forego rich (deserts, desserts).
2. There is a vast (desert, dessert) in the western part of our country.
3. It is an arid, (desert, dessert) region, thinly populated.
4. Children prefer (desert, dessert) to the nourishing dishes of a dinner.

CHECK YOUR LEARNING—*answers to test 47*

1. desserts   2. desert   3. desert   4. dessert

B. The Grammar of Allowable "Errors"

I *would* like to see you tonight.

By the same rules which—theoretically—govern the use of *shall* and *will*, the pronouns *I* and *we* (first person, singular and plural) require the auxiliary *should* in preference to *would*.

This requirement is as obsolete as the puristic distinctions between *shall* and *will*.

If you generally say *I should like* and *we should like*, by all means go on doing so. If it has become your habit, on the other hand, to say, *I would like* and *we would like*, make no effort to change.

"I *would* speak to him if he were here," and "we *would* be happier if we were richer," are just as good English, just as correct, just as acceptable as "I should speak . . . ," and "We should be . . ."

Furthermore, the use of *would* in such constructions is more popular, more current, less stilted, in informal speech.

Should, as a tense sign of the conditional tense, is gradually falling into disuse. Or, as a professor of mine used to like to phrase it, *should* is falling into a state of innocuous desuetude.

In modern English, *should* is mainly used to indicate compulsion, moral obligation, or the like.

As in the case of the panhandler who approached the bejeweled dowager in depression days.

"I haven't had a bite to eat in two days," the beggar announced.

"My good man," responded the matron, "you should force yourself!"

PRO AND CON

Q. Many modern grammarians maintain that *"Would you like to join us?"* is correct, idiomatic English, established by common usage among educated people. Do you agree? Would you use the expression in your everyday speech? [Prescriptive grammar demands *should* in such a question, because the expected form of the answer is *I should*—assuming the person answering is also a devotee of purism.]

Pro

A. I prefer the phrase "Would you . . ." rather than "Should you . . ."

—Paul Denis

Mr. Denis formerly conducted the radio column of the New York *Post*.

Con

You ask me for my opinion on the correctness of the sentence, "I *would* be happy to see him." My own view is that the correct way to say this would be, "I *should* be happy to see him." It may be as you say, "many modern grammarians maintain that 'I *would* be happy to see him' is correct, idiomatic English, established by common usage among educated people." I am afraid that I cannot comment upon this. I realize that good English can be established by usage, but, for my part, I prefer *should* to *would*.

—Harold L. Ickes

Harold Ickes was Secretary of the Interior in President Franklin D. Roosevelt's administration.

C. The Grammar of Correct Usage

Those kind of apples *are* too sour, *or*
That kind of apples *is* too sour?

This sentence represents a grammatical point that is still somewhat debatable. Following a strict interpretation, of course, *that* and *is* would be called for, since *kind* is indubitably singular. But *That kind of apples is too sour*, correct as it may be, sounds almost affected. The simple way to be correct without sounding unnatural is either to make the noun after *of* singular (*That kind of apple is too sour*), or to recast the sentence (*Apples of that kind are too sour, Such apples are too sour*, etc.).

Similarly, sentences like the following can be changed as indicated:

UNACCEPTABLE UNDER STRICT RULES	PREFERABLE
I don't like *those* kind of people.	I don't like *that* kind of *person, or,* I don't like such people, etc.
These kind of books *are* too deep for me.	*This* kind of *book* is too deep for me, *or,* Such books are too deep for me, etc.
Those kind of men can't be trusted.	*That* kind of *man* can't be trusted, *or,* You can't trust men like them, etc.
Those sort of women *are* bad medicine.	*That* sort of *woman* is bad medicine, *or,* Women like her are bad medicine, etc.

chapter 22 HOW TO SPLIT AN INFINITIVE

1. *The Problem*

What is a "split infinitive"? When, if ever, may we split an infinitive?

2. *The Solution*

An infinitive, we have learned, is the verb preceded by the preposition *to:*

to use	to eat
to plan	to be

Infinitives are not true verbs even though, as we shall see in a moment, they have tense and voice.

The infinitive, though one of the four moods of a verb (the other three are *subjunctive, indicative,* and *imperative*), always functions in a sentence as a noun, an adjective, or an adverb.

To solve this paradox of a verb which is not a verb, we call an infinitive a verbal.

There are three types of verbals in English grammar—infinitives, participles, and gerunds.

Every verbal is a verb which is not a verb; verbals have the force of verbs, they may have tense and voice, but they function within a sentence as some other part of speech.

Participles function as adjectives.
Gerunds function as nouns.
Infinitives function as nouns, adjectives, or adverbs.

An infinitive has voice and tense.

PRESENT ACTIVE INFINITIVE: to see
PRESENT PASSIVE INFINITIVE: to be seen
PERFECT ACTIVE INFINITIVE: to have seen
PERFECT PASSIVE INFINITIVE: to have been seen

"Splitting an infinitive" means placing an adverb between the preposition *to* and the rest of the infinitive.
To wit:

to quickly see
to thoroughly understand
to completely grasp
to first be considered

A genuine split infinitive contains the adverb directly after the preposition. If the adverb comes between any of the verbal parts of the infinitive, we are not dealing with a split infinitive.
These are *not* split infinitives:

to be favorably known
to have satisfactorily completed
to have quickly ended

Splitting an infinitive is no crime. It is not a violation of grammatical rule.
Although a few textbooks forbid the practice, the best people split infinitives.
Robert C. Pooley, professor of English at the University of Wisconsin, in his excellent book *Teaching English Usage* (Appleton-Century), points out:

The question as to whether one may "split" an infinitive by placing an adverbial modifier between the *to* and the infinitive form of the verb has been hotly debated for a century. . . . In spite of the quantities of print on the subject, and the definitive statements of linguists and grammarians, the textbooks still cleave to the nineteenth-century aversion [to the split infinitive].

Professor Pooley labels the so-called rule against the split infinitive "little more than pedantic rubbish" and then recites a list of reputable American authors who were infinitive splitters: Benjamin Franklin, Whittier, Washington Irving, Nathaniel Hawthorne, Theodore Roosevelt, and Woodrow Wilson, among others.

Pooley offers these examples from literature:

Theodore Roosevelt, *The Winning of the West:* "He stood high in the colony, was extravagant and fond of display, and, his fortune being jeopardized, he hoped *to more than retrieve it* by going into speculations in western lands."

Herbert Spencer, *Philosophy of Style:* "To an active mind it may be easier to bear along all the qualifications of an idea than *to first imperfectly conceive* such an idea."

Woodrow Wilson: "When I hear gentlemen say that politics ought to let business alone, I feel like inviting them *to first consider* whether business is letting politics alone."

Notice how stilted these sentences would become if the adverbs were placed before the preposition, as some strait-laced textbooks suggest:

". . . he hoped more than to retrieve it . . ." (In fact this sentence not only becomes stilted; it actually alters its meaning.)

". . . than first imperfectly to conceive such an idea." (The meaning is intact, but the language has become woefully schoolteacherish.)

". . . I feel like inviting them first to consider . . ." (Again a shift of the adverb out of the infinitive alters the meaning of the sentence.)

The alternative suggestion for avoiding a split infinitive, according to the same textbooks, is to place the modifier *after* the verb. In the first two sentences quoted, such a position will be seen to be impossible—the idiom of the language is too grossly violated. In the third sentence, Wilson might have phrased his thought ". . . I feel like inviting them to consider first whether . . . ," but surely the emphasis he was aiming at would have been completely lost.

Charles Carpenter Fries, professor of English at the University of Michigan, in the standard reference work for English teachers, *American English Grammar*, quotes these instances of split infinitives from the writing of educated people:

I desire *to so arrange* my affairs . . .

. . . his ability *to effectually carry on* . . .

. . . that he may help me *to properly support* my family . . .

. . . would incur such delay as *to almost defeat* the purpose . . .

. . . in such a manner as to enable him *to properly perform* his work . . .

. . . training is desired in order *to better acquaint* myself with the problems of . . .

. . . *to adequately prepare* myself for this examination . . .

If you attempt to revise these sentences by placing the adverb either before or after the infinitive, you will see how the effectiveness and emphasis of the adverbs are considerably diminished.

"The evidence in favor of the judiciously split infinitive is sufficiently clear to make it obvious that teachers who condemn it arbitrarily are wasting their time and that of their pupils." So concludes grammarian Sterling Andrus

Leonard, in his survey of current English usage for the National Council of Teachers of English.

Bear in mind that a rule of grammar is valid so long as educated users of English generally abide by that rule. Since the best writers and speakers split their infinitives whenever they feel that clarity of meaning is improved by such a practice, the student of grammar will decide that the split infinitive is current, established, and reputable English.

Don't, of course, go out of your way to split an infinitive.

On the other hand, don't hesitate to split one if you feel that your thought is best served by doing so.

3. *The Rule*

To deliberately split an infinitive, puristic teaching to the contrary notwithstanding, is correct and acceptable English.

PRO AND CON

Q. Many modern grammarians maintain that "It is necessary to accurately check each answer" (split infinitive) is correct, idiomatic English, established by common usage among educated people. Do you agree?

Pro

A. To accurately check is awkward but correct. *To check accurately* does not mean exactly the same.

Moses brought no rule against the split infinitive from the thunders of Sinai.

—Alvin Johnson

Alvin Johnson is president emeritus of the New School for Social Research, New York.

But what is correct grammar? Often it is nothing but rules set up by schoolteachers to stop the language from going where it wants to go. English, like all other languages, tends toward simplification. Simple language devices are gradually worked out in popular speech. Naturally, they are different from earlier, more complicated ways of saying the same thing; and so the grammarians call those new forms incorrect and everyone who uses them, uneducated.

Three hundred years ago the grammarians protested against the new form *its* and against the new passive infinitive formed with *being*. Today they are fighting against such things as prepositions at the end of a sentence, split infinitives, or using *them* and *their* after indefinite pronouns like *everyone* or *anybody*.

Let's find some witnesses for the defense of the split infinitive. They are surprisingly enthusiastic. Professor J. Hubert Jagger, in *English in the Future*, writes:

> There is no doubt that the split infinitive will in the end succeed because of its superiority to any other arrangement of the words in many sentences.

And George Oliver Curme, in his *Syntax*, says simply:

> The split infinitive is an improvement of English expression.

James Thurber, not a philologist, has put it even better:

> Word has somehow got around that the split infinitive is always wrong. This is of a piece with the outworn notion that it is always wrong to strike a lady.

It is not hard to find examples where the split infinitive is the only simple way of saying it. Curme quotes "He failed to entirely comprehend it" and Fowler, in *Modern*

English Usage, uses: "Our object is to further cement trade relations." Here is one I found in the AP story of MacArthur's landing in the Philippines:

Striking at a point where he is in position to quickly cut off the Island of Luzon . . . on which Manila is situated, from Mindanao on the South, MacArthur poured supplies ashore . . .

(The publisher's editor found another example on page 14 of this book. He was against it, but I won.)
—Rudolph Flesch, *The Art of Plain Talk* (Harper)

Pro

The 1886 Law on Succession to the Presidency makes it clear that the practice of Presidential succession is recognized in the United States Code of Laws. Anybody entering "on the Execution" of the President's office swears *to* "*faithfully execute* the Office of President," not the office of Vice President substituting for the President.
—*Newsweek*

as easy as A B C

A. What is the difference between *persecute* and *prosecute?*

B. Is it correct to say, "He had an *awful* cold"?

C. Which is preferable: "Do your work *like* I told you to," or "Do your work *as* I told you to"?

A. The Grammar of Meanings

Persecute, Prosecute

You belong, we will assume for the sake of argument, to a racial or religious minority. As a result, you suffer from a nightmare of petty, annoying, undignified experiences. You are, in a word, *persecuted*.

Or you are, to continue the same trend of thought, the victim of some psychopath's undying hate. The gentleman in question spends a full working day every week figuring out methods to harass, inconvenience, and molest you. He *persecutes* you.

Or let us say that during the war your landlord wanted you to vacate your apartment so that his newly married favorite cousin could move in. Federal laws, however, protected your tenancy. No fool, your landlord knew that if he made your occupancy sufficiently intolerable you would eventually seek other quarters. He started a systematic campaign of *persecution*.

The victim of *persecution* is generally innocent and inoffensive; his tormentors usually inhuman, illogical, and psychotic.

Paranoia is a mental affliction whose victims imagine themselves always to be the objects of *persecution.* Some historians claim that Germany suffers from a mass-*persecution* complex.

On the other hand, if you commit a crime, or in some less serious way breach the legal code of the community, you will be *prosecuted,* but not, it is to be hoped, *persecuted.*

DO YOU GET THE POINT?—*test 48*

1. The district attorney will (persecute, prosecute) the case himself.
2. The Nazis made a fine art out of (persecuting, prosecuting) the Jews.
3. Americans are sometimes guilty of (persecuting, prosecuting) certain native minorities.
4. People who break the law must expect to be (persecuted, prosecuted).

CHECK YOUR LEARNING—*answers to test 48*

1. prosecute 2. persecuting 3. persecuting 4. prosecuted

B. The Grammar of Allowable "Errors"

He had an *awful* cold.

In informal speech, *awful* is a respectable, idiomatic synonym for *severe, very bad, unusually great,* etc. It rarely means *awe-inspiring,* although this was its original signification.

Similarly, *awfully,* as a synonym for *very,* is permissible in speech, as in:

We had an *awfully* bad siege of illness this winter.

Lately, *awfully* has even been used as an adverb which intensifies adjectives of pleasant meaning, as in:

We had an *awfully* good time tonight.
She's *awfully* pretty.

The latter use is still somewhat frowned upon, even by liberal grammarians, and is not entirely current in cultivated speech, perhaps because of its sheer and humorous illogicality.

To use *awful* as an adverb is close to the illiterate level of speech. The following examples have little currency in educated language patterns:

We had an *awful* good time.
She's an *awful* pretty girl.
It's an *awful* lovely dress.
It's an *awful* cute puppy.

Nevertheless, *awful* as an adjective, or *awfully* as an adverb, with an unpleasant or unhappy signification, is permissible in spoken English. The following are *not* incorrect:

an *awful* cold
an *awfully* hot day
an *awfully* severe winter
an *awful* experience
awfully sarcastic

PRO AND CON

Q. Many modern grammarians maintain that "It was an *awfully* boring evening" is correct, idiomatic English, established by common usage among educated people, and completely acceptable in informal conversation. Do you agree?

Pro

A. In reply to your inquiry we can assure you that *awfully* as an intensive is encountered frequently in colloquial speech. Expressions such as "an awfully boring evening," "I'm awfully glad," and "I'm awfully sorry" are idiomatic and in common use among educated people. Aldous Huxley, in *Those Barren Leaves* (George H. Doran), 1925, page 14, uses the following sentence: "He was just one of those *awfully* nice, well-brought-up, uneducated young creatures. . . ." Sinclair Lewis, *Main Street* (Harcourt, Brace), 1920, page 338, uses the expression "you're awfully educated." Henry James, in *The Wings of the Dove* (Scribner's), 1923, page 240, uses the phrase "the awfully rich young American. . . ." Examples could readily be multiplied.

—Edward A. H. Fuchs

Dr. Fuchs was a member of the editorial staff of G. &. C. Merriam Co., publishers of the Merriam-Webster *New International Dictionary*.

Q. Many modern grammarians maintain that "He has an *awful* cold" is correct, idiomatic English, established by common usage among educated people. Do you agree? Would you use the expression in your everyday speech?

Pro

A. Yes I see nothing awful about it.

—Earl Wilson

Mr. Wilson is a columnist on the New York *Post* and author of *I Am Gazing into My Eight-Ball* and *Pike's Peak or Bust.*

C. The Grammar of Correct Usage

Do your work *like* I told you to, *or*
Do your work *as* I told you to?

We feel *like* a carload of jeeps had run over us, *or*
We feel *as if* a carload of jeeps had run over us?

Strictly speaking, *like* is a preposition and should not be followed by a clause; the use of *like* in the two sentences above is, on any but a very liberal basis, not entirely established or reputable, and therefore I cannot in all honesty recommend its use.

The following sentences are correct:

Work *as* hard *as* I.
Act *as* a man acts.
He thinks about her *as* I do.
Her husband reacted just *as* she did.
She reacted *as* you would have expected her to.
We feel *as if* a carload of jeeps had just run over us.
Just *as* all other mammals have sweat glands, so does a human being.

To be absolutely safe, use the versions above, which are somewhat preferable to the following:

Work hard, *like* I do.
Act *like* a man acts.
He thinks about her *like* I do.
Her husband reacted just *like* she did.
She reacted *like* you would have expected her to.
We feel *like* a carload of jeeps had run over us.
Just *like* all other mammals have sweat glands, so does a human being.

(Advertising agencies exhibit a growing fondness for *like* as a conjunction. For example, *Winstons taste good like a cigarette should*, and *Nobody's got a wagon like Valiant's got a wagon*.)

PRO AND CON

Q. Do you ever use in your informal conversation a sentence similar to the following: "He does it like I told him to"? In other words do you ever use the word *like* as a conjunction? Do your friends or associates ever use it? What is your opinion of the usage?

One View

A. No. In Brooklyn I've never heard anyone use *like* as a conjunction. They do not use it in this part of the South (Chapel Hill, North Carolina) either. I never use it that way. I don't care for the word *like* in any form. It's too pastel for my blood.

—Betty Smith

Betty Smith is author of *A Tree Grows in Brooklyn.*

Another View

Here is a sustaining show which is conscientious, and perceptive. It does not try to pass off goody-goody platitudes under the elegant guise of "public service," *like* so many others do.

—Paul Denis, in his radio column
in the New York *Post*

chapter 23 HOW TO LET YOUR
PARTICIPLES DANGLE

1. The Problem

What is a "dangling participle"? When is it permissible to let participles dangle?

2. The Solution

A participle is one of the three classes of *verbals*.
Along with infinitives and gerunds, it is a verb which is not a verb.
Like an infinitive, it has voice and tense.

PRESENT PARTICIPLE: seeing
PERFECT ACTIVE PARTICIPLE: having seen
PERFECT PASSIVE PARTICIPLE: having been seen, *or* seen

Present participles end in *-ing:* going, coming, spending, having, knowing, etc.
Gerunds also end in *-ing.*
Gerunds and present participles are identical in form—they differ in function.
Words like *seeing, going, coming, eating,* may be either participles or gerunds—depending on their use in a sentence.
A gerund is always a noun.
Here are some gerunds functioning as subjects of verbs:

The *going* is rough.
His *coming* was unexpected.

Spending is going on at a terrific rate.
Having money is nice.
Knowing Betty Grable is nicer.

Here is a gerund which is a predicate nominative:

Seeing is *believing*.

Here are some gerunds which are objects of verbs:

I enjoy *working*.
I like *swimming*.
I hate *rowing*.

And here are gerunds functioning as objects of prepositions:

We do not believe in *growing* old.
The work consists of *washing* and *ironing*.

As you can see, a gerund fulfills the same functions as does a noun: subject of a verb, object of a verb, predicate nominative, or object of a preposition. Since a gerund fulfills the functions of a noun, it is a noun, despite its very definite verbal force.

A participle is always an adjective, with a single exception to be noted shortly:

Seeing me, he turned pale.
Going home, she met a wolf.
I saw her *coming* down the street.
Spending at this rate, you will soon be broke.
Knowing Betty Grable, he envied Harry James.

The exception to the rule that a participle is always an adjective: A present participle may be part of a verb phrase, as in the progressive tenses:

He is *seeing* a play.
He was *going* home.
He will be *coming* in later.
He has been *spending* his capital.

Or a perfect participle may be part of a verb phrase in a perfect tense:

He has *had* a cold.
He had *known* her years ago.
He would have *been* insulted by your remark.

When the participle is part of a verb phrase, it is, of course, a true verb, not a verbal. So when the term "participle" is used, reference is usually made to the adjectival, not the verbal, use of the participle—that is, to the verbal, not to the verb.

Since a participle is an adjective, it must modify a noun.
That is a characteristic of adjectives you must constantly keep in mind—they modify nouns (or pronouns, of course, the latter being substitute nouns). Interrogative adjectives, descriptive adjectives, indefinite adjectives, numerical adjectives, participial adjectives—they all, without exception, modify nouns or pronouns.
Let us see how this works out.
In the five participles illustrated above (*Seeing* me, he turned pale, etc.):

seeing modifies *he,*
going modifies *she,*
coming modifies *her,*
spending modifies *you,*
knowing modifies *he.*

Or consider this sentence:

Walking down Liberty Avenue, the oldest section of New
    Rochelle, you will suddenly come upon a row of small,

compact, new homes, incongruously surrounded by ancient and rambling mansions built not long after the Huguenots landed.

This sentence, despite its length, has only one true verb—*will come;* and one subject—*you.*

However, it boasts three participles—*walking, surrounded, built.*

There is, of course, a considerable amount of verbal force in *walking, surrounded,* and *built;* for participles, like all verbals, have verbal force.

But *walking, surrounded,* and *built* are not verbs—not in this particular sentence. They are adjectives.

If the sentence read, "He was walking down Liberty Avenue," *walking* would be a verb, or part of one.

If the sentence read, "The new houses were surrounded by old ones," *surrounded* would be a verb, or part of one.

If the sentence read, "The old houses were built by the Huguenots," *built* would be a verb, or part of one.

But as the sentence read originally, *walking, surrounded,* and *built* are all participial adjectives. *Walking* modifies *you, surrounded* modifies *homes, built* modifies *mansions.*

If you wish to get on friendly terms with participles; you must learn to appreciate this clear-cut distinction between the verbals *walking, surrounded, built,* and the verbs *walking, surrounded, built.*

Further illustrations may help to make the distinction clear:

VERBS	VERBALS (PARTICIPLES)
She was *walking* in her sleep.	*Walking* in her sleep, she fell out of the window.
The soldiers *surrounded* the fort.	The fort, *surrounded* by the soldiers, had no choice but to surrender.
The fort was *surrounded.*	
The house was *built* in 1946.	*Built* in 1946, the house is completely modern.
She was *lying* awake.	*Lying* awake, she worried about money.

299

She was *worrying*.	She lay awake, *worrying*.
The words have been *spoken*.	These words, *spoken* softly, can be very effective.

To make sure that you are developing the ability to determine when a participle is a participle, and not a true verb, try your hand at the following exercise.

DO YOU GET THE POINT?—*test 49*

Directions: Label the italicized words in each sentence as either verbs or participles:

1. Time once *lost* (*a*) is impossible to regain.   *a*......................
2. Money which is hard come by is usually not *spent* (*b*) foolishly.   *b*......................
3. Money easily *earned* (*c*) is often *spent* (*d*) foolishly.   *c*......................
                                                                                       d......................
4. *Working* (*e*) hard all day, he *forgot* (*f*) to have lunch.   *e*......................
                                                                                       f......................
5. He was *working* (*g*) hard all day and completely *forgot* (*h*) about eating.   *g*......................
                                                                                       h......................
6. His lunch *forgotten* (*i*), he went right on with his work, *trying* (*j*) to finish before nighttime. *i*......................
                                                                                       j......................
7. "*Getting* (*k*) and *spending* (*l*), we lay waste our powers."   *k*......................
                                                                                       l......................
8. She was *spending* (*m*) it as fast as her husband was *earning* (*n*) it.   *m*......................
                                                                                       n......................

CHECK YOUR LEARNING—*answers to test 49*

a. participle	*f.* verb	*k.* participle
b. verb	*g.* verb	*l.* participle
c. participle	*h.* verb	*m.* verb
d. verb	*i.* participle	*n.* verb
e. participle	*j.* participle	

If you made a perfect or near perfect score, you're ready to go on to learn how participles dangle.

(If your score was low, study the answers carefully, trying to get the "feel" of participles.)

As we have said, participles are adjectives.

And adjectives modify nouns or pronouns.

Let us list at this point the sentences we have been working with and determine which noun or pronoun each participle modifies.

1. *Walking* in her sleep, she fell out of the window.

Participles have the force of verbs, though they are not true verbs—hence you will find an implied action in each participle. Determine to whom, or to what, that action applies, and you have the noun or pronoun which the participle modifies. In this sentence, the action of walking applies to *she*—she was doing the walking when she fell out of the window. The participle *walking* modifies the pronoun *she*.

2. The fort, *surrounded* by the soldiers, had no choice but to surrender.

Be careful here. What is described as *surrounded?* Not the soldiers, who are responsible for the action of *surrounding;* but the *fort,* which was *surrounded*. The participle *surrounded* modifies the noun *fort*.

3. *Built* in 1946, the house is completely modern.

Built modifies ....?
What is described as *built?* The house. *Built* modifies *house*.

4. *Lying* awake, she worried about money.

Lying modifies ....? The answer will be found at the foot of the page.

4. she

5. She lay awake, *worrying*.

Worrying modifies ....?

6. These words, *spoken* softly, can be very effective.

Spoken modifies ....?

7. *Walking* down Liberty Avenue, the oldest section of New Rochelle, you will suddenly come upon a row of small, compact, new homes, incongruously *surrounded* by ancient and rambling mansions *built* not long after the Huguenots landed.

a. *Walking* modifies ....?
b. *Surrounded* modifies ....?
c. *Built* modifies ....?

The noun or pronoun which a participle modifies is called the *antecedent* of the participle. This is, I admit, an illogical term, as so many grammatical terms are. *Antecedent* strictly means *coming before*—yet in many sentences, as you have noticed, the *antecedent* follows the participle. Nevertheless it is an antecedent—and every participle must have one.

Participles which are found in sentences without the benefit of antecedents are as illegitimate as children born of parents who are "married" without the benefit of law. You know the name applied to such illegitimate children —illegitimate participles are called "dangling participles." Here is an example:

Listening to the radio, my car went right through the stop sign.

The meaning, on a little analysis, is clear enough. I was listening to the radio and not paying too much attention to the road, so I drove my car right through a stop sign.

5. she   7a. you   7c. mansions
6. words   7b. homes

302

That is the implication of the sentence, looked at from any sane point of view. However, insane as this may sound, the sentence as it is now worded claims that my car was listening to the radio, for *car* is the only logical noun in the sentence which the participle can modify. Since the word to which the action of the participle is intended to apply (namely *I*) is unexpressed, the participle is said to be dangling—the noun to which it is anchored in logic is missing. There is no support—the participle dangles. To eliminate the dangle, we might reword the sentence somewhat as follows:

While I was listening to the radio, my car went right through the stop sign.

Here are some further examples of dangling participles:

Coming out of my house, a horse ran over a child.
Was the horse coming out of my house? Correctly revised:
Coming out of my house, I saw a horse run over a child.

Looking far and wide, only trees can be seen.
Were the trees looking far and wide? Correctly revised:
Looking far and wide, one can only see trees.

Born in the summer, his mother did not have to buy warm clothes for him.
Who was born in the summer—his mother? Correctly revised:
Since he was born in the summer, his mother did not have to buy warm clothes for him.

Running down the street as fast as he could, the cop nevertheless caught him.
Who was running—the cop? Correctly revised:
Running down the street as fast as he could, he was nevertheless caught by the cop.

Having finished the dishes, the front door bell rang.
Who finished the dishes—the front door bell? Correctly revised:

> After she had finished the dishes, the front door bell rang.

Working hard, the time sped by.
Was time working hard? Correctly revised:
As he was working hard, time sped by.

> Driving through New Rochelle, many fine homes can be seen.

Are fine homes driving through New Rochelle? Try your hand at revising this sentence.

> Standing on his feet all day, corns and calluses soon resulted.

What makes the participle dangle? How would you revise the wording?

> Believing in Japan's integrity, Pearl Harbor came as a shock to him.

Where's the dangle? How would you revise?

> Having been dried out by lack of rain, the gardener could not make the grass grow again.

Revise the sentence so that it sounds sane.

Illegitimate children can be useful and law-abiding citizens—but society frowns upon them. Similarly, sentences with dangling participles may be clear enough in meaning if some attention is given to an analysis of the probable intention of the speaker or writer. But since there is always a certain vagueness and ambiguity in a sentence with a dangling participle, such sentences are considered stylistically inferior and grammatically objectionable. Good writers, careful speakers, frown upon the use of a dangling participle.

3. The Rule

The logical antecedent of a participle should be expressed in a sentence, and should occur in such a place within the sentence that there can be no possible doubt as to the connection between participle and antecedent. In other words, avoid dangling participles.

as easy as A B C

A. What is the difference between *beside* and *besides*?

B. Is it correct to say, "I feel *badly*"?

C. Which is preferable: "She is one of those women who *run their husbands* ragged," or "She is one of those women who *runs her husband* ragged"?

A. The Grammar of Meanings

Beside, Besides

You sit *beside* a babbling brook, as the poets would say. You sit *beside* your wife; she sits *beside* you.

The meaning of *beside* (without the *s*) is thus clear enough: *next to, along side of, at the side of.*

You are wealthy, young, handsome, a spirited conversationalist and skillful dancer. *Besides*, you are unmarried. Do you wonder that the single girls find you irresistible?

No, you claim, you have not been invited to her party; and *besides*, you wouldn't go even if you were invited!

Besides (with the *s*) obviously means *in addition, moreover, also, what's more.*

DO YOU GET THE POINT?—*test 50*

1. She was sitting (beside, besides) her aunt.
2. They walked (beside, besides) each other in silence.
3. (Beside, Besides) chocolate, you will also need a second flavoring in the cake.
4. He is ill, unhappy, and irritable; (beside, besides,) he is too old for you.

1. beside   2. beside   3. besides   4. besides

B. *The Grammar of Allowable "Errors"*

I feel *badly*.

Although no one in his right mind ever says "I feel sadly," "I feel happily," or "I feel uselessly," the adverbial sounding form *badly* is often heard, from educated people, after the verb *feel*, generally with the sense of mental distress, thus:

He feels *badly* about their misfortune.
He felt *badly* when he heard of your loss.

Occasionally, *badly* is also used in reference to health, as in:

I feel *badly* this morning; I believe I need a strong laxative.

According to strict grammatical principles, the adjective *bad* should always be used after the verb *feel*, since *feel* is a copulative verb, and is equivalent in meaning and use to the copulative verb *be*. Copulative verbs regularly require predicate adjectives, not adverbs, as "He is *strong*" (not *strongly*); "The flower smells *sweet*" (not *sweetly*); "The soup tastes *bad*" (not *badly*). However, to feel *badly* is an accepted, current, idiom in American speech, and when *badly* is thus used, it becomes an adjective, despite its apparently adverbial ending. Perhaps one reason for the affection that many speakers have for *feel badly* is that *feel bad* seems to imply wickedness or naughtiness.

PRO AND CON

Q. Many modern grammarians maintain that "Don't feel *badly* about his death" is correct, idiomatic English,

307

established by common usage among educated people. Do you agree? Would you use the expression in your everyday speech?

Pro

A. I have often used "badly" in this sense—and also find myself occasionally saying "Don't feel too *bad* about this." Constant idiomatic usage of words takes precedence with most people, in my opinion, over stern, unyielding grammatical dictates. It's so much better that way too. Close adherence to the book of rules makes for stuffy, stilted speech.

—Louis Sobol

Mr. Sobol is a columnist on the New York *Journal-American.*

Pro (*with reservations*)

I use the expression "Don't feel *badly* about his death." I believe it is incorrect but it is like a good many expressions in common speech; we use the incorrect expression so as not to appear to be awkwardly correct.

—Walter A. Knittle

Professor Knittle was, before his death, director of the Adult Education Department of the College of the City of New York.

C. The Grammar of Correct Usage

She is one of those women who *run their husbands* ragged, *or*
She is one of those women who *runs her husband* ragged?

Who, as we have already discovered, agrees with its antecedent in number. In this sentence, *who* is plural because
308

its antecedent *women* is plural, and therefore takes plural forms. *One* is not the antecedent of *who;* antecedents are usually located in geographical proximity to the relative pronoun.

If you wish to look at it logically instead of grammatically, you analyze it as follows:

She is one of those women.

What women?

Those women who run their husbands ragged.

PREFERABLE FORMS:

She is one of those women who *run their husbands* ragged.

He is one of those authors who *turn* out a new book every year—each one worse than the preceding one.

It is one of those books which *are* very easy to read.

It is one of those things which *drive* people crazy.

He is one of those people who *are* never satisfied.

Are you one of those lucky ones who always *get* a seat on the Long Island Railroad?

chapter 24 HOW TO BE ILLITERATE

1. The Problem

What is wrong with the grammar of "Don't do nothing I wouldn't do"?

2. The Solution

The grammar of our language is not a body of divinely inspired rules.

We are dealing, when we venture into the confines of English grammar, with no set of immutable laws, with no absolute distinctions.

Grammar is not like mathematics.

In arithmetic, one and one is two; [1] in geometry, the sum of the squares of the arms of a right triangle equals the square of the hypotenuse; [2] in algebra, $(a - b) (a + b)$ equals $a^2 - b^2$. These are facts which no one in his right mind would care to argue. They have been demonstrated to be true and are accepted the wide world over. There is simply no ignoring or changing them.

Grammar is not like the natural sciences.

In physics, a body falls *down*—no human power has any influence on the law of gravity; in chemistry, water freezes at 32° Fahrenheit and boils at 212° Fahrenheit, whether we like it or not; and in biology, the one-celled amoeba reproduces by a process called binary fission.

These are all incontrovertible facts; they were true thousands of years before man discovered them and they

[1] Or, of course, one and one *are* two.
[2] If you are not familiar with this interesting geometric law, just take my word for it. High school sophomores struggle with it under the formidable name of "the Pythagorean theorem."

will continue to be true as long as the earth turns. Exact sciences like mathematics, physics, chemistry, and biology are thus seen to be comparatively dull and static, unlike grammar, in which there is constant change.

Grammar deals with one of the higher activities of human beings (the translation of thoughts into words) and is as dynamic, as unreliable, and as unpredictable as human beings themselves.

When you deal with a study (like grammar or history or semantics or psychology) which is deeply involved with the human equation you will be wise to expect no exact laws, you will do best if you look askance at all arbitrary and unqualified conclusions, you will be safe only if you maintain an open mind and an attitude of alert skepticism.

English grammar, as a science, attempts to make an accurate record of what people say and write, of how they phrase their thinking into sentence patterns. Just as chemistry and physics and biology study and record the phenomena of nature, so grammar analyzes the phenomena of human communication.

The grammar of a living language takes note of any usages that have currency. Thus an expression is part of English grammar if it is used by a considerable number of people whose native language is English.

For example, "Go you to the school?" is not part of English grammar. It is neither good grammar nor bad grammar, neither right nor wrong, neither correct nor incorrect, neither acceptable nor unacceptable—it is simply nonexistent. No considerable number of people who speak English as a native tongue ever phrase their thought into such a pattern as "Go you to the school?" although such is the phrasing in French (*Allez-vous à l'école?*).

But if we examine a pattern like "Don't do nothing I wouldn't do," we are forced to admit that such a usage is indeed part of English grammar. Hundreds of thousands of persons whose native language is English would so phrase the thought. We call such a pattern *the double negative,* since negation is expressed both by the adverb *not* (in the contraction *don't*) and again in the indefinite pronoun *nothing*.

The double negative is widely used in English. "No, I won't go" is a double negative of whose grammatical standing there is no question. "I didn't see it nowhere," "I can't wait no more," and "I ain't done nothing" are, on the other hand, often called "incorrect" grammar.

But why? What makes a pattern correct or incorrect?

Is the double negative an integral part of the English language—that is, does it have currency? In a certain type of speech it has the widest sort of currency; indeed, it supersedes any other way of expressing the same idea.

Does the double negative express a thought without confusion or ambiguity—that is, is it clear?

Most elementary-school teachers attack the usage on the grounds that it is unclear because it is illogical. Two negatives, they claim, make an affirmative. If you say "I didn't do nothing" you mean "I did something," for if you did *not* do *nothing*, you must have done something. Tommyrot! An expression means exactly what the person who hears that expression understands it to mean. When someone says to you, "I didn't do nothing," you have a very poor grasp of the English language if you understand him to mean that he did *something*. If a person "didn't go nowhere" he stayed home; if he "didn't eat no candy" he avoided the candy box.

Now in certain instances in which a speaker intends two negatives to signify an affirmative, they do indeed have such a significance to a listener. If a speaker says "It is *not impossible*" he means, obviously, that it *is* possible. If you accuse your wife of letting the lamb stew burn by doing nothing to stop it from burning you might say: "But you did nothing while it burned!" And your spouse, in justifiable anger, might answer: "I did *not* do *nothing*—I kept stirring it all the time!" Here indeed are two negatives which make an affirmative because your wife intends them to have a very decided affirmative meaning, and not because there is a grammatical law to that effect.

To attack the double negative because it seems, on analysis, to be illogical, is to show no appreciation whatever of the frequent illogic of language in general and of English in particular. Many expressions to which the most puristic of schoolmarms would have no grammatical objections are fantastically illogical if you descend to analyzing them. Is it logical to say "We will take the trolley home" when we really mean that we will let the trolley take us home? Is "She swept the room with her eyes" logical? Or "He holds my religion against me"? Or "He jumped down my throat when I said that"? Expressions can be grammatical and correct (and often picturesque) without having even a bowing acquaintance with logic.

"Don't do nothing I wouldn't do" is called "incorrect" because *such a grammatical pattern is not customarily used by educated people.*

Common usage among educated speakers is the sole yardstick by which correctness in grammar is judged. "Laws of grammar" by themselves have no validity unless they are based on educated custom, usage, habit, convention. As convention in language changes (and it often does), the "laws" change also. In this connection it is, I think, most interesting to note that the double negative—with a negative meaning—was "correct" during the time of Shakespeare—people of cultivation then used it freely.

The kind of double negative which our chapter problem illustrates is one of the customary grammar patterns on the lowest, or basement, level of American speech—a level usually called "illiterate," a not very felicitous description since many of the users of this level of language can certainly read and write, even though they do not subscribe to *Harper's* and *The Atlantic Monthly* nor buy *The New York Times* on their way to work in the morning.

Customary as is the double negative (of the type illustrated in the chapter-problem) on the lowest level of American speech, so is it rare to the point of nonexistence on any higher level of speech. Never in reputable writing, almost never in the speech habits of people of the slightest linguistic sophistication, is such a type of double negative found.

And that is the reason why the double negative—of the type referred to—is "incorrect"; it is used almost exclusively on the lowest level of language.

Patterns which are *exclusively* found on the basement level of grammar are incorrect on any other level—and since grammar itself is generally viewed from the educated level, illiterate patterns are usually, but loosely, called ungrammatical, though they are perfectly grammatical (because they are current and normal) on their own level.

Why are people of little linguistic sophistication so addicted to the "incorrect" type of double negative? One of the principles operative in illiterate speech is *emphasis by repetition*. The speaker is not sure, probably subconsciously rather than consciously, that *I see none* can sufficiently impress a listener with its negative force. So he emphasizes the negative force by making the verb as well as the pronoun negative—"I don't see none." He stresses the negative implication of *hardly* and *scarcely* by combining them (quite unnecessarily, according to the educated speaker) with negative verbs: "I couldn't scarcely believe my ears"; "I can't hardly hear him." To his mind, *from* is not sufficiently emphatic; he prefers *off of:* "He took the pen off of me"; "We got the money off of him."

The demonstrative adjectives *this* and *that* are too weak; he reinforces them with the locational adverbs *here* and *there: this here man, that there woman. Regardless* he intensifies by adding a negative prefix to the already adequate negative suffix: *irregardless.* By the same principle, *equally good* becomes *equally as good,* and adjectives are made comparative both fore and aft: *more slower, more quicker, more happier, more better.*

This first principle of illiterate speech—emphasis by repetition—is evident not only in grammatical patterns but also in phraseology; the basement-level speaker frequently iterates an idea and then immediately reiterates the very same idea in slightly different words. He is not quite sure you will understand him until he has said a thing at least twice.

The second principle of illiterate speech is either *an intellectual inability or an instinctive unwillingness to make certain distinctions.*

For example, when the present tense of the verbs *do* and *be* are negative, the "illiterate" speaker fails (or perhaps refuses) to distinguish among the variant forms for different subjects. Although he will use the affirmative of these verbs correctly (I *do;* you *do;* he, she, it *does;* we, they *do* —I *am;* he, she, it *is;* you, we, they *are*), he has a single negative form for all subjects, namely *don't* and *ain't:*

I don't	it don't	I ain't	it ain't
you don't	we don't	you ain't	we ain't
he don't	they don't	he ain't	they ain't
she don't		she ain't	

Now if you view this phenomenon objectively, you will admit that a single negative form for all subjects is sensible, economical, and perfectly clear, but—and this is the important point—it is customary only on the illiterate level. So, by that criterion, it is "wrong."

Similarly, the unsophisticated speaker usually uses the single comprehensive verb *was* for all subjects in the past tense, both affirmative and negative:

I was	I wasn't
you was	you wasn't
he, she, it was	he, she, it wasn't
we was	we wasn't
they was	they wasn't

In educated patterns of grammar, the possessive pronoun is used to combine with the suffix -*self* (myself, yourself, yourselves, ourselves) except in the third person, in which the objective pronoun is substituted (himself, herself, themselves). But in illiterate grammar, the possessive is used throughout: myself, yourself, hisself, herself, ourselves, yourselves, theirselves.

Again, in educated patterns, *learn* and *teach*, *lay* and *lie*, *good* and *well*, *invite* and *invitation*, *leave* and *let*, *owe* and *own*, *these* and *them* are carefully and unquestioningly distinguished. In illiterate patterns, on the contrary, one of each of these pairs of words is entirely discarded and the other expresses the meaning of both. The unsophisticated speaker relies exclusively on *learn*, *lay*, *good*, *invite*, *leave*, *own* and *them*. He will say:

I learn grammar, *and* Can you learn me grammar?
I lay my clothes away, *and* I am laying down for a nap.
I am good, *and* I see good.
I invite him, *and* I received an invite.
I'll leave you now, *and* Leave me go.
I own that car, *and* I'll own you five dollars.
I see them, *and* I see them books.

The linguistically immature person is somewhat baffled by the use of the apostrophe, and so to play safe generally puts it where it is not required, substituting *who's* for *whose*, *it's* for *its*, and even *boy's* for the simple plural *boys*. Inconsistently, on the other hand (and inconsistency is another characteristic of illiterate grammar), he will omit the apostrophe in verbal contractions, writing *dont*, *doesnt* (or, more likely, *dosent*), *wont*, etc.

Now on any level above the illiterate, the distinctions here discussed are universally honored.

To wit:

I learn grammar, *but* Someone teaches me grammar.
I lay my clothes away [transitive], *but* I am lying down for a nap [intransitive].
I am good [adjective], *but* I see well [adverb].
I invite him [verb], *but* I received an invitation [noun].
I'll leave you now [departure], *but* Let me go [allow].
I own that car, *but* I owe you five dollars.
I see them [pronoun], *but* I see those books [adjective].
Whose books [possessive], *but* Who's coming [contraction for *who is*].

Its paws [possessive], *but* It's raining [contraction for *it is*].

In illiterate grammar, the past participle of some verbs is used in place of the simple past, as in *I seen it, I done it;* inconsistently, the simple past of other verbs is used in place of the past participle, as in:

I have gave	*we have rang the bell*
I have went	*have you ran the water*
I have drank	*has she sang the song*
I have swam	*have you stole the money*
I have saw	*the car is broke*
it has broke	*the coat is tore*
I have ate	*have you spoke*
the bird has flew the coop	*I have wrote*
we have rode	

In most verbs, the past tense and the past participle are of course identical, but not in special irregular, or "strong," verbs. And the unsophisticated speaker does not make distinctions.

In a compound subject of which one part is a pronoun, the "illiterate" speaker invariably uses the objective case: "Me and John are going," or "Her and him ain't on speaking terms"; and when a pronoun is part of a compound object he uses the nominative case: "This is for he and I"; "This satisfies my partner and I." (Curiously enough, a kind of distinction is observed here, but directly opposite to the proper one.)

A third, somewhat minor, principle can be discovered in illiterate speech—*an inability to use the auxiliary "have" correctly. I should of* (or *I shoulda*) substitutes for *I should have; had ought* takes the place of *ought;* and *If I hadn't have done it* is used for *If I hadn't done it.*

A fourth and over-all principle in unsophisticated speech

317

is that *illiterate patterns are rarely found in isolation*. That is, the speaker habituated to one or two of the forms discussed is very likely to use a large number of them. Conversely, if some of these patterns are absent in a speaker's language, probably most of them are.

So, if you read the latter part of this chapter with a certain faint amusement and an increasing feeling of virtuousness (because the expressions described are foreign to your own speech habits) you are safe in skipping the rules and test which will follow shortly. However, if you felt a creeping sense of guilt as you read, and recognized as your own a number of the patterns illustrated, it is possible that —consciously or unconsciously—you have many habits of illiterate grammar, and if so, you would do well to practice quite painstakingly on the material which concludes this chapter.

3. The Rule

The following characteristic patterns of illiterate grammar should, by practice and thought, be avoided. Substitute the indicated educated pattern in each instance.

ILLITERATE PATTERNS	EDUCATED PATTERNS
Don't take *no* rubber nickels.	Don't take *any* rubber nickels.
She won't work *no* more.	She won't work *any* more.
I can't find it *nowhere*.	I can't find it *anywhere*.
It *ain't no* use.	It *isn't any* use.
We *can't* hardly finish on time.	We *can* hardly finish on time.
They *couldn't* scarcely earn enough to pay the rent.	They *could* scarcely earn enough to pay the rent.
He took my best coat *off of* me.	He took my best coat *from* me.
This here country	*This* country
That there attitude	*That* attitude
Irregardless	*Regardless*

ILLITERATE PATTERNS	EDUCATED PATTERNS
This here pen is *equally as good* as *that there* one.	*This* pen is *as good as that* one, *or* These two pens are equally good.
More slower	*Slower*
More better	*Better*
More quicker	*Quicker*
More safer	*Safer*
He *don't* live here *no* more.	He *doesn't* live here *any* more.
She *don't* do it *good*.	She *doesn't* do it *well*.
That there book *don't* make *no* sense.	*That* book *doesn't* make *any* sense.
It *don't* add up.	It *doesn't* add up.
You *ain't* going *nowhere*.	You *aren't* going *anywhere*.
I *ain't* talking.	*I'm not* talking.
It *ain't* right.	It *isn't* right.
You *wasn't* doing it right.	You *weren't* doing it right.
We *was* here on time.	We *were* here on time.
They *was* my buddies.	They *were* my buddies.
They *wasn't* listening.	They *weren't* listening.
We *wasn't* paid for today.	We *weren't* paid for today.
Was you there?	*Were* you there?
He can take care of *hisself*.	He can take care of *himself*.
They can take care of *theirselves*.	They can take care of *themselves*.
Can you *learn* me how to skate?	Can you *teach* me how to skate?
Lay down	*Lie* down
I didn't get *no invite* to the party.	I didn't get *an invitation* to the party.
I *own* him a dollar.	I *owe* him a dollar.
Them there books *ain't no* good.	*Those* books *aren't any* good.
The man *who's* wife	The man *whose* wife
It hurt *it's* foot.	It hurt *its* foot.
I *seen* it.	I *saw* it.
I *done* it.	I *did* it.

ILLITERATE PATTERNS	EDUCATED PATTERNS
I *have gave*	I *have given*
I *have went*	I *have gone*
I *have drank*	I *have drunk*
I *have swam*	I *have swum*
I *have saw*	I *have seen*
It *has broke*	It *has broken*
I *have ate* (*et*).	I *have eaten*.
The bird *has flew*	The bird *has flown*
We *have rode*	We *have ridden*
We *have rang*	We *have rung*
Have you *ran*	*Have* you *run*
She *has* already *sang*.	She *has* already *sung*.
Have you *stole* . . . ?	*Have* you *stolen* . . . ?
The car is *broke*.	The car *is broken*.
The coat is *tore*.	The coat is *torn*.
You *have spoke*	You have *spoken*
I *have wrote*	I have *written*
Me and you are through.	*You and I* are through.
Send my wife and *I* a copy.	Send my wife and *me* a copy.
I should *of* went.	I should *have* gone.
You *hadn't ought to of* done that.	You *ought not to have* done that.
If I *hadn't have* seen it	If I *hadn't* seen it

A SPECIAL WORD

To readers who believe they habitually use some of the illiterate expressions recorded above:

Illiterate patterns, as you have seen, are so basic and involve expressions which occur so frequently in a normal day's conversation that you will need to develop a super-consciousness of your faults before you can hope for any success in eliminating them from your speech.

I tried an interesting experiment recently with a group of four students who had some of the typical illiterate grammar patterns, most conspicuous of which were the double negative and the substitution of *don't* for *doesn't* (as in

He don't). To achieve as nearly unacademic an atmosphere as possible, we went out for some coffee after class one evening, and I explained that I was interested in determining whether the double negative and the substitution of *don't* for *doesn't* could be eliminated from their speech patterns by means of a few weeks of practice. They expressed the greatest willingness to co-operate, and we discussed the possible methods of exorcising these two errors. We decided, finally, to try sheer will power as a first method. For the remainder of our conversation—which dealt, of course, with nongrammatical subjects—my students were embarrassingly self-conscious, fearful that they would inadvertently double their negatives or use the improper form of the verb *do*. A few times they fell into error but immediately corrected themselves.

Next week, we again stopped for some after-class refreshment. I purposely avoided the subject of grammar, and we shortly fell into a spirited political discussion. Not at all to my surprise, negatives were doubled and *don't* was used with third person singular subjects. Later on, I asked my students how they were getting along with their use of will power to eliminate the two errors which we had discussed the previous week. They assured me without hesitation that the method was working to perfection!

So for our third meeting over the coffee cups I brought with me eight index cards on each of which I had typed two phrases, thus:

DOESN'T

HE ~~DON'T~~ WORK HERE

ANY

I DON'T SEE IT ~~NO~~ MORE

I asked each of my students to take two cards, place one in his wallet right next to his money, and paste the other on the top of his bathroom mirror so that he would not fail to see it when he shaved in the morning.

By these means, I insured that my students would be reminded several times each day that they were trying to rid themselves of certain errors in their speech. They knew what the errors were and how to correct them, and the sight of the card in the early morning and again each time they extracted a bill from their wallets was enough to keep the subject on the conscious level of their minds.

The following week I was gratified to note, during the conversation over coffee, that *doesn't* had largely superseded *don't* with a third person singular subject, and that the double negative had become conspicuously rare.

The first step in eliminating an error in grammar that has become habitual with you is the conscious recognition that the error exists in your speech. Do you believe that you are addicted to some of the violations tabulated in the charts on pages 318-320. Check the ones you think you make most frequently. Take, then, the next step in eliminating habitual errors—invent some means to keep the error in your conscious mind. The card method worked for my four students—it may work for you. Or you may devise some other method more applicable to your way of living. In any case, a few days of superconsciousness of the existence of the error in your speech should serve to eradicate it.

4. The Test

DO YOU GET THE POINT?—*test 51*

1. I can't (ever, never) get along with your brother.
2. She (isn't, ain't) working here (any, no) more.
3. We (have, haven't) hardly begun to fight.
4. He took my pencil (from, off of) me.
5. I like (this, this here) car better.
6. You must finish your work (regardless, irregardless).

7. (That, That there) way of talking (isn't, ain't) going to get you (anywhere, nowhere).
8. If you get the brakes adjusted, you'll be (safer, more safer).
9. He (don't, doesn't) work (well, good).
10. You (weren't, wasn't) even listening to me!
11. He has to get hold of (himself, hisself).
12. Please (teach, learn) me how to read faster.
13. (Lay, Lie) down for a few minutes.
14. I hope I get an (invite, invitation) to the dance.
15. You (own, owe) me ten cents.
16. (Them, Those) people are always making trouble.
17. Is your coat (tore, torn)?
18. The light is (broke, broken) again.
19. His money was (stole, stolen).
20. You and (me, I) are good friends, (ain't, aren't) we?
21. I wish you'd invite (he, him) and Dorothy to the party.
22. (Them, They) and (us, we) can't get along (no, any) more.
23. (Leave, Let) us go.
24. You should (of, have) seen her.
25. Have you (et, ate, eaten)?

CHECK YOUR LEARNING—*answers to test 51*

1. ever	9. doesn't, well	18. broken
2. isn't, any	10. weren't	19. stolen
3. have	11. himself	20. I, aren't
4. from	12. teach	21. him
5. this	13. lie	22. they, we, any
6. regardless	14. invitation	23. let
7. that, isn't, any-where	15. owe	24. have
8. safer	16. those	25. eaten
	17. torn	

as easy as A B C

A. What is the difference between *council* and *counsel?*

B. Is it correct to say, "I *only* see him once a week"?

C. Which is preferable: "It is I who *am* tired," or "It is I who *is* tired"?

A. The Grammar of Meanings

Council, Counsel

These two words, identical in pronunciation, are naturally confusing. The distinction is as follows:

A *council* is a group of men (or women, or some of each), as a legislative council, The National Council of Teachers of English. A *councilor* is, of course, a member of a council.

Counsel, on the other hand, means either advice or an attorney (or group of attorneys). An attorney is also called a *counselor,* as is any person who gives advice (personal relations counselor).

Counsel may be used as a verb, meaning to advise. *Council,* however, does not ever function as a verb; it is only a noun.

B. The Grammar of Allowable "Errors"

I *only* see him once a week.

Logically, you mean that you see him *only* once a week, and it is on the basis of its illogicality that many texts warn against placing *only* before the verb, contending that if you only *see* him once a week, you do not *hear, feel, smell,* or *taste* him.

Such hair-splitting is of course unadulterated tommyrot. Nobody but a professional "schoolmarm" would misunderstand you (and she would do so deliberately), if you say "I only go there on Sundays," "We only eat meat twice a month," or "I only wish I had your luck."

Professor Porter G. Perrin, of the University of Washington, reports in his *Writer's Guide and Index to English:* "The importance of the position of *only* has been greatly exaggerated. . . . Placing *only* before the verb is a characteristic and reputable English idiom." Professor Perrin then quotes from Ernest Hemingway and Bertrand Russell to show that the use of *only* before the verb is well established in writing. The truth is, of course, that in ordinary, informal speech, *only* is naturally placed before the verb by all educated speakers.

PRO AND CON

Pro

Certainly they don't spend very much time with the members of their unions or with the members of other unions. In fact, I have become convinced that they must *only* associate with each other.

—Howard Lindsay

Mr. Lindsay is coauthor of the Broadway stage hit *State of the Union,* and star of *Life with Father.* This excerpt, like the one on page 213, is from a guest column Mr. Lindsay wrote for the New York *Post.*

Pro

Quinidine, one of the derivatives of cinchona, could *only* be prescribed in small amounts for certain types of cardiac patients for whom the drug was an essential therapy, and often necessary to preserve the lives of these patients. No raw cinchona has yet come out of the East Indies since the war.

—Editorial columns of *The New York Times*

Pro

Albert E. Koonz, of 1650 Bogart Avenue, the Bronx, a mechanical dentist, also got 100%, but, since he included fewer details, he will *only* receive the bronze medal for second place.

—*The New York Times*, July 21, 1947

Q. Modern grammarians maintain that "He *only* has ten cents left" (position of *only*) is correct, idiomatic English, established by common usage among educated people and completely acceptable in informal conversation. Do you agree? Would you use the expression in your everyday speech?

Con

A. It doesn't mean that I am right, of course, but I would say "He has only ten cents" because the *only* seems to me to refer to the *ten cents* and not to the *has*. I think you want to lessen the ten cents rather than the verb.

—Lillian Hellman

Miss Hellman is the noted playwright, author of *The Little Foxes, Watch on the Rhine,* and other Broadway successes.

Q. Modern grammarians maintain that "He only spoke once" (position of *only*) is correct, idiomatic English established by common usage among educated people and completely acceptable in informal conversation. Do you agree? Would you use the expression in your everyday speech?

A. Yes, I would say "He only spoke once"—if he were the *only* one who spoke. But if I wanted to convey the idea that he spoke *only* once (just one time) then I'd say "He spoke *only* once."

However, I intend to start a League Against Split Infinitives, regardless of the current vogue for them, so I may be just a fuss-pot! Or maybe that eighth grade English teacher I had really scared me for keeps.

—Marian Young

Marian Young conducts the Martha Deane program over WOR and the Mutual network.

Pro

"I *only* have one company," Hughes began, then checked himself with a laugh. "I guess I have more than one, at that."

—Earl Wilson, New York *Post* columnist, reporting an interview with Howard Hughes, millionaire moving-picture producer and airplane manufacturer.

C. The Grammar of Correct Usage

It is I who *am* tired, *or*
It is I who *is* tired?

The relative pronoun agrees with its antecedent in number and person. In this sentence, *I* is the antecedent of *who*. Since *I* is first person singular, *who* is also first person singular, and takes a first person singular verb, *am*.

Note in each of the following sentences how the antecedent of the relative pronoun indirectly governs the verb of which *who* is the subject:

You can't speak that way to me, who know more about
you than you do yourself.

It was not she who was to blame, but her husband.

It is I who have made the error.

I am the one who has made the error.

It is they who have caused all the trouble.

It is they who are lonely.

It is I who am lonely.

PREFERABLE FORM:

It is I who am tired.

chapter 25 HOW TO TALK LIKE
A HUMAN BEING

You have to come to terms with grammar.

You have to bear in mind that the rules of grammar are not the revealed word of God. The various and numerous "thou shalt nots" with which many speech manuals scare the daylights out of their readers are not divine commandments, nor are infractions of such "laws" punishable by fines of $10,000 or two years in jail, or both. Nor even by social ostracism, as the speech manuals intimate.

You can—take my word for it—lead a normal, happy life even if you do not faithfully follow the austere restrictions of pedantic or puristic grammar. Indeed, the chances for living such a happy, normal life are far better if you relax and use, whenever the occasion demands or the mood suits, some or all of the expressions on which purists and precisians frown.

In my adult classes at New York University, many of my pupils are confused, and a few are shocked, when they learn that the idioms for which their high school teachers rapped their knuckles or slapped their wrists (but which they and their friends always use anyway) are perfectly correct, acceptable, standard English.

What idioms, for instance?

Some of them have already been covered under the rambling section called "The Grammar of Allowable 'Errors' ":

He *got* sick. (Outmoded restriction: He *became ill.*)
Don't get *mad* if I tell the truth. (Outmoded restriction: Don't *become angry* if . . .)
I'll come *providing* you let me. (Outmoded restriction: . . . *provided. . . .*)

The reason I love you is *because* you are so pretty.)
(Outmoded restriction: ... *that* ...)

Can I have a piece of cake? (Outmoded restriction: *May* ...)

That dress is different *than* mine. (Outmoded restriction: ... *from* ...)

It's a *nice* day. (Outmoded restriction: ... *pleasant* ...)

He is not *as* tall as he looks. (Outmoded restriction: After a negative verb, use *so*.)

She was most *aggravated*. (Outmoded restriction: ... *exasperated*.)

It's *liable* to rain. (Outmoded restriction: ... *likely* ...)

The *above* remarks ... (Outmoded restriction: *Above* is only an adverb.)

Have you *got* my book? (Outmoded restriction: *Have you my book?*)

Due to the telephone strike ... (Outmoded restriction: *Owing to*, or *because of* ...)

Everybody stood up and shouted at the top of *their* lungs. (Outmoded restriction: ... *his* lungs.)

I *will* write to him tonight. (Outmoded restriction: I *shall* write ...)

I *would* like to see you tonight. (Outmoded restriction: I *should* like ...)

He had an *awful* cold. (Outmoded restriction: ... a *severe* cold ...)

I feel *badly* about his death. (Outmoded restriction: I feel *bad* ...)

Go *slow*. Come *quick*. (Outmoded restriction: Go *slowly*. Come *quickly*.)

I *only* see him once a week. (Outmoded restriction: I see him *only* once a week.)

The restrictions listed are unrealistic. The grammar of any language is founded upon the current and reputable use of that language by its educated speakers. And if you will keep your ears wide open you will hear educated people saying *mad* (meaning *angry*); *nice* (meaning *pleasant*); *awful* (meaning *severe*); and *aggravating* (meaning *exas-*

perating). You will hear them saying *different than* and *have you got*. And you will see, in reputable books, magazines and newspapers, *liable, above, further, due to,* and similar "errors" in the very type of sentence patterns railed against by the speech manuals.

Is such a liberal attitude toward grammar accepted by the schools of the country? That depends partly on the school, partly on the community, and very largely on the individual teacher. There are conservatives and reactionaries in teaching and in grammar just as there are in politics. Many teachers prefer to teach only what they themselves were taught—no more and no less—whether such teaching is in accord with the latest findings of educational researchers or not; whether such teaching is realistic and honest and sensible, or not.

And what are the latest findings of educational researchers?

In 1932, a professor at the University of Wisconsin, Dr. Sterling Andrus Leonard, set out to discover, scientifically, the standing of some of the expressions deplored by purists.

Under the sponsorship of the National Council of Teachers of English, he set about obtaining what he called a "consensus of expert opinion" about controversial questions of grammatical usage. Selecting 230 expressions "of whose standing there might be some question," he mailed a questionnaire to 231 judges. These judges were:

30 linguistic specialists
30 well-known editors
22 established authors
19 business executives
50 college teachers of English
50 high school teachers of English
30 speech teachers

These experts, who represented a diverse and very capable cross section of American life, were asked to indicate what, to their minds, was the standing of each of the controversial expressions. "Score, please," they were told,

331

"according to your observation of what is actual usage rather than your opinion of what usage should be."

Here, then, was a wonderful test of American usage—a true laboratory test to be freed, theoretically, of subjective reactions and ethical considerations. Obviously, Dr. Leonard was totally uninterested in what grammar books preached about correct usage or what the judges thought *ought* to be correct usage. His one concern was to discover what the majority of educated American speakers and writers were actually doing with their language.

The results of this questionnaire are most interesting.[1] Thirty-eight of the 230 items were rated almost unanimously as *illiterate* usages. Among these, were such expressions as:

I have*n't hardly* any money.
The kitten mews whenever it *wants in*.
All came except *she*.
My Uncle John, *he* told me a story.
I must go and *lay* down.
I have *drank* all my milk.
That there rooster is a fighter.
You *was* mistaken about that, John.
Just *set* down and rest awhile.

This was much to be expected. Your average high school freshman will tell you that such expressions are "bad" grammar—they are the kinds of expressions which, when used by Sunday night comics, draw hearty laughs from radio audiences.

The revolutionary aspect of the Leonard study concerns those expressions which a majority of the judges considered established, correct, and fully acceptable English. Close to 50 per cent of the test items (150), were so rated. Let us glance at some of them:

1. *None* of them *are* here.
2. I felt I could walk no *further*.

[1] *Current English Usage*, National Council of Teachers of English.

3. We will *try and get* it.
4. I've absolutely *got* to go.
5. We can expect the commission *to at least protect* our interests.
6. You'd better go *slow*.
7. There are some *nice* people around here.
8. *Will* you be at the Brown's this evening?
9. We *only* had one left.
10. This room is *awfully* cold.
11. It is *me*.
12. *Who* are you looking for?
13. *Can* I be excused from class?
14. Everyone was here, but *they* all went home early.

Of the 230 expressions, 85 are unaccounted for. On these there was not enough agreement among the experts to permit Dr. Leonard to label them either as *established* or as *illiterate*.

Unfortunately, Dr. Leonard lost his life by drowning before he could carry out the next logical step of his project. This was left to two other members of the council, Albert H. Marckwardt and Fred G. Walcott. This step was to discover how prevalent among established and distinguished authors of the past was each of the expressions with which the Leonard questionnaire was concerned. This check was made possible by systematic reference to the *Oxford English Dictionary*, the Merriam-Webster *New International Dictionary*, second edition, Jespersen's monumental *Modern English Grammar*, Hall's *English Usage*, and other volumes. Marckwardt and Walcott stress that their work was purely scientific and objective, that they were not trying to establish a justification for the Leonard work, that they expected to draw no conclusions from their findings. Their one interest was to see how popular the two hundred thirty expressions were in the works of well-known authors. But we may draw our own conclusions from the researches of Marckwardt and Walcott, which, very briefly, show the following:

1. All but six of Leonard's established usages were found so frequently in the works of such authors as Shakespeare, Macaulay, Pepys, Bunyan, Defoe, Burke, and Sheridan—literary giants all—that one is forced to consider them perfectly acceptable and literary English. The six exceptions appear in such a way that they may be considered "colloquial"—that is, acceptable in informal speech, and not by any means "incorrect."

2. Some of the "disputable" usages were also found in the works of these authors.

3. Most of the "illiterate" usages were not found.

The second investigation substantiated the first.

Many of the constructions at which purists and puristic grammar texts rail have been accepted literary or colloquial tradition for centuries.

There are other natural, idiomatic expressions which, judging by the criteria which Professor Leonard set up, you may use with a clear conscience. They are not ungrammatical. They are not incorrect. They are not illiterate. At worst, some of them are "colloquial," but remember that colloquial English bears no stigma—it is simply the English used by educated people in everyday conversation, and in informal writing, even if it is not entirely appropriate to dignified or "literary" occasions.

The following expressions are part of the structure of English grammar—they have the blessings of the National Council of Teachers of English and of cultivated speakers throughout the country:

He *graduated from* Princeton. (Outmoded restriction: He *was graduated from* . . .)

I don't know *if* I can find the time. (Outmoded restriction: *whether* I can find . . .)

Can you *loan* me a dollar? (Outmoded restriction: *lend* for the verb; *loan* only for the noun, as in "He made me a small *loan*.")

That's a *pretty* dangerous statement. (Outmoded restriction: *Pretty* means attractive, nothing else.)

Pro (*with reservations*)

As a qualifier of adjectives, "pretty" has apparently achieved currency (and recognition) in colloquial speech. Situation ought probably to determine its use. I do not think it is acceptable in formal discourse. And certainly it is out of place—even colloquially—in phrases like "pretty confused," "pretty inaccurate," "pretty false and misleading." There the sense of the adjectives is so strong that the qualifier appears like a weak-kneed compromise—almost like saying "pretty absolute," which is nonsense. Style and attention to meaning would alike limit the use of the word as adverb very much, I should think.

—Margaret Schlauch

Dr. Schlauch was formerly a professor of English at New York University and is the author of *The Gift of Tongues*.

Q. Many modern grammarians maintain that "He *graduated from* Princeton in 1938" is correct, idiomatic English, established by common usage among educated people. Do you agree? Would you use the expression in your everyday speech?

Pro

A. I believe that "He graduated from Princeton in 1938" is correct, idiomatic English, established by common usage.

—Freda Kirchwey

Miss Kirchwey was formerly editor of *The Nation*.

Keep it on ice till it's *good and cold*. (Outmoded restriction: *good and* is bad English.)
Go and finish your work.
Come and see me soon.

Try and do it better. (Outmoded restriction: Substitute *to* for *and*.)

The two children were playing with *one another*. (Outmoded restriction: Use *one another* only when more than two are involved. Use *each other* for two.)

Don't. *blame it on* me. (Outmoded restriction: Don't *blame me for* it.)

Can you *fix* my car? (Outmoded restriction: *fix* means keep in one place, not *repair*.)

What was the reason for *him* talking that way? (Outmoded restriction: . . . for *his* talking . . .)

The treaty was concluded *between* the four powers. (Outmoded restriction: . . . *among* the four powers.)

He came in *around* four o'clock. (Outmoded restriction: . . . *about* four o'clock.)

PRO AND CON

Q. Is "Come and see me" acceptable English?

Pro

A. "Come and see me" is a common idiomatic locution.
—Edward A. H. Fuchs

Dr. Fuchs was a member of the editorial staff of G. & C. Merriam Co., publishers of the Merriam-Webster *New International Dictionary*.

Pro

The phrase "Don't blame it on me" is certainly idiomatic English and I've heard many educated persons use it in informal conversation.

I am not a stickler for the fine distinctions in English— I prefer English as it is spoken to the English written by many a pedant.
—Albert Mitchell

Albert Mitchell and his collaborator Bruce Chapman were "The Answer Man" over WOR, New York; WGN, Chicago; and KSD, St. Louis. Mr. Mitchell is the author of *Here's the Answer*.

Now, if for personal reasons of your own, you prefer to observe the restrictions described in this chapter, by all means do so. Following such restrictive laws will not make your English any less effective—but, and this is the point to keep in mind, neither will it make your English any better, more effective, more nearly correct, or more acceptable.

Bear in mind that there are two kinds of grammar: *traditional,* which aims at the perpetuation of usages which conform to those principles of word-patterns which were set by eighteenth-century scholars; and *scientific* (to use Professor Charles Carpenter Fries's term), which adopts the experimental approach and considers correct all usages which are currently found in the speech and writing of educated people.

The traditional concept views language as unchanging— what pleased the ears of our great-great-grandfathers must not be deviated from, not one jot, by speakers of our modern day. Any attempt to improve or simplify is heresy of the most dangerous sort.

On the contrary, say our modern language scholars, there is only *one* criterion of good English: Do most educated people use an expression? If they do, that expression is accepted, established, and correct English; and if rules are violated, then the rules, not the speakers, are wrong.

This modern philosophy is tersely summarized by the eminent linguist, H. C. Wyld, in his *Elementary Lessons in English Grammar,*[2] as follows:

> A grammar book does not attempt to teach people how they ought to speak, but on the contrary, unless it is a very bad or a very old work, it merely states how, as a matter of fact, certain people do speak at the time at which it is written.

[2] S. E. Stechert & Co.

The same thought is phrased in different words by the scholars Grattan and Gurrey in their excellent volume *Our Living Language:* [8]

> The grammar of a language is not a list of rules imposed upon its speakers by scholastic authorities, but is a scientific record of the actual phenomena of that language, written and spoken. If any community habitually uses certain forms of speech, these forms are part of the grammar of the speech of that community.

There is no other sensible standard by which to judge correct grammar, and if it is feared that such a radical and revolutionary philosophy will result in the scuttling of all those musty grammar manuals which you and I struggled so patiently with in school, then—and this attitude is echoed by every modern grammarian—the quicker the manuals are scuttled the better it will be for everyone concerned.

It may be argued that this is a dangerous way to live. If enough people violate a law, shall we scrap the law? Or would it not be far safer and wiser to reprimand, or discipline, or, if necessary, jail the violators?

Well, for one thing, you cannot build enough jails to house all the violators of an unpopular law, as witness what happened when prohibition was in effect. And for another, just as laws of government depend for their power on the consent of the governed, so also laws of grammar depend for their value on the universal consent of the speakers of the language.

If you may be wondering whether this scientific approach to grammar may not eventually result in a slovenly and backwoods kind of language, set your doubts at rest. Modern English is the richest, most powerful language in the world. And it gains its richness and power from its complete and contemptuous avoidance of straitlaced rules and regulations. If "lawlessness" and change were not the potent factors that they are in shaping our native tongue,

[8] Thomas Nelson and Sons.

we would all still be speaking the language used by Geoffrey Chaucer—a wonderful language, but somewhat incomprehensible to the twentieth-century ear, as you know if you have ever tried to read an unmodernized version of *The Canterbury Tales*.

You are probably thinking: "Don't most English teachers in elementary and high schools still force their students to hew strictly to the lines of traditional grammar?"

Yes, many of them do. But there is evidence of strong pressure to make such teachers view grammar from a more liberal point of view. The following excerpt, for example, is from an article by Professor Roy P. Basler, chairman of the Department of English of the George Peabody College for Teachers, which appeared in the June, 1947, issue of the *Coronet Teaching Guide:*

This is what a noted linguist, Professor C. C. Fries, has to say about the teaching of English in our schools:

"Unfortunately, from the point of view of modern linguistic science, much of this work [teaching of grammar and usage] is not only wasted time, but harmful practice, as well. It is wasted time because it employs methods and materials that could not possibly attain the ends desired, no matter how much time was given to English. It is harmful practice because the habits set up and the views inculcated turn the students away from the only source of real knowledge—the actual language of the people about them. Our students are practically never given the tools of observation and analysis necessary to the use of these resources." ("Implications of Modern Linguistic Science," *College English,* March, 1947.)

Anyone familiar with the teaching of English in our schools and colleges may recognize that the weakest phase of instruction in English is in language study. The teachers themselves are often ill prepared. Seldom do we find a teacher who has, in the course of acquiring a degree in English, taken as much as one tenth of his work in language courses as compared to literature courses. Beyond "freshman composition"—in itself seldom attentive to the scientific facts of English—the college student majoring in English with the purpose of becoming a teacher usually devotes his attention solely to literature, literary history, and criticism. Furthermore, the English curriculum in elementary and secondary schools is largely devoted to the study of literature, and that portion which is devoted to language study is often skimped by a teacher who finds the teaching of language "uninteresting to students," and incompatible with his own training and interests. In so far as attention is given to grammar and usage, as Professor Fries points out, the work is concentrated on drill in identifying parts of speech and learning the terminology of a pre-scientific, prescriptive grammar, and on further drills in the recognition of prescribed "right" or "wrong" usage. It is, indeed, an unusual classroom in which one finds students studying "the actual language of the people about them."

Professor Basler's paper is one of the many which have appeared in professional journals, all of them urging teachers to adopt a more scientific, more liberal, more realistic attitude toward English grammar. With this kind of pressure, and with a greater emphasis on linguistics now apparent in teacher's colleges and universities we may eventually expect modern teachers to turn out students less shackled by the puristic approach to grammar than was true in the case of members of your generation and mine.

as easy as A B C

A. What is the difference between *luxurious* and *luxuriant?*

B. Is it correct to say, "Let's not walk any *further* today"?

C. Which is preferable: "The manager wants you and *I* to open the store tomorrow," or "The manager wants you and *me* to open the store tomorrow"? Also, which is preferable: "He thought us to be *them*," or "He thought us to be *they*"? Finally, which is preferable: *"Whom* did you think him to be?" or *"Who* did you think him to be?" (These are all facets of the same problem.)

A. The Grammar of Meanings

Luxuriant, Luxurious

A forest can grow *luxuriantly,* a person can have *luxuriant* black hair or a *luxuriant* imagination. A building can be characterized by *luxuriant* ornamentation and soil can be *luxuriant.*

On the other hand, cars, yachts, servants, mansions, and mink coats add to *luxurious* living. You may dine *luxuriously* on lobster thermidor, champagne, and nesselrode pie, and you may live *luxuriously,* even in times of inflation, on $200,000 a year (after federal income taxes).

The two words are thus seen to be quite different in implication. *Luxuriant* refers to rich growth, fertility, lushness, abundance. *Luxurious* refers to things which are expensive, rare, and pleasurable. *Luxurious* things are usually man-made, while *luxuriant* things are natural.

1. The tropics contain (luxuriant, luxurious) vegetation.
2. Her (luxuriant, luxurious) black hair is the most beautiful I have ever seen.
3. He owns a (luxuriant, luxurious) yacht.
4. Coral grows (luxuriantly, luxuriously) on that reef.
5. He spent a (luxuriant, luxurious) month at the Waldorf.
6. He embezzled $50,000 and lived (luxuriantly, luxuriously) for two weeks on the money.

CHECK YOUR LEARNING—*answers to test 52*

1. luxuriant	3. luxurious	5. luxurious
2. luxuriant	4. luxuriantly	6. luxuriously

B. *The Grammar of Allowable "Errors"*

Let's not walk any *further* today.

Further, say some texts, may be used only in reference to time or to figurative distance, as, "Let's explore the matter *further,*" or "The *further* we go in our study, the more confused we get." *Farther* should be used in all actual, or spatial, distance (according to these texts), as in "Let's ride a little *farther* up the road before we part." However, dictionaries without exception call *further* and *farther* synonymous. (*Merriam-Webster:* "farther: beyond the present point; further"; *Funk and Wagnalls:* "further: more remotely, farther.") In actual usage, *further* is gradually displacing *farther* in the language, and *farther,* like *shall,* is being less and less employed.

PRO AND CON

Q. Modern grammarians maintain that "Let's walk a little *further* before we turn back" is correct, idiomatic English, established by common usage among educated people and completely acceptable in informal conversation. Do you agree? Would you use the expression in your everyday speech?

Pro (*with reservations*)

A. In my everyday speech I might say *further* but I would regret not having said *farther;* in my writing I would say, *walk a little farther.* I have no better justification than habit and hence auditory preference.

—Paul Klapper

Dr. Klapper was president emeritus of Queens College, the author of numerous textbooks on methods of teaching, and professor of education at the College of the City of New York.

Pro (*with reservations*)

Whereas in my own speech and writing, I probably make an effort to distinguish between *further* and *farther,* I do not feel disposed to be fussy about this distinction and should certainly not react negatively to the interchangeable use of these two words.

—Eason Monroe

Dr. Monroe is professor of education and director of the Reading Clinic at Pennsylvania State University.

C. The Grammar of Correct Usage

The manager wants you and *I* to open the store tomorrow, *or*

The manager wants you and *me* to open the store tomorrow?

This is a more complicated problem than it may at first seem.

By now you are sufficiently sophisticated when it comes to problems of English grammar to be able to choose the correct form in the above sentence. Of course you would say, "The manager wants you and *me* to open the store tomorrow."

But why?

You and me is not the compound object of the verb *wants*. The manager does not want *you and me*.

You and me is not the object of a preposition. There is no preposition in the sentence except *to*, which you recognize as the sign of the infinitive *to open,* and not the introductory word in a true prepositional phrase.

So why the objective pronoun?

First, look at the infinitive, *to open*. Who's going to do the opening? *You and me*. (This sounds ungrammatical, but, as you will presently see, isn't at all.)

An infinitive, while not a true verb, has the force of a verb. And a pronoun which initiates the action of a verb is usually the subject of that verb. (The exception, you recall, occurs when the verb is passive, as in "America was discovered by Columbus," in which the initiator of the action is *Columbus* but the subject is *America*.)

So—

You and me is the subject of the infinitive *to open*. Yes, infinitives may have subjects, even though they are not true verbs. (They are called, you will remember, verbals.)

Consider:
I want *you* to stop beating your wife.
Who is to stop? *You*.
You is the subject of the infinitive *to stop*.

Consider:
I'll force *her* to obey, or know the reason why.
Who is to obey? *Her*.
Her is the subject of the infinitive *to obey*.

Consider:
We want *them* to cut out all that noise.
Subject of the infinitive *to cut out*? *Them*.

344

Consider:

He expects *us* to believe his lies.

Subject of the infinitive *to believe? Us.*

An infinitive may have a subject. In what case is such a subject? Look back—*her, them, us.*

So—

The subject of an infinitive is in the objective case.

Therefore, of course, a compound subject of the infinitive is also in the objective case.

CORRECT FORMS:

The manager wants you and *me* to open the store to-morrow.

I want you and *him* to stop annoying the children.

I bet I can make Gerbrand and *her* obey me.

Do you want *him* and his wife to come in now?

We expect Nellie and *him* to come for supper.

Now, knowing that the subject of an infinitive is in the objective case, we're ready for our last principle in English grammar.

Think about this problem:

He thought us to be *them, or* He thought us to be *they?*

And about this one:

Whom did you think him to be? *or*
Who did you think him to be?

Very likely you will be tempted to make an unhappy choice in these two sentences.

You think the correct forms are: "He thought us to be *they,*" and "*Who* did you think him to be?"

Well, you're wrong.

You are probably thinking: "But *to be* is a copulative

345

verb, and *they* and *who* are the complements of the copulative verb and so should be in the nominative case!"

Very good—you've learned your lessons well.

However, I've held back, until this very last moment, the fact that there is one exception to that rule you've just quoted.

Yes—the complement of a copulative verb *is* in the nominative case—

Except when the copulative verb is in the infinitive form *and* when said infinitive has a subject.

Then (and then only) the complement of a copulative verb agrees in case with the subject of the infinitive.

And in what case is the subject of an infinitive? In the objective case, as we decided only a page or so back.

So here is one last rule to complete your understanding of English grammar:

When the infinitive of a copulative verb has a complement, the complement agrees in case with the subject of the infinitive—if the infinitive has a subject, and *only* if the infinitive has a subject.

Now don't get discouraged. This is hard, I know. That is why I left it to the last.

Let's go over it again:

If the copulative verb is in the infinitive form, say "to be"—

And if the infinitive has a subject, say, "He thought *us* to be"—

Then, the complement of the copulative verb is in the objective case, agreeing in case with the subject (*us*) of the infinitive: "He thought *us* to be *them*."

Have you got it straight now?

Consider the problems with which we started:

He thought us to be *them* (or *they*).
INFINITIVE: to be (a copulative verb)
SUBJECT OF THE INFINITIVE: us (objective case)
COMPLEMENT OF THE COPULATIVE INFINITIVE: *them* (objective case)

Whom (or *Who*) did you think him to be?

INFINITIVE: to be (a copulative verb)

SUBJECT OF THE INFINITIVE: him (objective case)

COMPLEMENT OF THE COPULATIVE INFINITIVE: *whom* (objective case)

But wait!

Remember that the copulative infinitive must have a subject before you put this new rule into effect.

There must, to rephrase the idea, be a subject of the infinitive before the complement of the infinitive goes into the objective case.

Suppose the copulative infinitive does not have a subject?

In such a contingency, the earlier rule still applies, namely: *The complement of a copulative verb is in the nominative case.*

Note that in the following sentences the copulative infinitive will not have a subject with which the complement must agree. Therefore, by our earlier rule, the complement of the copulative infinitive will be in the nominative case:

I would like to be *he.* (*I* is the subject of *would like,* not of *to be.*)

Who do you want to be? (*You* is the subject of *want,* not of *to be.*)

You have begun to realize by now that the subject of an infinitive must *immediately* precede the infinitive.

Now—

Just to make sure you have the two rules under control, let us contrast them.

EARLIER RULE: The complement of a copulative verb or infinitive is in the nominative case.

NEW RULE: The complement of a copulative infinitive is in the objective case, agreeing with the subject of said infinitive, *if* the infinitive has a subject.

That's the whole story—see if you understand the distinctions between the two rules by taking a quick test.

347

1. (Who, Whom) would you like to be if you weren't yourself?
2. (Who, Whom) did you think him to be?
3. Would you like to be (we, us)?
4. Did you think them to be (us, we)?
5. I thought the General to be (he, him).
6. I thought the nurse to be (she, her).
7. We thought the criminals to be (they, them).
8. We expected the murderer to be (him, he).
9. The murderer turned out to be (she, her).
10. I want you and (she, her) to help me.

CHECK YOUR LEARNING—*answers to test 53*

1. who	5. him	9. she
2. whom	6. her	10. her
3. we	7. them	
4. us	8. him	

chapter 26 HOW TO MEASURE YOUR PROGRESS—A FINAL TEST OF YOUR GRAMMATICAL ABILITY

Did it really hurt so much, after all?

Becoming an expert in English grammar turned out, I trust, to be a lot easier than you had dared hope.

Easier, and pleasanter, and certainly less gruesome than your previous experiences with the subject might have led you to believe.

You have come away from your intensive study of grammar with certain prime abilities and with healthy, liberal attitudes.

You know when to make a personal pronoun nominative and when to make it objective—and why.

You have a complete familiarity with the simple rules governing the distinctions between *who* and *whom*.

You are no longer stumped by *lay* and *lie.*

You know when a verb should be plural, and when it is preferably singular.

You have a running acquaintance with all the important rules that form the framework of English grammar—and, more important, you know that you may violate some of those rules if the occasion demands.

You have freed yourself from any vestiges of a guilt complex over using expressions upon which purists frown but which are, notwithstanding, correct, established, idiomatic English.

You can, in a phrase, handle with rare expertness and artistry the multitudinous complexities of our amazing, contradictory, expressive language.

You know the word to use under any circumstances—and why to use it.

If all these statements do in truth apply to you, then

you have gotten out of this part of the book precisely what was put into it—and you are ready for a final test of your grammatical ability.

A Final Test of Your Grammatical Ability

Directions: Check, in each sentence, the word which you believe is grammatically preferable.

1. Now, how does Marilyn Monroe (affect, effect) you?
2. And your wife produces the same (affect, effect) of course?
3. The earth (continually, continuously) moves around the sun; if it ever stopped, human beings would be in a devil of a fix.
4. What's the sense (of, in) getting drunk?
5. If you (let, leave) your children speak naturally, they will not grow up with language inhibitions.
6. What (sort of, sort of a) grade do you think you will make in this test?
7. The Federal Savings and Loan Society now pays 3½ per cent on your (principle, principal).
8. The spy was (hanged, hung).
9. He has somehow managed to keep on good terms with his (brothers-in-law, brother-in-laws).
10. He offered one (incredulous, incredible) excuse after another for coming home late.
11. Mix two (cupsful, cupfuls, cups full) of flour with a cupful of sugar.
12. Do you (imply, infer) that I am lying?
13. The lion licked (its, it's) chops when the first Christian entered the arena.
14. No one but (I, me) would believe you.
15. There's something going on between Judy and (him, he).
16. Everyone except (she, her) was on time.
17. Was the letter addressed to you and (I, me) or only to you?

18. He (robbed, stole) my watch.
19. (Those, That) criteria (are, is) not valid.
20. Allan Kleinwax expects you and (I, me) to come to the Lincoln Studio to have our pictures taken tomorrow at ten.
21. What is a good (preventative, preventive) of rickets?
22. Many curious (passer-bys, passers-by) stopped, but no one offered to help him.
23. Would you like to take a walk with Estelle and (I, me)?
24. The price of books (is, are) getting higher and higher.
25. How (is, are) your mother and father today?
26. One of my best friends (is, are) practicing chiropody.
27. The manager of the Social Security office, with his assistants and secretaries, (is, are) coming to check over your payroll today.
28. Jules as well as Allan (is, are) having lunch with us today.
29. English, like French and Latin, (contain, contains) case forms.
30. When either of your manuscripts (is, are) rejected, let me know.
31. Each of your sisters (is, are) very pretty.
32. Boatload after boatload of soldiers (is, are) landing.
33. Neither of your reasons (is, are) sufficient.
34. Margie, unlike her parents, (has, have), a calm, sweet disposition.
35. His ability and experience (is, are) of great value to his company.
36. Congress or the President (has, have) to tackle this job before it's too late.
37. Neither your aunt nor your uncle (has, have) left you any money.
38. Either Eden or Evan (is, are) sure to phone you tomorrow.

39. Her (childish, childlike) innocence is most refreshing.
40. I think one or two of your accounts (has, have) canceled their orders.
41. (He, Him) and Myrtle are our best friends.
42. Did you visit (he, him) and Myrtle last Sunday?
43. You look bored and (uninterested, disinterested).
44. A number of bottles (was, were) broken when the shipment arrived.
45. I'd like to (lie, lay) down for a few minutes.
46. (Lie, Lay) your coat on the bed.
47. The wounded man (lay, laid, lied) in the street for over an hour before the ambulance arrived.
48. Where have you (laid, lain) my things?
49. The baby has (laid, lain) in the carriage all morning.
50. The checks were (laying, lying) on my desk all morning.
51. In which room did you (lie, lay) the red rug?
52. He (laid, lay) his hat on the table and started to talk.
53. "(Lay, Lie) the baby on the bed and I'll examine her," said the doctor.
54. "Conducting, in short, is a form of government for which instinct as well as skill (is, are) required." (Jacques Barzun, in *Harper's Magazine*)
55. Two-thirds of the work (is, are) finished.
56. A majority of your friends (is, are) married.
57. It was (I, me) you were talking about, wasn't it?
58. A drop in spending together with a boost in prices (has, have) caused a mild recession.
59. Was it (he, him) who answered the phone?
60. (Who, Whom) does he think he is?
61. The man (who, whom) you're referring to has left our employ.
62. I'll invite (whoever, whomever) wants to come to the party.
63. Her sister, (who, whom) he divorced after a year of marriage, is looking for a new husband.

64. (Who, Whom) would you like to be?
65. I met the man (who, whom) you thought could manage my business.
66. (Who, Whom) did you wish to see?
67. He can talk even faster than (I, me).
68. But you can talk just as fast as (he, him).
69. Neither I nor he (is, are, am) able to help you.
70. Neither the art teachers nor the supervisor (was, were) at the faculty meeting.
71. Have you (drank, drunk) the Tom Collins yet?
72. I would (of, have) had my picture taken at Lincoln Studios if I had been in New Rochelle.
73. It is a lovely (sensuous, sensual) poem.
74. He talks as if he (was, were) her husband.
75. Many liberals wish that Roosevelt (was, were) still alive.
76. You wouldn't act that way if your wife (was, were) here.
77. If the doctor (was, were) in, why didn't he see you?
78. He drove through the (dessert, desert) for nearly an hour.
79. The Nazis (persecuted, prosecuted) the Jews because, say the historians, the government needed to offer a scapegoat to take the people's minds off their troubles.
80. No one is here besides (we, us).
81. (Beside, Besides) the dishes, you also have to wash the silverware.
82. He is one of those men who (has, have) no consideration for others.
83. I (can, can't) scarcely see the stage.
84. (Irregardless, Regardless) of what you say, I'm going anyway.
85. I'm not talking about (that, that there) man.
86. That (doesn't, don't) make such sense.
87. I would rather work for the Browns than for (she, her) and her husband.
88. I thought you (was, were) my friend!

89. We would like an (invite, invitation) to your party.
90. She (don't, doesn't) look very well to me.
91. Have you any (council, counsel) for a misguided youth?
92. Can you (teach, learn) me grammar?
93. It is I who (is, am) more interested in your welfare than you are yourself.
94. The (luxurious, luxuriant) vegetation makes passage almost impossible.
95. We have work for (whoever, whomever) wants to work.
96. Are you willing to venture a (prophecy, prophesy) about building costs next year?
97. What I want (is, are) more pictures.
98. Ten cents a piece (is, are) too much for that candy.
99. We thought the General to be (he, him).
100. (Who, Whom) did you think her to be?

ANSWERS

1. affect	17. me	35. are
2. effect	18. stole	36. has
3. continu-ously	19. those, are	37. has
	20. me	38. is
4. in	21. preventive	39. childlike
5. let	22. passers-by	40. have
6. sort of	23. me	41. he
7. principal	24. is	42. him
8. hanged	25. are	43. uninterested
9. brothers-in-law	26. is	44. were
	27. is	45. lie
10. incredible	28. is	46. lay
11. cupfuls	29. contains	47. lay
12. imply	30. is	48. laid
13. its	31. is	49. lain
14. me	32. is	50. lying
15. him	33. is	51. lay
16. her	34. has	52. laid

53. lay	69. is	85. that
54. is	70. was	86. doesn't
55. is	71. drunk	87. her
56. are	72. have	88. were
57. I	73. sensuous	89. invitation
58. has	74. were	90. doesn't
59. he	75. were	91. counsel
60. who	76. were	92. teach
61. whom	77. was	93. am
62. whoever	78. desert	94. luxuriant
63. whom	79. persecuted	95. whoever
64. who	80. us	96. prophecy
65. who	81. besides	97. is
66. whom	82. have	98. is
67. I	83. can	99. him
68. he	84. regardless	100. whom

SCORING

Each correct choice counts 1 point.

Your score should be in the 90's if you have successfully understood all the material in the book.

YOUR SCORE ON THE FINAL TEST: .... (Record the result on page 13.)

PART 2 *Correct Pronunciation*

chapter 27 WHAT IS CORRECT
PRONUNCIATION?

You have heard about the woman who was making a purchase at the meat counter. "I want a pound of kiddlies, please," she said.

The butcher was momentarily perplexed. "Don't you mean *kidneys*, madam?" he asked.

And the woman answered, "Well, I *said* kiddlies, did'll I?"

Of course, this is only a joke. But it admirably illustrates that you often do not realize how you sound to others.

There is the case of the little New York urchin who was sitting in school one April day. The sun was shining, the windows were open wide, summer was in the air. Suddenly a robin hopped on the sill.

"Look!" the child cried. "A boid!"

"No, Johnnie," admonished the teacher, who could not permit her appreciation of nature to interfere with her job, "that's not a *boid*—it's a *bird*."

The boy was frankly astonished. "That's funny," he said. "It *looks* like a boid!"

It is true there are people in New York who say "boid" and "foist," "erl" and "fried ersters." They are, as it happens, in the minority—but they have no conception that their speech is different from that of other New Yorkers. To them, their pronunciation sounds perfectly natural—just as natural as it sounds to a Midwesterner to say "Hairy" for "Harry" and "airogant" for "arrogant." The Bostonian pronounces words like *park* and *parson* in a way not heard anywhere else in the country, yet no Bostonian is conscious of a "Boston accent."

359

A common password during the Pacific islands fighting, in World War II, was "lallapalooza." Why "lallapalooza," of all things? Because Japanese infiltrators who discovered the password still couldn't say it—the closest they could manage was "rarraparooza." *L* is an alien sound to the Japanese, just as *R* is to the Chinese. When a waiter in a Chinese restaurant suggests "flied lice" for your dinner, have no fear of the edibility of what he wishes to serve you. He means "fried rice," a most palatable dish. The point is, neither the Japanese nor the Chinese is conscious of his mispronunciation.

The average person's deafness to his own speech peculiarities is graphically evident when you make a phonograph recording of his voice and play it back to him. Now, for the first time, he is listening to himself from the outside. And how does he react? Generally with utter disbelief. "Is this the way I sound? Impossible!"

You too may be unaware of how you sound to others when you speak. When you mispronounce a word, you are usually the one person who doesn't know it. When you use an illiterate or affected pronunciation, you are usually completely unconscious of its effect on your listeners. Yet your pronunciation, especially of certain common and frequently used English words, is often the means by which people form their first impressions of your educational and cultural background, of your ability and intelligence, perhaps even of your personality. That this is so is unfortunate and in many instances probably completely illogical—what a man says is admittedly a vastly more reasonable criterion of his worth than how he says it. But human nature is not always reasonable, and listeners tend to jump to sweeping conclusions from quick, surface impressions of the way a person speaks.

Your pronunciation, for this reason, always either adds to, or detracts from, the power and persuasiveness of your ideas.

Consider the importance of pronunciation from another point of view. The effectiveness of a spoken thought stems not alone from its intrinsic value or from the words in which it is presented, but also, often even more so, from the self-assurance of the speaker. *Confidence and security about the correctness of your pronunciation can therefore be a vital factor in helping you put your ideas across successfully.*

And so Part Two of this book has a number of related purposes:—To give you practical training in the educated and preferable pronunciations of the most troublesome words in the English language.

—To root out of your speech, permanently and completely, most of the unconscious errors you may now make.

—To settle any doubts or confusion you may have about those pronunciation demons that harry the average speaker.

—And thus, in total, to produce a tremendous increase in your self-assurance whenever you give spoken expression to your ideas and thinking.

But let us settle first a very important question, namely:

What *is* correct pronunciation?

Is it what actors and actresses use on the Broadway stage?

Is it what the members of the social register use?

Is it what the English professors at the great universities use?

Is it what the dictionaries recommend?

Is it what the people use in Boston? Or in the Middle West? Or along the Atlantic seacoast? Or in the South? Or in London, England?

Or is it, perhaps, what your teachers taught you to use in high school and college?

Correct pronunciation is none of these, exclusively; yet it is a combination, in part, of all of them.

Correct pronunciation is the pronunciation used by the great majority of educated people throughout the country. This definition is agreed upon by all language scholars. It is the principle which governs the pronunciations offered in your dictionary. It is the criterion by which a skillful speaker is judged.

Correct pronunciation, in other words, is no more nor less than *current* pronunciation. The *proper* way to say a word, by this token, is simply the way educated people are saying it at the moment.

Correct pronunciation has no relationship whatever to phonetic beauty. The broad sound *ah* may, to some, sound lovelier than the flat sound ă, as in *at*. Yet, though perhaps prettier, *bahth* is incorrect, while băth is correct—because most educated people say it that way.

Correct pronunciation has no exclusive relationship to spelling. *Warm* and *farm* are spelled similarly, but pronounced differently. *Fur* and *her* and *myrrh* are spelled differently but, except for the initial consonant, pronounced the same. In *psalm* there is a *p* in the spelling but none in the pronunciation, while in hiccough (pronounced *hĭk-up*) there is a *p* in the pronunciation but none in the spelling.

Correct pronunciation has no exclusive relationship to clearness. In *handkerchief, vegetable,* and *comfortable* the correct pronunciations are those which run all the syllables together.

Correct pronunciation is not exclusively charming, nor impressive, nor clear, nor cultured, nor glamorous; it is only two things—*current* and *acceptable*.

The effective way to pronounce a word is the popular way. Unpopular pronunciations, no matter what authority or reasons you have for using them, are ineffective pronunciations that rob your speech of power, not add power to it.

There is no Supreme Court of Speech, no final arbiter to rule on the constitutionality or legality of a pronunciation. The dictionaries, to which we refer when we are in doubt about a pronunciation, or when a controversy occurs, generally offer an authoritative answer, but dictionaries do not rule on how you must speak, nor do they make any pretense of doing so. They do no more than record how most educated people are currently speaking—and the multitudinous changes which are introduced into each new edition of a dictionary will serve to convince a skeptic that dictionaries do not try to establish trends in pronunciation, but only record those trends as accurately as they can.

Let us turn, now, to an analysis of the most important of these trends.

chapter 28 TRENDS IN AMERICAN PRONUNCIATION

1. Long A

Shall we say *dayta* or *datta* for the word *data? Ignoraymus* or *ignorammus* for *ignoramus? Staytus* or *stattus* for *status?*

The answers to these questions depend almost completely on the business or profession in which the speaker is engaged. Lecturers, authors, educators, editors, lawyers, actors, journalists, commentators, and others whose work demands an unusual degree of skill in the language arts are almost completely committed to the long *A* (*ay*) in these and similar words. Millions of other people of equal education—doctors, dentists, executives—whose daily activities do not impose upon them the same need for linguistic sophistication, use the flat *A* (as in *at*). Hence, it is obviously impossible to label either of the two possible forms as "correct" or "incorrect." What can be said is that authorities have generally favored the long *A* up to recent times, but are now becoming more charitably inclined toward the flat form; many dictionaries now accept the flat *A* in words like *data, ignoramus, status, gratis, apparatus*, etc., generally as a second choice.

In this matter, as in so many others, you must let your ears be your guide. Do you personally, in your own business or professional circles, more frequently hear long *A*'s than flat ones? Then you should use long *A*'s also. Do so many of your associates use flat *A*'s that it will sound as if you are being affected when you do otherwise? Your course of action is then obvious.

Here is a fairly complete list of the words which many skilled speakers pronounce with a long *A*:

data	aviator	desideratum
fracas	ignoramus	pro rata
status	radiator	verbatim
ultimatum	stratum	gratis
implacable	erratum	apparatus

Ultimatum is frequently heard with a broad *A* (*ul-ti-mah'-tum*), most commonly with a long *A,* and only rarely with a flat *A.*

2. *The Broad* A

American English is clearly tending away from the broad *A* in many groups of words. Pronunciations like *vahst* (vast), *lahf* (laugh), *cahn't* (can't), *exahmple* (example), *chahnce* (chance), *ahfter* (after), etc. now sound peculiarly un-American, and except from someone with a marked British accent, absurdly affected. Even in the following words, popular trends strongly favor the somewhat flat *A* of *gather;* the broad *A* of *father* is heard today with diminishing frequency.

WORD	POPULAR AND CURRENT PRONUNCIATION	LESS POPULAR PRONUNCIATION
almond	ăm'-'nd	ahm'-'nd
rather	ră'-ther (rhyme with gather)	rah'-ther (rhyme with *father*)
drama	dră'-ma	drah'-ma
khaki	kă'-kee	kah'-kee
plaza	plă'-za	plah'-za
patio	pă'-tee-o	pah'-tee-o
salve	săv (rhyme with *have*)	sahv
tomato	to-may'-to	to-mah'-to
aunt	ănt (rhyme with *slant*)	ahnt
vase	vayz (rhyme with *ways*)	vahz

However, *llama,* the South American animal, and *lama,* the Tibetan monk, are both pronounced only with the broad *A: lah'-ma.*

3. Words Ending in -ABLE

In effective and educated speech the following words receive the accent on the first syllable:

am′icable	for′midable
hos′pitable	rev′ocable
lam′entable	pref′erable
ex′plicable	rep′arable
ap′plicable	rep′utable
com′parable	des′picable

In the negative form the accent is retained on the same syllable on which it falls in the positive form:

inhos′pitable	irrev′ocable
inex′plicable	irrep′arable
inap′plicable	disrep′utable
incom′parable	

An important exception to this principle is *disputable*, which may be accented on either the first or second syllable:

dis′putable　　　　or　　　　dispu′table

The negative follows suit:

indis′putable　　　　or　　　　indispu′table

4. Words Ending in -AGE

In eight common words the ending *-age* contains the consonant sound represented by the letter *S* in pleasure. This sound is formed by the mouth in the same way that *SH* is, but it is a *voiced* rather than a *breathed* sound. The phonetic symbol generally used to represent this sound is *ZH*. These are the words:

barrage	ménage
camouflage	persiflage
massage	corsage
garage	espionage

Prestige (press-teezh′) and cortege (kor-tezh′) contain the same sound. Guard against *presteedge* and *kortedge*.

5. Hard and Soft G

Before *E, I,* and *Y*, the letter *G* is usually soft, as in *gem;* at other times it is generally hard, as in *gum*. Short words, of Anglo-Saxon origin, are the most frequent exceptions to this rule.

Soft G	*Hard G*
orgy (or′jee)	go
gill (measure)	guard
giblets	game
gesture (jes′-ture)	gust
gesticulate (jes-tic′-u-late)	glint
manger (mayn′-jer)	grass
gibe (jibe)	prodigal
gibberish (jibberish)	
harbinger (har′-bin-jer)	
intelligentsia (in-tel-i-jen′-see-a)	
longevity (lon-jev′-i-tee)	
turgid (tur′-jid)	
orgiastic (or-jee-ass′-tik)	
gibbet (jibbet)	

6. Words Ending in -ILE

The American tendency, as distinguished from the British, is to pronounce the suffix *ile* as if it were spelled *ill*. The following common words follow this principle:

fragile	imbecile	juvenile	mercantile
servile	puerile	textile	domicile
versatile	hostile	docile	agile
fertile	sterile	virile	futile

Puerile is pronounced *pyoo'-er-ill;* and *juvenile, textile, mercantile,* and *domicile* are also acceptable with a final syllable that rhymes with *mile.*

The following words are exceptions to the rule, the ending being pronounced as if it were spelled *aisle:*

infantile	bibliophile
francophile	profile
anglophile	exile
crocodile	reconcile
senile	turnstile

7. *How to Pronounce* s

S, like *G*, has two principal sounds: *Z* as in *reside*, and *S* as in *sit*. Here are the major words which cause confusion:

S (*sit*)	*Z* (*reside*)
absurd	usurp
absorb	venison
gasoline	resilient
vaseline	abysmal
vise	because
	demise (de-mize')

8. -ITIS

Diseases ending in *-itis* are preferably pronounced *eye'-tiss*, not *ee'-tis*.

appendicitis	laryngitis
arthritis	meningitis

bronchitis	neuritis
colitis	pharyngitis
gastritis	tonsillitis

9. The Sharp U

Like the broad *A*, the sharp *U* (as in *few, mule,* etc.) is also gradually falling into a state of disuse. After the consonants *D, L, N, S,* and *T,* a frank ōō sound, somewhat less protracted than that heard in *moon,* is now characteristic of standard American pronunciation. For example:

allure	lure	stupid
assume	lurid	superb
astute	new	superior
dude	news	tuba
due	nuisance	tube
duel	numerous	tune
during	nutrition	tumor
duty	stew	Tuesday
ludicrous	student	

(Contradictorily, however, for *avenue, av-en-yoo,* rather than *av-en-oo* is the preferable and more popular form.)

In words ending in *-ture,* the last syllable is popularly and correctly pronounced *chŏŏr,* rather than *tyŏŏr.* For example, *feature, literature, nature, pasture,* etc.

On the other hand, the consonants *B, C, F, G, H, K, M, P,* and *V* are regularly followed by the sharp *U,* as in *bureau, cute, fuse, gewgaw, humor, kudos, mural, pure, view,* etc.

10. American vs. British Pronunciation

In a number of instances, the British pronunciation of a word contains definite differences when compared with the general American version. Some of the words in which our pronunciation differs from that of our English cousins are:

American Pronunciation	British Pronunciation
organization	organ-eye-zation
civilization	civil-eye-zation
fast	fahst
laff (laugh)	lahff
secreterry (secretary)	secret'ry
conservatoary (conservatory)	conservat'ry
laboratoary (laboratory)	labor'-at'ry
project	proe'ject
progress	proe'gress
process	proe'cess
ate	et
ski	shee
skedyool (schedule)	shedyool
medicine	medsin
circumstănce	circumst'nce
bin (been)	bean

It is no wonder that English is a difficult language to pronounce, even for its most educated speakers. Consider some of the pitfalls always present in the path of the unwary:

I. Spelling is no criterion.
   a. *Warm* and *harm* are similar in spelling. Note how differently they are pronounced.
   b. *tough, through, though, cough, bough,* all end in *ough*. In each case this suffix has a different pronunciation.
   c. Consider how perplexed a foreigner learning English would be by pairs like these:

   > *ghost* and *guest*
   > *palm* and *thumb*
   > *plumber* and *hammer*
   > *hymn* and *dim*

   d. Often the spelling of a word is not even remotely connected with its pronunciation. Consider:

   > *victuals* (vittles)
   > *colonel* (kernel)
   > *quay* (kee)
   > *solder* (sodder)
   > *phthisic* (tizik)
   > *Sioux* (soo)

II. A tremendous part of the vocabulary of English comes from foreign languages. Every language on the face of the earth is represented: ancient languages, modern languages, dead languages, living languages. Hebrew, Latin,

Greek, Sanskrit, Hawaiian, Japanese, Chinese, French, and Icelandic, to mention just a few, have contributed tens of thousands of words to our present-day dictionaries. Some of these foreign words are Anglicized when they are taken over into English; some are Anglicized years later; some always retain their foreign flavor.

For example:

  a. From the French, *sachet* is still pronounced in a Gallic manner (sa-shay′); *valet* has been Anglicized (val′-et).
  b. *Sotto voce,* from the Italian, has not been Anglicized (sot-to voe′-chay); *viva voce,* from the Latin, has been (vye′-va voe′-see).
  c. *Weltschmerz* and *wanderlust* are both from the German. The former is still truly Teutonic in sound (velt′-shmertz); the latter is now pure English (wahn′-der-lust).

III. Sometimes *TH* is soft as in *th*e, li*th*e, bli*th*e; sometimes hard, as in *th*ing, hear*th*, ei*th*er; sometimes like *T,* as in *th*yme. And no rule can be relied on to tell us which is which.

IV. Sometimes *H* is silent, as in *h*onor; sometimes pronounced as in *h*umor or *h*eart.

V. *OO* may be heard one way, as in b*oo*k; or quite differently, as in m*oo*n.

VI. *CH* may be *tsh,* as in *ch*air; *sh,* as in ma*ch*ine; or *k,* as in pa*ch*yderm.

VII. *S* may be *sh,* as in *s*ugar or *s*ure; *s,* as in *s*inecure; *z* as in re*s*erve; or *zh* as in plea*s*ure.

VIII. *Ine* may be *īne* as in fel*ine;* or *in,* as in genu*ine.*

IX. Letters may be silent, as in malign (*ma-line′*) or viscount (*vye′-count*); or they may require an entire syllable for themselves, as in coyo*te* (*kye-o′-tee*), or ag*ue* (*ay′-gyoo*).

These nine principles do not by any means exhaust the peculiarities and idiosyncrasies of English pronunciation.

They are sufficient, however, to indicate the great complexity of our language. An educated Frenchman, or German, or Spaniard can pronounce perfectly any word in his languages with which you may wish to confront him—and this statement holds whether he's ever seen the word before or not. Pronunciation hews obediently to definite rules in these and other languages; the exceptions, if any, are infrequent and unimportant.

But English stands in a class by itself—its pronunciation is contradictory, confusing, intricate almost beyond belief. Consider, for example, the following groups:

1. The following words contain letters which careless speakers often ignore.

arc*t*ic (ark'-tik)
su*g*gest (sugg-jest')
epitom*e* (e-pĭt'-o-mee)
dilettan*t*e (dĭl-a-tăn'-tee)
canap*e* (kan-a-pay')
fla*c*cid (flak'-sid)
a*c*cessory (ak-sess'-or-ee)

ag*u*e (ay'-gyoo)
gover*n*ment (guv'-ern-ment)
stren*g*th (stren*k*th)
len*g*th (len*k*th)
wi*d*th (wi*d*-th)
brea*d*th (bre*d*-th)
su*c*cinct (suk-sinkt')

2. Other words, on the contrary, contain letters which are *silent*.

indi*c*t (in-dyte')
mali*g*n (ma-lyne')
poi*g*nant (poyn'-int)
ches*t*nut (chess-nut)
boa*ts*wain (bōs'n)
com*p*troller (kon-trole'-er)
gun*w*ale (gunnel)
ba*g*nio (băn'-yo)

fore*h*ead (forrid)
so*l*der (sodder)
vi*s*count (vye'-count)
kil*n* (kill)
*h*erb (erb)
of*t*en (offen)
imbro*g*lio (im-brole'-yō)

3. Words ending in *-ine* are pronounced in one of three ways: long *I* (ī), short *I* (ĭ), or long *E* (ē).

ĭ (in)	ī (ine)	ē (een)
aquiline	alkaline	submarine
genuine	asinine	peregrine
heroine	canine	nectarine
saccharine	concubine	nicotine
gelatine	turpentine	benzine
	leonine	gasoline
	saturnine	cuisine
	serpentine	(kwee-zeen')
	feline	guillotine
	bovine	(gil-o-teen')

4. A large proportion of our two- and three-syllable words ending in *-et* have come from French. In French, the digraph *et* is always pronounced *ay*. Some of these words retain their Gallic flavor—some have been Anglicized.

Anglicized (*et*)	*Gallic* (*ay*)
valet (val'-et)	sachet (să-shay')
bayonet	sobriquet (soe-brĭ-kay')
cadet (ka-det')	cabaret (kab-a-ray')
coronet	bouquet (boo-kay')
tourniquet (turn'-i-ket)	cabriolet
martinet (mar'-ti-net')	Chevrolet
	gourmet (goor-may')

5. *TH* may be hard, as in *th*ing, or soft, as in *th*e. Here are the few confusing forms:

Hard (*thing*)	*Soft* (*the*)
youth	lithe
cloth	blithe
baths	thence
	youths
	bathes
	swathe (swaythe)

374

6. *QU* is occasionally pronounced as a simple *K*, most often as a *KW*.

K	*KW*
liquor	banquet (bang′-kwit)
piquant (pee′-k'nt)	quote
piqué (pee-kay′)	querulous (kwer′-ŏŏ-lus)
quay (kee)	quaint
risqué (riss-kay′)	acquiesce
bouquet (boo-kay′ or boe-kay′)	loquacious (etc.)
lacquer (lak′-er)	
parquet (par-kay′ or par-ket′)	

7. A few words which have come from the French retain the Gallic pronunciation of *on* for *EN:*

ennui (on′-we)	en rapport (on ra-pore′)
en route (on root′)	entr'acte (on′-tract)
ensemble (on-sahm′)	entree (on′-tray)
enceinte (on-sant′)	en famille (on fa-mee′)

8. *H* is silent in many words. In the following, however, careful speech requires its sounding:

> *h*omage, not 'omage
> *h*umble, not 'umble
> *h*otel, not 'otel
> *h*uman, not 'uman
> *h*umane, not 'umane
> *h*umor, not 'umor
> *h*umorous, not 'umorous

In the following, *H* is preferably silent:

ve~~h~~ement
pro~~h~~ibition
ve~~h~~icle
~~h~~erb

9. *CH* has three possible pronunciations: *TSH* as in *ch*air; *K* as in *ch*aos; *SH* as in ma*ch*ine. Generally, *TSH* is found in words of Anglo-Saxon origin, *K* in words of Greek derivation, and *SH* in words of French origin.

TSH	*K*	*SH*
chair	archangel	champagne
chase	archeology	chauvinism
arch	hierarchy	chagrin
archbishop	Archimedes	chic
champion	chaos	chicanery
	chasm	(shi-kay'-ne-ree)
	epoch	
	archaic	
	archipelago	
	chiropodist	
	chimera	
	(ki-mee'-ra)	

Bach, the composer, retains a German pronunciation: *a* as in *f*ather, K a gargling sound.

10. Rule for Pronunciation of *NG:*

A. *NG at the end of a word is never exploded.*
   lon(g), sin(g), win(g), han(g).
B. When *NG* occurs in the body of a word, drop all the letters following it. If a real word is then left, do not explode the *G*.
   Example 1: singer; drop *er. Sing,* a real word, remains. Hence: *sin(g)er.*

Example 2: linger; drop *er. Ling,* a non-existent word, remains. Hence: *lingger.*

Exceptions:
1. longer (lon*g*ger) and longest (lon*g*gest)
2. younger (youn*g*ger) and youngest (youn*g*gest)
3. stronger (stron*g*ger) and strongest (stron*g*gest)

Practice on these:

Explode the NG		*Nasalize the NG*	
finger	spangle	singing	lung
longest	dangle	hangar	clinging
youngest	angle	hanging	tang
linger	tingle	wringer	twang
English	wangle	wringing	song
angry	angler	long	songster
anger	bungle	strong	bringing
angered		young	losing
		clang	ring
		Long Island	ringer
		working	ringing

Read this paragraph aloud, pronouncing each *NG* correctly:

The *singer* was born in *Long* Island. She was *younger* and *stronger* than her sisters, and could produce *longer* notes than any other *songstress* I remember *having* listened to. Her *English* was perfect, her voice was *soothing* and sweet, and she could *sing songs* in many *languages.* She had an attractive *languid* appearance, but, like many of the artists with whom she *mingled,* frequently had fits of *anger. During* the summer she liked *living* in a *bungalow* and *working* on her *singing, spending* all her week ends *shopping* at the local stores and *talking* over her problems with her *gangster* husband.

11. A fairly reliable rule is that *ate,* as a suffix in *nouns* or *adjectives,* is pronounced almost like the word *it;* as a suffix in *verbs,* it is pronounced *ayt.*

Verb—(ayt)	*Adjective or Noun—(it)*
graduate	graduate
aggregate	aggregate
alternate	alternate
animate	animate
appropriate	appropriate
approximate	approximate
articulate	articulate
associate	associate

Note these exceptions:

The following, though nouns or adjectives, are pronounced with long a—*ayt.*

candidate	potentate
irate (eye'-rate)	prostrate
magnate (mag'-nate)	reprobate
ornate	sedate
	inmate

The verb *acclimate* may be pronounced either *ac-clye'-mit* or *ack'-li-mayt.*

chapter 30 CHECK UP ON YOUR PRONUNCIATION

This chapter is simply a list of words. Some of them are tricky because they are "reading" rather than "speaking" words. That is, you will come across them over and over on the printed page, but actually say them infrequently. Hence, you may easily have blundered into mental mispronunciations and never have had the opportunity to check yourself or be checked by your listeners.

A number of words in particular are those which lend themselves all too easily to careless articulation. Others sound so different from the way they are spelled that mispronunciation is often extremely tempting.

And still others may be in that large class of words which have two pronunciations, one infinitely preferable to the other.

The best and most helpful way to go through this chapter is to cover the right-hand column, in which the phonetic respellings are offered, with a blank card. Say each word in the left-hand column, aloud. Check at once with its pronunciation by shifting your card one line. If your pronunciation and the one offered check, well and good. If they do not, mark the word and continue. When you have finished each list, study the words that gave you trouble.

A few have already been discussed in previous chapters; most are offered for the first time.

Group 1

Is your enunciation accurate, clear, and easily understandable? Or is it garbled, indistinct, and illiterate? The list that follows contains twenty-five words which will provide you with a valid yardstick for measuring the clarity of your speech. Keep your pencil handy, and check for future practice any word you mispronounce. If you make no more than four or five errors, your speech is free of slovenliness. Consider a large number of mistakes as a warning that careless and illiterate mannerisms are detracting from the effectiveness of your speech.

Word	Pronunciation
1. government	1. goverɴment, not gover'ment nor gov'ment
2. just	2. just, not jist
3. kept	3. kept, not kep'
4. library	4. lye'-bra-ry, not li'-berry
5. attacked	5. at-takt, not at-tak-ted
6. American	6. American, not Amurrikan
7. arctic	7. arctic, not artic
8. Italian	8. ĭ-tal'-ian, not eye'-tal-ian
9. wrestle	9. ressle, not rassle
10. elm	10. elm, not ell-um
11. film	11. film, not fill-um
12. law	12. law, not lore
13. asked	13. askt, not ast
14. potato	14. po-tay-toe, not per-tay-ter
15. window	15. win-doe, not win-der
16. accurate	16. ak'-yōō-rit, not akkerit
17. manufacture	17. man-yōō-facture, not manafacture
18. particular	18. pertikyōōler, not pertikkaler
19. regular	19. reg-yōō-ler, not reggaler
20. poem	20. po'-'m, not pome
21. ruin	21. roo-in, not roon
22. recognize	22. rek-og-nize, not rekkernize
23. question	23. kwess-chin, not kwesh-in
24. believe	24. be-leev', not bleev
25. figure	25. fig-yōōr, not figger

380

Group 2

Word	Pronunciation
1. bade	1. băd
2. forbade	2. forbăd
3. route	3. rōōt (in army or commercial parlance, *rowt* is allowable)
4. brooch	4. broach
5. squalid	5. squah-lid
6. nausea	6. naw'-sha, not naw'-zee-a
7. nauseate	7. naw'-she-ate
8. fjord	8. fyord
9. finis	9. fye'-niss, or, as second choice, fin'-iss; not fee-nee'
10. egregious	10. e-gree'-jiss
11. zoology	11. zoe-ol'-o-jee
12. virago	12. vir-ay'-go
13. falcon	13. fawl'-kin
14. quay	14. kee
15. plebeian	15. ple-bee'-in
16. sacrilegious	16. sac-ri-lee'-juss
17. nonpareil	17. non-pa-rěl'
18. flaccid	18. flak'-sid
19. decade	19. děck-āde
20. suave	20. swahv

Group 3

Word	Pronunciation
1. with	1. with (th as in *the*, not as in *th*ink)
2. associate	2. a-so'-she-ate
3. association	3. a-so'-see-ay'-shun
4. appreciate, appreciation	4. ap-pree'-she-ate ap-pree'-she-ay'-shun
5. pecan	5. pe-căn, not pe-cahn'
6. travail	6. trăv'-ayl

7. radiator	7. ray'-dee-ay-ter, not răd'-ee-ay-ter
8. comparable	8. com'-par-a-ble, not com-par'-able
9. illustrate	9. il'-lus-trate, not il-luss'-trate
10. orgy	10. or'-jee, not or'-gee
11. often	11. offen, not off-ten
12. coupé	12. coo-pay' preferable to cōōp
13. coupon	13. koo'-pon preferable to kyoo'-pon
14. exquisite	14. eks'-kwiz-it or eks-kwiz'-it
15. pomegranate	15. pum-gran'-it
16. vanilla	16. va-nil'-la, not vi-nel'-la
17. romance	17. ro-mance' preferable to ro'-mance
18. secretive	18. se-cree'-tiv preferable to see'-cre-tiv
19. dirigible	19. dir'-ij-ible, not di-rig'-ible
20. scourge	20. skûrj
21. clandestine	21. clan-dess'-tin, not clan'-de-styne
22. posthumous	22. poss'-chu-mous
23. gaol	23. jail
24. harass	24. harris preferable to ha-rass'

Group 4

Word	Pronunciation
1. absolutely	1. ab'-so-loot-lee
2. isolate	2. eye'-so-late, not iss'-o-late
3. positively	3. poz'-i-tiv-lee
4. bicycle	4. bye'-sickle
5. poniard	5. pon'-yerd
6. vineyard	6. vĭn'-yerd
7. ignominy	7. ig'-no-minny
8. ignominious	8. ig-no-min'-ee-uss
9. impious	9. im'-pee-uss
10. era	10. ee'-ra
11. enigma	11. e-nig'-ma
12. amateur	12. am'-a-cher or am'-a-tur
13. caricature	13. car'-i-ca-chŏŏr, not car-ic'a-chŏŏr
14. perfunctory	14. per-funk'-ter-ee

Word	Pronunciation
15. clique	15. cleek, not click
16. divan	16. dye'-van
17. irony	17. eye'-ron-ee, not eye-er-nee
18. strength, length	18. strĕn*k*th, lĕn*k*th; not strĕnth, lĕnth
19. width	19. widd-th, not with
20. culinary	20. cyoo'-li-nerry
21. grimy	21. grye'-mee
22. panacea	22. pan-a-see'-a

Group 5

Word	*Pronunciation*
1. bronchial	1. bronk'-ee-il, not bron'-ik-'l
2. mischievous	2. miss'-chi-viss, not miss-chee'-vee-us
3. grievous	3. gree'-vuss, not gree'-vee-us
4. faucet	4. fawset, not fasset
5. intricate	5. in'-trik-it, not in-trik'-it
6. modern	6. mod'-urn, not mod'ren
7. municipal	7. mu-niss'-i-p'l, not mu-ni-sip'-l
8. deficit	8. def'-i-sit, not de-fiss'-it
9. accept	9. ak-sept', not a-sept'
10. drowned	10. drownd, not drownded
11. February	11. Feb'-roo-ary, not Feb'-you-erry

Notes on the Pronunciation of Certain Interesting Words

ABDOMEN: *Ab'-do-men* was once frowned upon by the authorities (they preferred *ab-do'-men*), but it has become so popular that most dictionaries now list it as first choice.

ABSOLUTELY: Except for emphasis, the accent falls on the first syllable (*ab'solutely*). The same rule applies to *positively* (*pos'itively*).

ABSORB: Preferably hiss the *S*, rather than buzzing it. The same suggestion applies to *absurd*.

ACCLIMATE: *Ac-kly'-mit* is the more scholarly form, but *ac'-li-mayt* is equally correct.

ADDRESS: Say either *ad'-dress* or *a-dress'* for the place where a person lives, only *a-dress'* for a formal speech or lecture. The verb, no matter what the meaning, is always accented on the second syllable.

ADULT: Say either *a-dult'* or *ad'-ult*.

ADVERTISEMENT: *Ad-ver'-tiz-ment* or *ad-ver-tize'-ment*. They're equally good.

AGAIN, AGAINST: In poetry, of course, these words are often required by the rhyme scheme to be pronounced *agayne* and *agaynst*. But in ordinary conversation, such pronunciations sound stilted.

APRICOT: *Ăp'-ri-cot* is more popular, though some people say *ay'pri-cot*.

ATHLETIC: Three syllables only, not four.

AWRY: *Aw-rye'* only!

BECAUSE: Buzz the *S*, don't hiss it.

BONA FIDE: Enough speakers silence the final *E* (*bona fyed*) to make it acceptable, though some authorities entreat you to add that extra syllable (*bona fy'dee*).

CHAUFFEUR: *Sho-fur'*, the older form, is rapidly giving ground to the common and preferable *sho'-fer*.

CHIC: *Sheek* is the preferable and recommended pronunciation, although both *shick* and *chick* are often heard on less educated levels.

CLIQUE: *Cleek* is preferable, although *click* admittedly has some currency.

COMBATANT: Accent the first syllable, skip lightly over the second: *com-b'-t'nt*. In best usage, *combat*, whether a verb or noun, is also accented on the *com*.

DEBUT: The fully Anglicized form *de-byoo* is the easiest to say and the one most commonly heard.

DISHABILLE: Also completely Anglicized (*diss-a-beel'*).

EITHER: The controversy between *eether* and *eyether* has raged for years and will probably never abate. Both forms are correct, and both are current, but to some people *eyether* sounds a bit affected. It is suggested, therefore, that unless *eyether* is completely natural in your speech habits and is prevalent in your social group or geographical locality, it might be wiser to avoid it. (These comments apply equally to *neether* and *nyether*.)

The late C. A. Lloyd, noted language scholar and professor of English at Biltmore College, Asheville, North Carolina, used to tell a characteristic anecdote in this connection:

"In the early days of the Far West a citizen of a small town encountered a crowd of cowboys who were dragging a man behind them, with the evident intention of lynching him.

" 'Wait a minute, boys,' he said. 'What's he done?'

" 'Stole a horse,' was the answer.

" 'Well, that's pretty bad, boys,' said the citizen, 'but we need more law in this town. Why not turn him over to the sheriff and give him a fair trial?'

"'Yes, pardner, but he shot the man that the horse belonged to, besides,' replied the cowboys.

"'That's terrible, boys, but it's not your place to settle with him. Let the law do it.'

"'Yes, but besides all that, he says "eyether" and "neyether"!'

"'Oh, well, take him on out, boys.'"

ENVELOPE: C. A. Lloyd puts it as follows: "'Envelope' comes from the French, though it is now spelled 'enveloppe' in that language. Its English pronunciation may be 'ENvelope' or 'ONvelope,' or even 'enVELop,' when it is spelled without the final 'e.' Of these three 'ENvelope' is undoubtedly the most reasonable and the most widely used. If those who use the other pronunciations could just agree to drop them and center on 'ENvelope,' the cause of uniformity would be greatly aided and a needless source of possible irritation removed."

EPITOME: Four syllables. This is a somewhat bookish word and should be pronounced properly: *e-pit'-o-mee.*

EXILE: Hiss the *X* in this word and also in *exit* and *exhibition.*

FIANCÉ: Man or woman, he or she is a *fee-ahn-say'.* The feminine form is spelled *fiancée.*

INCOGNITO: *In-cog-nee'-to* was once frowned upon, but is gaining in popularity. *In-cog'-ni-to* is the more scholarly pronunciation.

INFAMOUS: Here, as in *impious* and *impotent,* the accent falls on the first syllable.

INQUIRY: There's no stigma attached to *in'-kwĭ-ree,* though many skillful speakers prefer *in-kwy'-ree.*

IODINE: No matter how you say this word, you're bound to be correct. There are three possible pronunciations and they're all acceptable.

KILN: The *N* is preferably silent.

LICORICE: We still hear *likkerish* occasionally, but mainly from kids who are buying a penny's worth of it. Say *lick'-er-iss.*

LIVELONG: In this word the *I* is short (*lĭv-long*) but in *long-lived* it's long (*long-lyved*).

MODERN: Say it as it's spelled—*mod'-ern*, not *mod'-ren.*

PANACEA: *Pan-a-see'-a.*

PERFUME: Accent either syllable.

POTPOURRI: You have to keep the French flavor of this term: *poe'-poo'-ree'.*

PREFACE: Noun or verb, stress the *pref.*

QUAY: *Kee* is the only proper way to say it.

REMONSTRATE: It's *re-mon'strate,* even though it's *dem'-on-strate.*

RIBALD: Short *I: rib'-ld.*

ROBUST: Preferably rhyme it with "Go bust'!"

STRENGTH: Here, as also in *length,* the *G* should be pronounced, and with almost the same sound as you would ordinarily give to a *K* (*strenkth, lenkth*).

SUITE: With that *E* at the end, we've got to say *sweet.*

TACITURN: The *C* is soft: *tass'-i-turn.*

THYME: Silence the *H: time.*

VAGARY: Accent the second, not the first, syllable—*va-gair'-ee.*

VICTUALS: It doesn't look like it, but this is just plain *vittles.*

ZOOLOGY: Because of the shortened form *zoo,* we're tempted to call it *zoo-ol'-o-gy,* but the preferable pronunciation is *zoe-ol'-o-gy.*

chapter 32 A RESTATEMENT OF
PRINCIPLES

It is not difficult to improve your pronunciation. On the contrary, it is one of the easiest—and quickest—kinds of linguistic improvement you can aim at. If you will follow the simple principles you have studied in these pages, you should very shortly begin to feel completely self-assured about the effectiveness of your pronunciation.

Let me restate the most important of these principles under three headings:

1. *Make sure to avoid so-called illiterate speech habits.*

Check up on yourself. Are you careful of your *TH*'s? Do you ever say *dis* for *this, dat* for *that, de* for *the?* Most people who do are never conscious of their error—until they begin to listen critically to themselves.

Do you ever drop your final *G*'s, and say *askin, talkin, workin, doin? ING* words are used a hundred times a day in the course of normal conversation—are you careful of them?

Check to see whether you occasionally omit letters that should be articulated. Do you say *strenth* for *strenGth, lenth* for *lenGth, with* for *wiDth, goverment* for *goverN-ment, ast* for *asKed, assessory* for *aCcessory, fith* for *fiFth, kep* for *kepT,* or *pitcher* for *piCture?*

Or, do you on the other hand, obtrude unnecessary letters where they do not belong? Do you say *ath-a-letic, ath-a-lete, drowned-ed, griev-ee-ous, mischiev-ee-ous, across-t, attacked-ted, burg-u-lar, el-um, fil-um,* or *once-t,* for *athletic, athlete, drowned, grievous, mischievous, across, attacked, burglar, elm, film,* and *once?*

Does an *R* creep in where none is called for? Do you ever say *lawr, sawr, idear, yeller?*

Do you ever get your syllables confused, saying *ir-rev-e-lant* for *irrelevant, larnyx* for *larynx, mod-ren* for *modern, pat-ren* for *pattern, per-scription* for *pre-scription* and *pres-piration* for *perspiration?*

2. *Be careful to avoid speech mannerisms that may make you sound as if you are the product of a class in diction.*

Do not broaden your *A*'s unless you are of British origin or hail from one of the few sections of the United States where the broad *A* is customarily heard. Do not say *bahth, ahsk, ahfter, commahnd,* or *lahst* solely because you think such pronunciations sound impressive. They don't—they are more likely to sound affected.

Watch especially such words as *chauffeur, either, neither, vase, tune, student, tomato, rather, again,* and *aunt.* Some speakers do not sound artificial when they say *sho-FUR, eyether, nyether, vahz, tyoon, styoodent, tomahto, rahther, agayne,* and *ahnt,* but most people are wise to avoid these pronunciations unless they are natural and customary in their particular social groups or geographical sections.

3. *Take care not to mispronounce words which most edu-cated people pronounce correctly.*

For example, there are a number of words ending in *-able,* in which the accent is preferably placed on the first syllable. Among these are:

com'-parable	hos'-pitable
for'-midable	pref'-erable
rev'-ocable	lam'-entable
rep'-utable	ap'-plicable

Be wary of the letter *A.* While it is unwise to say *ahsk,* it is equally frowned upon to say *âsk (Â* as in *âir),* or *cândy, mân,* or *hând.* Pronounce these words with the flat *A* sound of *hat.*

On the other hand, do not flatten the *A* when it is preferably long. Say *AYviator* and *AYviation,* not *AVViator* and *AVViation, RAYdiator,* not *RADiator.*

Do not slide over an *H* where most educated people give it full value. Avoid *wear, watt, wen, wy, weather* for *where, what, when, why,* and *whether.* And especially don't drop the initial *H* sound in *human, humid, humorous, huge,* and *humble.*

Don't be tripped up by a *G.* Sometimes it's soft, as in *gesture, gesticulate,* and *orgy,* in which words it has the sound of *J.* Sometimes it has the sound of *ZH,* like the *S* of *pleasure* or *measure.* Say *pleasure,* watching particularly how the *S* sounds, and give that same sound to the *G* in *garage* (second *G* only), *rouge, loge, mirage, prestige, corsage,* etc.

In many words, a *K* sound is followed by a *Y* sound, as in *cute, curious, cube.* But stay on guard against temptation in these three words:

coupon—koopon, preferably, not kyoopon
escalator—ess-ka-lator, not ess-kya-lator
percolator—per-ko-lator, not per-kyo-lator

Sometimes the sharpest distinction between educated and uneducated speech lies in the position of the accent. In these words, the accent belongs on the *first* syllable: *IMpious, INfamous, IMpotent, PERmit* (noun only), *INtricate,* and *IGnominy.* On the following words, the accent is preferably placed on the *second* syllable: *griMACE, roBUST, reMONstrate, eNIGma,* and *vaGAry.* On the other hand, words like *address* (i.e., residence), *adult, inquiry, acclimate,* and *exquisite* may with equal correctness be accented either on the first or second syllable.

The effective speaker, then, takes care to avoid three dangerous pitfalls—illiterate patterns; affected and pedantic forms; and common mispronunciations. He develops habits of pronouncing words correctly without sounding *too* correct or *too* precise; he speaks well because he has not lost the common touch.

PART 3 *Correct Spelling*

chapter 33 THE THIRTEEN HARDEST
WORDS TO SPELL

The novelist F. Scott Fitzgerald was a notoriously poor speller; Andrew Jackson, seventh President of the United States, was even worse, and is remembered for his ingenious excuse that "It's a darned poor mind that can think of only one way to spell a word!"

Thorstein Veblen, noted economist, felt equally vehement. "English spelling," he said, "is archaic, cumbrous, and ineffective."

So archaic and cumbrous is it, in fact, that most present-day Americans, even those of considerable education, find themselves baffled, confused, and irritated by the spellings of a great number of fairly common English words.

But perhaps you are an exception? Let us put it to a test.

Below are the thirteen words most frequently misspelled by literate adults. Top score made by a random selection of high school graduates was only *five;* a similarly chosen group of college graduates could do no better than *seven.* So if you think your spelling ability is better than average, this test will be in the nature of a challenge.

If you're prepared to accept the challenge, study the various patterns of each word below, checking the one you trust. Consider yourself quite normal if you make a correct choice only four or five times; better than average if you can score up to eight; and a superior speller if you can check ten or more proper forms.

1. (a) all-right, (b) alright, (c) all right, (d) allright
2. (a) supercede, (b) supersede, (c) superceed, (d) superseed

3. a) embarrassment, (b) embarrasment, (c) embarassment, (d) embarressment, (e) embaressment
4. (a) drunkedness, (b) drunkeness, (c) drunkenness, (d) drunkness, (e) drunkardness
5. (a) desiccate, (b) dessicate, (c) desicate, (d) dessiccate
6. (a) occurance, (b) occurrence, (c) occurence, (d) occurrance
7. (a) ecstasy, (b) ecstacy
8. (a) tyrrany, (b) tyrranny, (c) tyranny, (d) tyrany
9. (a) disippate, (b) disapate, (c) dissapate, (d) dissippate, (e) dissipate
10. (a) innoculate, (b) inocculate, (c) inoculate
11. (a) cooly, (b) cooley, (c) coolly, (d) coolley
12. (a) irresistable, (b) irresistible
13. (a) anoint, (b) annoint

Key: 1-c, 2-b, 3-a, 4-c, 5-a, 6-b, 7-a, 8-c, 9-e, 10-c, 11-c, 12-b, 13-a.
Score: Number of correct choices out of 13: ....

Can You Learn from Your Errors?

Below, in different order, are the thirteen words you have just studied, each one misspelled. Cross out the incorrect spelling and, without referring to the preceding key, rewrite each word correctly. Can you materially improve your previous score?

Incorrect Spelling	*Correct Spelling*
ecstacy	....
dessicate	....
disapate	....
irresistable	....
alright	....
embarassement	....
drunkeness	....
inocculate	....

396

Incorrect Spelling	Correct Spelling
annoint	....
supercede	....
occurance	....
tyrrany	....
cooly	....

Key: ecstasy, desiccate, dissipate, irresistible, all right, embarrassment, drunkenness, inoculate, anoint, supersede, occurrence, tyranny, coolly.

Score: Number right out of 13: ....

Another Test of Your Spelling

Here are twelve more words occasionally misspelled even by the most educated of adults. Can you choose the correct forms?

1. (a) repetition, (b) repitition
2. (a) irritable, (b) irritible
3. (a) indispensable, (b) indispensible
4. (a) despair, (b) dispair
5. (a) superintendent, (b) superintendant
6. (a) separate, (b) seperate
7. (a) recommend, (b) reccomend, (c) reccommend
8. (a) incidentally, (b) incidently
9. (a) development, (b) developement
10. (a) receive, (b) recieve
11. (a) weird, (b) wierd
12. (a) battalion, (b) batallion

Key: All (a) forms are correct.
Score: Number of correct choices out of 12: ....

Can You Learn from Your Errors?

Study any mistakes you may have made, then check your learning by once again crossing out the incorrect spellings listed below and rewriting each word in its proper form.

Incorrect Spelling	Correct Spelling
wierd	....
recieve	....
batallion	....
developement	....
incidently	....
reccomend	....
seperate	....
superintendant	....
irritible	....
repitition	....
dispair	....
indispensible	....

Key: weird, receive, battalion, development, incidentally, recommend, separate, superintendent, irritable, repetition, despair, indispensable.
Score: Number right out of 12: ....

chapter 34 TEN HANDY SPELLING RULES AND MEMORY AIDS

1. –*EFY*

A natural and extremely common ending in English spelling is -*ify*—it is found in hundreds of words, for example, *clarify, classify, mortify, codify, testify,* etc.

But in four words in which -*ify* seems to be the natural and sensible ending, only -*efy* is correct. These are the words:

1. liqu*efy*	3. stup*efy*
2. putr*efy*	4. rar*efy*

Particularly paradoxical is the fact that in the first three words, an *i* replaces the *e* in the associated forms *liquid, putrid,* and *stupid.* Other derived forms, such as *liquefaction, putrefaction, stupefaction, rarefaction, liquefied, putrefied,* etc. keep the *e.*

2. *K after C*

When a word ends in *c,* for example, *colic, frolic, picnic, mimic,* etc., a *k* is added before appending *e, i,* or *y;* for example, *colicky, frolicker, picnicker, mimicking,* etc. *C* ordinarily has the soft sound of *s before e, i,* and *y,* and the *k* is necessary to keep the *c* hard. Note these forms:

frolic*k*ing	picnic*k*ing
mimic*k*er	traffic*k*er
panic*k*y	traffic*k*ing

3. *E after C*

On the other hand, *e* must be retained after *c* before the ending *-able* in order to keep the *c* soft. Note these forms:

noti*c*eable	pea*c*eable
servi*c*eable	enfor*c*eable
embra*c*eable	pronoun*c*eable
repla*c*eable	tra*c*eable

4. *E after G*

E is kept after *g* before the endings *-able* and *-ous* in order to give the *g* the soft sound of *j*. Note these forms:

chan*g*eable	advanta*g*eous
mana*g*eable	coura*g*eous
char*g*eable	gor*g*eous

In *judgment, acknowledgment, lodgment, abridgment* and similar words containing *dg* before *-ment*, no *e* is necessary—the *d* serves to keep the *g* soft.

5. *–IZE, –ISE, and –YZE*

In the entire language, only two nontechnical words end in *-yze: analyze* and *paralyze*. A few technical terms, such as *catalyze, dialyze,* and *electrolyze* also have this ending, but otherwise your choice is between *-ise* and *-ize*. Generally, few people ever have any problem in making the proper choice. But watch *analyze* and *paralyze* and their derived forms, *analysis, paralysis, analytic, paralytic,* and *analyst.*

6. *IE and EI*

In choosing between *ie* and *ei*, bear in mind that *ei* is used immediately after the letter *c*:

rec*ei*ve	c*ei*ling
rec*ei*pt	conc*ei*t
perc*ei*ve	conc*ei*ve

The single exception is *financier*.

Ei is also used in words in which it has the sound of *a* in *freight*:

w*ei*ght	fr*ei*ght
w*ei*gh	n*ei*gh
n*ei*ghbor	v*ei*n
v*ei*l	r*ei*gn

Or the sound of *i* in *height*, *sleight* (of hand), *gneiss*, *stein* (of beer), *Fahrenheit*, etc.

Exceptions: *fiery, hierarchy, hieroglyphic*.

Ei is also used in these special words that merit careful study:

l*ei*sure	
s*ei*zure	*ei*ther
s*ei*ze	n*ei*ther
sh*ei*k	cod*ei*n
prot*ei*n	caff*ei*ne
w*ei*rd	

Siege, however, is spelled *-ie*.

Otherwise use *-ie*.

th*ie*f	br*ie*f
bel*ie*ve	gr*ie*f
f*ie*nd	cash*ie*r
n*ie*ce	ach*ie*ve
f*ie*ld	y*ie*ld

(etc.)

7. –CEDE, –CEED, and –SEDE

Only one word in the language ends in -*sede*: *supersede*. Three others end in -*ceed*: *exceed, proceed, succeed*. (But note the spelling of *procedure*.)

All others end in -*cede*: *accede, cede, concede, intercede, precede, recede, secede*, etc.

8. –LLY

Be careful of the -*lly* ending on these four words:

incidenta*lly*	coo*lly*
accidenta*lly*	rea*lly*

Note that we are simply adding the adverbial ending -*ly* to the adjectives *incidental, accidental, cool,* and *real*.

Adjectives which end in -*ic*, such as *lyric, scholastic, academic*, etc. add -*ally* to form the adverb: *lyrically, scholastically, academically*, etc. The only important exception is *publicly*.

9. –ABLE and –IBLE

The five most troublesome words in this category are *dependable, indispensable, irritable, inimitable,* and *irresistible*. For the first two, think that *able* men are usually depend*able* and indispens*able*. For the next two, think of the related forms irrit*ate* and imit*ate*. And for the last, let us assume that *lipstick* makes women irresist*i*ble.

10. –ENT and –ANT

The troublesome words ending in -*ent* are as follows:

superintend*ent*	persist*ent*
insist*ent*	depend*ent*

A memory trick that works for these words is: "The superintend*ent* collects the r*ent* in an apartm*ent* house; he is insist*ent* and persist*ent* about it, and the landlord is depend*ent* on him."

The nouns of -*ent* adjectives end of course in -*ence*: superintend*ence*, insist*ence*, persist*ence*, and depend*ence*.

Occurrence is also a frequently misspelled word—to remember the correct pattern, think of an oc*currence* as a *current* event.

Two troublesome words end in -*ant*, resist*ant* and defend*ant*, and one in -*ance*, persever*ance*.

Test Your Learning

Check the correct spelling of each word:

1. (a) liquefy, (b) liquify
2. (a) rarify, (b) rarefy
3. (a) picnicker, (b) picnicer
4. (a) enforcable, (b) enforceable
5. (a) changable, (b) changeable
6. (a) judgement, (b) judgment
7. (a) analize, (b) analyze
8. (a) receive, (b) recieve
9. (a) acheive, (b) achieve
10. (a) fiery, (b) feiry
11. (a) leisure, (b) liesure
12. (a) weird, (b) wierd
13. (a) seize, (b) sieze
14. (a) seige, (b) siege
15. (a) superceed, (b) supersede, (c) supercede
16. (a) exceed, (b) excede
17. (a) precede, (b) preceed
18. (a) cooly, (b) coolly
19. (a) accidently, (b) accidentally
20. (a) indispensable, (b) indispensible
21. (a) irresistable, (b) irresistible
22. (a) irritable, (b) irritible

23. (a) superintendant, (b) superintendent
24. (a) insistant, (b) insistent
25. (a) perseverance, (b) perseverence

Key: 1-a, 2-b, 3-a, 4-b, 5-b, 6-b, 7-b, 8-a, 9-b, 10-a, 11-a, 12-a, 13-a, 14-b, 15-b, 16-a, 17-a, 18-b, 19-b, 20-a, 21-b, 22-a, 23-b, 24-b, 25-a.

chapter 35 TRICKS TO REMEMBER
SPECIAL WORDS

Group 1

1. *tyranny*—one *r* and double *n*, as in the phrase "down with tyrants!" Similarly *tyrannous* and *tyrannical*.
2. *drunkenness*—*drunken* plus *-ness*, hence double *n*. *Suddenness* follows a similar pattern.
3. *definitely*—make sure *finite* appears in the word.
4. *vilify*—one *l*, as in the related word *vile*.
5. *descendant*—the opposite of *ancestor;* note the *an* at the end of one word and the beginning of the other.
6. *sacrilegious*—very different in meaning from *religious*, and the *e* and *i* are interchanged.
7. *iridescent*—one *r*, as in *iris*, both words being related to the Greek stem for *rainbow*.
8. *accelerate*—one *l*, as in the related word *celerity*.
9. *principal*—means *main;* note the *a* in both words.
10. *principle*—means *rule;* note the *-le* in both words.
11. *stationary*—means *standing* still; note the *a*.
12. *stationery*—means *paper;* note the *-er*.
13. *vacuum*—one *c*, as in the related word *vacant*.
14. *occasional*—only one *s*, as also in *pleasure, measure, treasure,* etc. in which *s* has the same sound.
15. *category*—*e*, not *a*, follows the *t;* think of the synonym *section*.
16. *balloon*—round, like a *ball*.
17. *all right*—two words, two *l*'s, like its opposite, *all wrong*.
18. *absence*—like the adjective *absent*.
19. *recommend*—the prefix *re-* plus *commend*.
20. *repetition*—the fourth letter is *e*, as in *repeat*.

Test Your Learning

Can you correct each misspelled word?

Incorrect Spelling	Correct Spelling
1. tyrrany	....
2. drunkeness	....
3. definately	....
4. villify	....
5. descendent	....
6. sacreligious	....
7. irridescent	....
8. accellerate	....
9. vaccuum	....
10. occassional	....
11. catagory	....
12. baloon	....
13. abscence	....
14. reccomend	....
15. repitition	....
16. alright	....

Key: 1. tyranny, 2. drunkenness, 3. definitely, 4. vilify, 5. descendant, 6. sacrilegious, 7. iridescent, 8. accelerate, 9. vacuum, 10. occasional, 11. category, 12. balloon, 13. absence, 14. recommend, 15. repetition, 16. all right

Group 2

21. *vicious*—like the form it derives from, *vice;* hence no *s* before the *c.*
22. *exhilarate*—one *l,* followed by *a,* as in the related word *hilarious.*
23. *anoint*—no double *n;* think of a*n o*il used in *anointing.*
24. *embarrassed*—two *r*'s, two *s*'s; think of "*two r*obbers emba*rr*assed in *S*ing *S*ing."

25. *fricassee*—made, often, in a *cas*serole; hence one *c*, two *s*'s.
26. *battalion*—often engaged in ba*tt*le; two *t*'s, one *l*.
27. *inoculate*—one *n*, one *c*, as in its synonym *inject*.
28. *ecstasy*—this word and *idiosyncrasy* end in -*sy*, not -*cy*.
29. *desiccate*—note the one *s* and double *c*.
30. *ukulele*—the third letter is *u*, not *e*.
31. *dissipate*—double *s*, one *p*.
32. *guttural*—*u* follows the double *t*.
33. *accommodate*—double *c*, double *m*.
34. *separate*—the fourth letter is *a*, not *e*.
35. *development*—no *e* following the *p*.
36. *privilege*—no *d* in the word.
37. *argument*—no *e* following the *u*, even though *argue* does have an *e*.
38. *truly*—drop the *e* in *true* before adding -*ly*.
39. *rhythmical*—note the *h* after the *r*.
40. *disappoint*—*appoint* plus the prefix *dis-*; *disappear* follows a similar pattern.

Test Your Learning

Can you correct each misspelled word?

Incorrect Spelling	Correct Spelling
1. viscious	....
2. exhillarate	....
3. annoint	....
4. embarrased	....
5. friccazee	....
6. batallion	....
7. innocculate	....
8. ecstacy	....
9. dessicate	....
10. ukelele	....
11. dissapate	....
12. gutteral	....

Incorrect Spelling	Correct Spelling
13. accomodate	....
14. seperate	....
15. developement	....
16. priviledge	....
17. arguement	....
18. truely	....
19. rythmical	....
20. dissapoint	....

Key: 1. vicious, 2. exhilarate, 3. anoint, 4. embarrassed, 5. fricassee, 6. battalion, 7. inoculate, 8. ecstasy, 9. desiccate, 10. ukulele, 11. dissipate, 12. guttural, 13. accommodate, 14. separate, 15. development, 16. privilege, 17. argument, 18. truly, 19. rhythmical, 20. disappoint.

Group 3

41. *assassin*—two sets of double *s*'s.
42. *assistant*—double *s*, followed by single *s*.
43. *benefited*—single *t*.
44. *comparative*—*a* follows *r*, despite the contradicting word *comparison*.
45. *dumfound*—preferable spelling omits the *b* after *m*.
46. *dessert*—meaning cakes, pies, etc.; think of *so sweet*, to remember the double *s*.
47. *desert*—think of the *Sahara desert* to remember one *s*.
48. *newsstand*—*news* plus *stand*, hence double *s*.
49. *bookkeeper*—*book* plus *keeper*, hence double *k*.
50. *possession*—two sets of double *s*'s.
51. *kidnaped*—in all forms of this word, one *p* is the preferable spelling; hence *kidnaper* and *kidnaping*.
52. *chagrined*—a single *n*, though double *n* would make more sense; likewise *chagrining*.
53. *sincerely*—*sincere* plus *-ly;* do not omit the *-e* after the *r*.
54. *whiskey, whisky*—domestic varieties spelled *-ey*, imported varieties spelled *-y*.

55. *villain*—double *l*.
56. *tranquillity*—double *l* is the preferable form.
57. *holiday*—one *l*.
58. *sheriff, tariff*—one *r*, double *f* in both.
59. *pursuit*—not *persuit*.
60. *despair*—not *dispair*.

Test Your Learning

Can you correct each misspelled word?

Incorrect Spelling	Correct Spelling
1. asassin	....
2. asisstant	....
3. benifitted	....
4. comparitive	....
5. dumbfound	....
6. newstand	....
7. bookeeper	....
8. posession	....
9. kidnapper	....
10. chagrinned	....
11. sincerly	....
12. vilain	....
13. tranquility	....
14. holliday	....
15. sherrif	....
16. tarriff	....
17. persuit	....
18. dispair	....

Key: 1. assassin, 2. assistant, 3. benefited, 4. comparative, 5. dumfound, 6. newsstand, 7. bookkeeper, 8. possession, 9. kidnaper, 10. chagrined, 11. sincerely, 12. villain, 13. tranquillity, 14. holiday, 15. sheriff, 16. tariff, 17. pursuit, 18. despair.

Index

Index

413

414

415